Safeguarding, Child Protection and Abuse in Sport

The safeguarding of children and young people participating in sport has become an increasingly prominent concern in policy-making and research communities around the world. Major organizations such as the IOC and UNICEF now officially recognize that children in sport can be at risk of exploitation and abuse, and this concern has led to the emergence of new initiatives and policies aimed at protecting vulnerable young people and athletes. This book is the first to comprehensively review contemporary developments in child protection and safeguarding in sport on a global level.

The book is divided into two parts. Part I critically analyses current child protection and safeguarding policy and practice in sport across a range of countries, including the US, Canada, the UK, Australia, China and Germany, providing a global context for current policy and practice. This represents one of the most comprehensive reviews to date of the landscape of child protection and safeguarding in sport and provides a starting point for critical international comparisons. Part II explores a range of issues related to child protection and safeguarding in sport, including many not covered in previous books, such as emotional abuse, injury and overtraining. While in many instances the impetus for policy in this area has arisen from concerns about sexual abuse, the second part of this book therefore opens up a broader, more holistic approach to child and athlete welfare.

By bringing together many of the leading researchers working in child and athlete protection in sport from around the world, this book is important reading for all advanced students, researchers, policy makers or practitioners working in youth sport, physical education, sports coaching, coach education or child protection.

Melanie Lang is a sociologist and former British international youth swimmer, swimming coach and journalist who now works at Edge Hill University, UK. Her research centres on the policy and practice of safeguarding and child protection in sport and her work has featured in *The Times* and *The Independent* newspapers and on BBC Radio as well as in leading academic journals. She has sat on the Child Protection in Sport Unit Research Evidence Advisory Group since 2009 and is on the editorial board of the *Irish Journal of Sociology.*

Mike Hartill is a sociologist and Senior Lecturer at Edge Hill University, UK. He conducts and publishes research on child maltreatment in sport. Recent publications include a review of this field for the *Directory of Sport Science* (6th edn) published by the International Council of Sport Science and Physical Education (ICSSPE). He has sat on the Child Protection in Sport Unit Research Evidence Advisory Group since 2003.

Routledge Research in Sport, Culture and Society

Safeguarding, Child Protection and Abuse in Sport

International perspectives in research, policy and practice

Edited by Melanie Lang and Mike Hartill

Routledge
Taylor & Francis Group

LONDON AND NEW YORK

First published 2015
by Routledge
2 Park Square, Milton Park, Abingdon, Oxon OX14 4RN

and by Routledge
711 Third Avenue, New York, NY 10017

Routledge is an imprint of the Taylor & Francis Group, an informa business

British Library Cataloguing-in-Publication Data
A catalogue record for this book is available from the British Library

Library of Congress Cataloging-in-Publication Data
Safeguarding, child protection and abuse in sport : international perspectives
in research, policy and practice / edited by Melanie Lang, Mike Hartill.
    pages cm. – (Routledge research in sport, culture and society)
    1. Sports for children – Safety measures. 2. Sports for children – Moral
and ethical aspects. 3. Sports for children – Research. 4. Sports for
children – Cross-cultural studies. 5. Child welfare – Cross-cultural
studies. 6. Child abuse – Cross-cultural studies. 7. Child sexual abuse –
Cross-cultural studies. 8. Abused children – Services for – Cross-cultural
studies. 9. Child abuse – Prevention – Cross-cultural studies. 10. Child
sexual abuse – Prevention – Cross-cultural studies. I. Lang, Melanie.
II. Hartill, Mike.
GV709.2.S28 2014
796.083–dc23   2014002767

ISBN: 978-0-415-82979-3 (hbk)
ISBN: 978-0-203-62851-5 (ebk)

Typeset in Times New Roman
by HWA Text and Data Management, London

For our parents
Frank and Margaret
and
Les and Mary

Contents

Contributors

Stiliani 'Ani' Chroni, PhD (Hedmark University College, Elverum, Norway) has a background in sport sciences and sport psychology and is a certified Sport Psychology Consultant in Greece and the USA. Her research falls under two themes: exploring the psychological safety and wellbeing of sport participants, including gender and equity issues with an emphasis on the sexual harassment of female athletes; and understanding the perceptions and responses of athletes that influence their persistence, performance and experience. Prior to moving to Norway in 2013, she coordinated the EU-funded programme 'Gender and Equity Issues' at the University of Thessaly in Greece, developed material on gender equity for a Greek school programme, organized the 1st International Forum on Youth Sport with a Gender Perspective in Greece, and served as a scientific advisor on the 2012 EU project Prevention of Sexualized Violence in Sport: Impulses for an Open, Secure and Sound Sporting Environment in Europe. Ani also serves as Secretary for WomenSport International.

Kristine De Martelaer, PhD (Vrije Universiteit Brussel, Belgium, and International Centre for Ethics in Sports (ICES), Ghent, Belgium) is Assistant Professor at the Faculty of Physical Education and Physiotherapy at Vrije Universiteit Brussel, where she is also the head of the Department of Movement Education and Sports Training. She teaches sport history and philosophy, didactics, the PE curriculum and first aid/basic life support. Her work centres around pedagogy, in particular focusing on didactical teaching approaches, the experiences and expectations of children and teachers/coaches within PE, youth sport and play, and ethics in (youth) sport.

Mike Hartill is a sociologist and Senior Lecturer at Edge Hill University. He conducts and publishes research on child maltreatment in sport. Recent publications include a review of this field for the Directory of Sport Science (6th edn) published by the International Council of Sport Science and Physical Education (ICSSPE). He has sat on the Child Protection in Sport Unit Research Evidence Advisory Group since 2003.

Fan Hong, PhD (University of Western Australia) is Winthrop Professor in Chinese Studies and academic editor of *The International Journal for the*

History of Sport. Her research interests are in the fields of gender and politics in sport in China and cross-cultural studies.

Gretchen Kerr, PhD (University of Toronto, Canada) is a Professor and Associate Dean in the Faculty of Kinesiology and Physical Education at the University of Toronto in Canada. Her research focuses on the psycho-social health of young people in sport, maltreatment in sport, and the role of coaches in advancing healthy athlete development. Gretchen also serves as the harassment officer for Gymnastics Ontario and Gymnastics Canada, the ethics committee chair for Gymnastics Ontario, and as an editorial board member for the *Canadian Journal for Women in Coaching*. In 2011, the Canadian Association for the Advancement of Women in Sport and Physical Activity named Gretchen one of the most influential women of the year, celebrating her impact on advancing sport and physical activity for women and girls.

Melanie Lang is a sociologist and former British international youth swimmer, swimming coach and journalist who now works at Edge Hill University. Her research centres on the policy and practice of safeguarding and child protection in sport and her work has featured in *The Times* and *The Independent* newspapers and on BBC Radio as well as in leading academic journals. She has sat on the Child Protection in Sport Unit Research Evidence Advisory Group since 2009 and is on the editorial board of the *Irish Journal of Sociology*.

Zhang Ling, PhD (Guangdong University of Foreign Studies, China) received her doctorate from University College Cork, National University of Ireland, and is now a Lecturer in Sports Studies at Guangdong University of Foreign Studies in China. Her research centres on Chinese sports policy and the Chinese sports system, specifically on elite athletes' education, training and re-employment.

Rhodri S. Lloyd, PhD (Cardiff Metropolitan University, Wales) is a Lecturer in Sport and Exercise Physiology at Cardiff Metropolitan University in Wales, where he also earned his doctorate. He is accredited with the UK Strength and Conditioning Association (UKSCA) and the National Strength and Conditioning Association. Rhodri serves on the Board of Directors for the UKSCA and is the inaugural convener of the UKSCA Youth Training Special Interest Group. He is also an Executive Council Board Member for the NSCA Youth Training Special Interest Group. He regularly delivers coach development workshops and advises sports organizations on their strategies for developing physical fitness in youths.

Donna A. Lopiano, PhD (Southern Connecticut State University, USA) is President of the consultancy firm Sports Management Resources and the former Chief Executive Officer of the Women's Sports Foundation (1992-2007). The *Sporting News* in the US has repeatedly listed her as one of 'The 100 Most Influential People in Sports,' and she has been nationally and internationally recognized for her leadership advocating for gender equity in sports. Donna received her bachelor's degree from Southern Connecticut State University, her masters and doctoral degrees from the University of Southern California, and is the recipient of five honorary doctoral degrees.

Guillaume Maebe, MA (Erasmushogeschool in Brussels, Belgium) graduated *magna cum laude* from Ghent University with a Master of Arts in history and is currently completing a Master's degree in journalism at the Erasmushogeschool in Brussels, Belgium. His work investigates the historical evolution of ethical awareness in Flemish sport legislation, particularly focusing on the Ethically Justified Sports Act enacted in 2008 by the Flemish government.

Montserrat Martin, PhD (University of Vic, Catalonia, Spain) is a lecturer in the Faculty of Education at the University of Vic in the Catalan region of Spain. Her research centres on women in sport and the narrative experiences of players across all levels, with a particular focus on team contact sports such as rugby. She also works on alternative ways of writing about the social world of sport. She is focused on implementing codes of ethics and good practice in sport organizations in Catalonia and Spain and on implementing education courses on preventing child sexual abuse in Catalan and Spanish Sport Unions. She has published in *Qualitative Inquiry* and in the *International Review for the Sociology of Sport*.

Aaron L. Miller, PhD (Kyoto University, Japan) is Assistant Professor and Hakubi Scholar at Kyoto University, affiliated with the Graduate School of Education, and Visiting Scholar at Stanford University Centre on Adolescence. His research explores the relationships between education, sports, discipline, and culture. Many of his publications can be downloaded from his website, www.aaronlmiller.com.

Atsushi Nakazawa, PhD (Hitotsubashi University, Japan) is Assistant Professor in the Graduate School of Social Sciences, Hitotsubashi University in Japan. His research explores the sociological and historical relationship between education and sport, especially focusing on school sport in secondary education in Japan, the USA and the UK.

Jimmy O'Gorman, PhD (Edge Hill University, England) is a Senior Lecturer in Sports Development at Edge Hill University and a part-time football coach at an academy of an English football league club. Jimmy's research and teaching interests centre on the organization and delivery of sport for young people, and he has researched and advised on aspects of safeguarding young people in football as part of an evaluation of the Football Association's Charter Standard scheme.

Jon L. Oliver, PhD (Cardiff Metropolitan University, Wales) is a Senior Lecturer in Exercise Physiology at Cardiff Metropolitan University in Wales, having completed his doctorate at the Children's Health and Exercise Research Centre at the University of Exeter in 2006. Jon has served as convenor of the British Association of Sport and Exercise Science paediatric exercise science interest group and has conducted extensive research on childhood and long-term athlete development. He has translated much of this knowledge to aid practitioners, with a continuous theme of considering the impact of training on the wellbeing of children and adolescents. His work in youth sport has included collaborations in elite youth soccer, rugby union and athletics.

Maria Papaefstathiou, MA (University of East Anglia, England) is completing a PhD at the School of Education and Lifelong Learning at the University of East Anglia on the experiences of competitive track and field child athletes in Cyprus and their understandings of child protection and abuse. She has an MA in Child Welfare and Protection in Sport and formerly worked as a primary school physical education and dance teacher in Cyprus.

Sylvie Parent, PhD (University of Laval, Quebec, Canada) is Assistant Professor in the Department of Physical Education at Laval University in Canada. Her research focuses on protecting young athletes against violence, and she is involved in developing an intervention framework in sport in Quebec to protect young athletes. Sylvie is also working on the development of a tool for collecting data on violence against young people in sport and on the analysis of a database representative of the Quebec population aged 12-17 dealing with their romantic journey and victimization experienced in this area (n=8000).

Elizabeth C. J. Pike, PhD (University of Chichester, England) is Head of Sport Development and Management, Reader in the Sociology of Sport and Exercise, and Chair of the Anita White Foundation at the University of Chichester. Her recent publications include the co-authored book (with Jay Coakley) entitled *Sports in Society: Issues and Controversies*, the co-edited book (with Simon Beames) *Outdoor Adventure and Social Theory*, and papers on ageing, gender issues, and the role of complementary and alternative medicines in sport. She is the President of the International Sociology of Sport Association and serves on the Editorial Boards of the *International Review for the Sociology of Sport*, *Leisure Studies* and *Revista ALESDE*.

Daniel J. A. Rhind, PhD (Brunel University, England) is a chartered psychologist. His work has been presented at a range of international conferences and has been published in leading journals. His research has been featured on BBC News and on BBC Radio 4 as well as in *The Guardian* newspaper and *Community Care* magazine. Daniel leads the Brunel International Research Network for Athlete Welfare and is a member of the Child Protection in Sport Unit's Research Evidence and Advisory Group. Daniel's research focuses on understanding the development and maintenance of (un)healthy and (in)effective relationships in sport.

Bettina Rulofs, PhD (German Sport University Cologne, Germany) is a member of the German National Working Group on Child Protection in Sport, a spokesperson for sport sociology within the German Association for Sport Sciences, and in 2011 she compiled guidelines for child protection in sport for the organization German Sport Youth. Her main areas of research are gender studies, social inequality, diversity management and child protection and the prevention of violence in sport.

Kate Russell, PhD (University of Sydney, Australia) is a Senior Lecturer at the Faculty of Education and Social Work at the University of Sydney, Australia. Her research interests and publications span the fields of child protection in sport, gendered identities in the sporting and educational context and the development of body image among sportswomen. Some of her most recent publications include the co-edited book *Youth Sport in Australia* (2011) and *Child Welfare in Football: An Exploration of Children's Welfare in the Modern Game* (2007), a co-authored series *Science Through Sport: Body Image I Middle Secondary* and *Science Through Sport: Body Image II Senior Secondary* (2009), and journal articles on gendered bodies in swimming (with Johnson 2012) and snowboarding (with Lemon 2012).

Nicolette Schipper-van Veldhoven, PhD (Netherlands Olympic Committee* Netherlands Sports Confederation, Netherlands) is programme manager of research at the Netherlands Olympic Committee*Netherlands Sports Confederation. Before this, Nicolette worked as a Physical Education teacher and Associate Professor. She is a research adviser on sexual harassment and abuse and sports pedagogy, and has extensive experience of designing and evaluating physical exercise programmes for children with special needs. Her main interests lie within the field of education and ethics in youth sport.

Andrea Scott, PhD (University of Chichester, England) is Senior Lecturer in the Sport Development and Management Department at the University of Chichester, where she teaches the sociology of sport. Her research interests are the management of pain and injury in sport, particularly the knowledge, working practices and social organization of healthcare professionals providing treatment within this context. Her work has been published in such journals as the *International Review for the Sociology of Sport*, *Social Science and Medicine*, and the *British Journal of Sports Medicine*.

Andy Smith, PhD (Edge Hill University, England) is Professor of Sport and Physical Activity at Edge Hill University, UK, where he is also director of the Centre for Youth Sport and Leisure Research. He is co-editor of the *International Journal of Sport Policy and Politics* and a co-author of *Sport Policy and Development* (with Daniel Bloyce), *Disability, Sport and Society* (with Nigel Thomas), and *An Introduction to Drugs in Sport* (with Ivan Waddington). His latest book (co-edited with Ivan Waddington) is *Doing Real World Research in Sports Studies*, also published by Routledge.

Ashley Stirling, PhD (University of Toronto, Canada) is a Lecturer in the Faculty of Kinesiology and Physical Education at the University of Toronto in Canada. Her research centres on athletes' experiences of maltreatment in sport and strategies for athlete protection. In 2007, Ashley received the Thesis Award from the Association for the Advancement of Applied Sport Psychology, and in

2009, she was awarded the Young Investigator Award by the European College of Sport Science for her research on the emotional abuse of athletes. In 2012, Ashley co-wrote a coach education module on creating positive and healthy sport experiences for the Coaching Association of Canada.

Jan Toftegaard-Støckel, PhD (University of Southern Denmark, Denmark) is a senior Lecturer at the Institute of Sport and Biomechanics at the University of Southern Denmark. He has been involved with policy development and public debate about sexual harassment and abuse in sport since 1997 and has published widely in this area. He is currently involved in a retrospective study of athletes' experiences of emotional, physical and sexual abuse in sport, research into the participation of at-risk children in organized sport, and intervention programmes for vulnerable young people.

Jan Tolleneer, PhD (KU Leuven University, Belgium, and Ghent University, Belgium) is Professor at both the Faculty of Kinesiology and Rehabilitation Sciences, KU Leuven University in Belgium, and the Faculty of Medicine and Health Sciences, Ghent University, Belgium, and also teaches at the National Training Academy of Flanders. He coordinates the Interfaculty Research Group on Sport and Ethics at KU Leuven University, which is involved in a government-funded inter-university research project on sport and sexual integrity in sport, and is a former board member of the International Society for the History of Physical Education and Sport.

Rudolph Leon Van Niekerk, PhD (University of Johannesburg, South Africa) completed his PhD in Psychology at the University of Johannesburg and completed a European Masters in Sport and Exercise Psychology at the Catholic University in Leuven, Belgium. He is a licenced Counselling Psychologist and works part time in private practice. He has worked with athletes from a variety of national teams on their psychological preparation and regularly presents his work at international and national conferences.

Tine Vertommen, MA, MSc (Collaborative Antwerp Psychiatric Research Institute (CAPRI), University of Antwerp (UA), Antwerp, Belgium, and Antwerp University Hospital (UZA), Antwerp, Belgium) is completing a PhD on the prevalence and consequences of harassment and abuse in sport at the University of Antwerp. She has been involved in projects analysing incident registration forms at the Netherlands Olympic Committee*Netherlands Sports Confederation helpline for sexual harassment in sport in the Netherlands, and in projects advising sport authorities on the development of child protection policies in Flanders in Belgium. Tine is a board member of the International Centre for Ethics in Sports (ICES) and also works as a criminologist at the University Forensic Centre in Antwerp, where she facilitates the treatment of sexual offenders in Flanders, Belgium.

Lieke Vloet (Netherlands Olympic Committee*Netherlands Sports Confederation, Netherlands) is senior advisor on sports policy and coordinator of the programme 'The Social Impact of Sport' at the Netherlands Olympic Committee*Netherlands Sports Confederation. She has been involved in work on fair play and diversity in sport policy and on developing sexual harassment policies in sport. Lieke previously worked as the coordinator for youth sport and the programme coordinator for the project 'Values and Norms in Sport' at the Netherlands Christian Sports Union.

Connee Zotos, PhD (New York University, USA) spent 22 years in US college athletics as an NCAA Division II and Division III coach and athletic director. She served on the NCAA Division III Management Council, on the Board of Directors of NACWAA, and as the President of the College Athletic Administrators of New Jersey. She has been the recipient of two Athletic Director of the Year award and the Garden State Award for substantial and enduring contributions to the development of intercollegiate athletics. Connee is currently a Clinical Associate Professor of Sports Management at New York University and is a senior associate for the consulting firm, Sports Management Resources.

Joca Zurc, PhD (College of Nursing Jesenice, Slovenia) is an Assistant Professor in Kinesiology and Health Promotion and Vice-Dean for Education at the College of Nursing Jesenice, Her research focuses on child wellbeing in aesthetic sports, especially gymnastics. She was on the scientific advisory committee of the EU project Prevention of Sexualized Violence in Sport: Impulses for an Open, Secure and Sound Sporting Environment in Europe and is a past recipient of the International Council of Sport Science and Physical Education's international scientific excellence award.

Foreword

Safeguarding and child protection are both relative newcomers to the research and policy agendas in sport. In some continents, however, there is still resistance to the idea that safeguarding is necessary. Safeguarding policy advocates have often found their voices silenced or their sport practitioners dismissive of the issue. In addition, researchers in this field have had to contend with denial of a problem that has all-too-often been defined as marginal to the 'proper' business of sport science. But, as the list of authors here reflects, there is an emerging international alliance of interests developing evidence-based policy to improve safety for athletes. Research needs to underpin policy and practice if sustainable improvements for young athletes are to be achieved, but it is a welcome hallmark of this field of enquiry that the research-policy divide has been so effectively bridged.

Much of the knowledge that does exist in this field comes from countries in the global North: this book therefore provides a welcome overview of the political geography of safeguarding in sport with especially important insights from African research. Finding an ethical balance between universal approaches to safeguarding – as embodied, for example, in the UN Convention on the Rights of the Child – and cultural relativism is no easy task. It would be tempting for the earliest safeguarding advocates in sport to see their work as one more element of globalization and to proselytize about the advances made in their own countries. But deep understanding of the issues involved comes only through personal and organizational learning related to local settings and local challenges. Of course we should share ideas, as this book sets out to do, but we should also avoid the trap of thinking that one solution to safeguarding in sport fits all.

The book widens the scope of some previous publications by addressing both adult and child protection in sport. In many respects, age boundaries are irrelevant in a field of activity like sport where elite performers might be in their low teens and beginners as old as 80. Whilst respecting that legal thresholds vary across international boundaries, we should also note that moral and human rights obligations apply to everyone, regardless of age.

The contributors here reflect the alliance mentioned above, between the research and policy communities, that characterizes this field. The close cooperation between those seeking new knowledge about abuse in sport and those seeking to implement abuse prevention measures is an excellent example of how to maximize the impact of research.

Professor Celia Brackenridge OBE
Brunel University, UK

Acknowledgements

The editors wish to thank Professor Celia Brackenridge OBE for her unwavering support for both editors during this and other projects and for kindly writing the foreword to this book. We sincerely thank all the contributors for their commitment to this project and their timely contributions despite very busy schedules, and our editors at Routledge for their advice and support. We would also like to express sincere thanks to Sharon Hartill and Steven M for providing the constant and crucial support that has made it possible for us to find time within our family lives to produce this book. Mike would also like to acknowledge Isaac (9) and Frances (8) who unselfishly offer a constant source of inspiration and distraction as required.

Introduction

What is safeguarding in sport?

Melanie Lang and Mike Hartill

Children's participation in sport is generally regarded as beneficial, a component of a healthy childhood and a long, healthy adulthood, both physically and mentally (US Department of Health and Human Services 2008; Brackenridge et al. 2010; Micheli et al. 2011). As well as being fun, sport and physical activity have the potential to positively affect health and fitness; increase bodily awareness and self-esteem; and teach rules, respect, sportsmanship and social interaction (Department of Health, Physical Activity, Health Improvement and Protection 2011; Micheli et al. 2011). Benefits have also been identified for wider society such as increased revenue for the world economy; improved educational attainment and productivity in the workplace; reduced congestion and pollution through active travel; and cost savings for health and social care services (Shibli 2007; Brackenridge et al. 2010; Department of Health, Physical Activity, Health Improvement and Protection 2011). Governments worldwide have been quick to recognize and seek to harness these benefits, placing youth sports participation high on the political agenda. In England, for example, the latest youth sport strategy (Department for Culture, Media and Sport 2012: 3) aims to 'increase consistently the number of young people developing sport' by, in the words of the report's title, 'creating a sporting habit for life'.

However, the performance-centred nature of modern organized sport can have negative implications for young participants that have only been recognized in the last two decades (Brackenridge et al. 2012). Critics suggest that competitive pressures engendered by adult supervision have robbed youth sport of its play and socialization values. David (1999: 53-4), for example, argues that modern organized sport is 'an environment in which the most respectable aspects of sports, such as its educative scope, sportsmanship and physical and mental wellbeing, are seriously threatened', with coaches 'no longer asking how sports could benefit children but rather how children could benefit sports'. In addition, young athletes are often viewed as miniature adults, as athletes first and children second, and as objects by the adults around them who have a stake in their success (Brackenridge 2001; Brackenridge and Kirby 1997; David 1999), all of which threaten the potential benefits to young people of participation in sport.

Increasingly, research on the impact of competitive sports on youth athletes is supporting these claims by highlighting the ease with which common sporting practices can cross the line into the realm of poor practice, abuse and exploitation. Areas of particular concern include injury, early specialization in sport and intensive training of youth athletes (American Academy of Pediatrics 2000; World Health Organization 1998); child labour (Donnelly 1993, 1997); disordered eating (Kerr et al. 2006; Sundgot-Borgen 2004); doping (David 1999); and physical and emotional abuse and sexual violence (Alexander et al. 2011; Brackenridge 1997, 2001; Brackenridge and Kirby 1997; Brackenridge et al. 2010; Donnelly 1999).

Despite the number of young people who take part in sport and physical activity globally, the traditional autonomy of the sports sector has made governments reluctant to intervene in sport, resulting in 'a legacy of traditionalism and resistance to change' (Brackenridge 2001: 10), including making sport slower than other institutions to adopt social reforms for child welfare. Consequently, as the chapters in this book illustrate, measures to safeguard children in sport are relatively recent additions to the British and international sport policy agenda (Brackenridge 2001).

Approaches to safeguarding children's welfare

Since measures to safeguard children's welfare in sport began to appear on the agenda of international governments and sports organizations over the past 20 years, terminology and approaches to child welfare among governments have shifted in reflection of changes to prevailing understandings of and values about children and their welfare. This evolution also indicates a change in how child welfare concerns are policed and who is responsible for children's welfare. A study of the social policies and professional practices across nine countries in the 1990s found governments tend to adopt one of two approaches to children's welfare – either a 'child protection approach', or a 'family service approach' (Gilbert 1997; Parton and Berridge 2011). Within a child protection approach, governments adopt a liberal, paternalistic attitude to children's welfare policies and practice – child abuse is framed as a moral issue caused by family dysfunction and pathological, violent individuals; interventions are aimed at protecting children by responding to and reducing harm with the state imposing sanctions to punish perpetrators (Gilbert et al. 2011; Parton 2011); and involvement in family life is broadly avoided unless absolutely necessary to 'rescue' children from abuse (Gilbert et al. 2011; Laird 2013; Lonne et al. 2009). Consequently, among countries within the child protection orientation, child welfare systems developed around evaluating the risks to children, legislating powers to react to child abuse allegations and identifying, reporting and investigating suspected child abuse. In other words, little attention is paid in this approach to proactively safeguarding children's overall wellbeing or promoting their holistic development.

This child protection orientation was, until recently, used in England, leading Lonne et al. (2009) to name it the 'Anglophone approach', and was replicated in the 1980s-2000s by other countries such as the USA, Canada and Australia, some of which modelled their child welfare policies and procedures on those in England

(Gilbert et al. 2011; Parton 2008). Elements of the 'Anglophone approach' have also been embedded in international law such as the United Nations Convention on the Rights of the Child (UNCRC) (Melton 2009). Article 19.2 of the UNCRC, for example, requires states to protect children from all forms of maltreatment through implementation of 'protective measures' such as 'identification, reporting, referral, investigation, treatment and follow-up of instances of child maltreatment' (United Nations General Assembly 1989).

Moreover, as several countries initially modelled their own child welfare systems on those of England, the 'Anglophone approach' arguably has significance way beyond the nation's borders (Melton 2009). Similarly in sport, England has been placed at the vanguard of protecting children from abuse in sport (see Chapter 1), with other countries and international organizations following the model used in the country. In 2012, for example, the United Nations Children's Fund (UNICEF) and partner organizations that form the International Safeguarding Children in Sport Working Group drafted a set of 11 standards to protect children in international sport and sport-for-development (International Safeguarding Children in Sport Working Group 2013). The international standards were compiled in conjunction with England's Child Protection in Sport Unit (CPSU) and are based on similar standards enacted by the CPSU in sport in the country.

Meanwhile, within a family service approach to children's welfare, child abuse is understood as resulting from social and/or psychological circumstances such as poverty and inequality, and early intervention by the state is proactive and supportive in nature, aimed at preventing future issues and strengthening family relations (Gilbert et al. 2011). In the 1990s, countries including Denmark, Sweden, Belgium, the Netherlands and Germany were identified as operating broadly within a family service orientation (Gilbert 1997).

However, in recent years a new orientation has also emerged – a 'child-focused approach' (Gilbert et al. 2011). Within this orientation, in recognition that societies need healthy and contributing citizens, unequal outcomes for children have become the primary cause for concern and interventions are encouraged at an early stage to promote children's wellbeing and equal opportunities (Gilbert et al 2011; Parton 2010). This approach goes 'beyond protecting children from risk to promoting children's welfare' (Gilbert et al. 2011: 252) and foregrounds children's rights over the rights of adults. Consequently, early intervention and preventative services are regarded as a positive way of helping maximize children's developmental opportunities, educational attainment and overall health and wellbeing, and interventions are 'not restricted to narrow forensic concerns about harm and abuse – rather the object of concern is the child's overall development and wellbeing' (Parton 2010) in order to prevent problems in later life. England, Finland, Norway, Germany and the USA have all begun over the last decade to adopt child-focused approaches, which reflects the fact they have all, except the USA, signed the UNCRC (United Nations General Assembly 1989). However, the extent to which this approach has made inroads within sport varies considerably, as the chapters on the context of policy and practice in sport in England, Germany, the USA and Canada, indicate (See Chapters 1, 5, 10 and 11).

Not everyone has welcomed this reconceptualization of children's welfare. Some argue it encourages a broader, more interventive and regulatory role for the state (Parton 2005, 2008). The concern is that this results in the emergence of a 'preventive-surveillance state' (Parton 2008: 166) that renders children the objects of intensive assessment and monitoring and creates the potential to erode human rights and civil liberties at the expense of according children control over their own lives (Parton 2005). Meanwhile, the evolution in safeguarding policy is not always evident in safeguarding *practice* and child protection often remains the key focus of many practitioners. In part, this may be because financial constraints in recent years have forced preventative measures onto the 'back burner' (Laird 2013), although a lack of understanding of the changes and/or a privileging of concerns about child maltreatment over broader welfare promotion may also be to blame. Indeed, in some cases the term 'safeguarding' is used interchangeably with 'child protection', with little apparent understanding of the differences between the terms, perhaps because legislation and practice to prevent and manage child abuse has a longer history and offers clearer, measurable outcomes than legislation and practice aimed a safeguarding children's welfare, and because the impacts of reacting to child abuse are quicker and easier to identify than the results from proactively safeguarding children.

Within England, the child-focused approach to children's welfare is encapsulated by the use of the term 'safeguarding'. The term began to appear in English policy documents in the mid-1990s (see for example, Department of Health 1995), and by the early 2000s the terms 'child protection', 'child abuse' and 'risk' – the buzz words of previous policy documents – were largely absent, replaced by the terms 'safeguarding', 'needs' and 'strengths' (Munro and Calder 2005). This is more than a simple change in terminology. In line with the child-focused orientation to children's welfare, it signals a reorientation of policy and practice away from predominantly reactive services for a small number of children considered at risk of abuse and towards a more preventative range of services for all children and the introduction of policies and practices to promote the welfare of children (Munro and Calder 2005):

> The main thrust of the safeguarding agenda is preventive: it is hoped that providing early intervention for family problems will help support parents and so reduce the number who become abusive.
>
> (Munro and Parton 2007: 9)

Specifically, safeguarding and promoting children's welfare includes:

> Protecting children from maltreatment; preventing impairment of children's health or development; ensuring that children are growing up in circumstances consistent with the provision of safe and effective care; and taking action to enable all children to have the best outcomes.
>
> (Department for Education 2013: 85)

The purpose of such an approach, then, is to intervene early to prevent social problems before they occur and promote children's wellbeing both in childhood and later in life (Parton 2008), specifically in terms of being healthy, staying safe, enjoying and achieving, making a positive contribution to society, and achieving economic wellbeing (Chief Secretary to the Treasury 2003; Department for Children, Schools and Families 2009). Concerns about protecting children from abuse did not disappear however, rather they were relocated within the new safeguarding agenda and wider concerns about promoting children's welfare (Parton and Berridge 2011). Similar moves towards a more child-focused, safeguarding orientation to children's welfare have also occurred elsewhere – for example in the USA and Canada (Parton 2010) – although the term 'safeguarding' is not always the terminology employed in such countries. Importantly, however, the growing move towards adopting a child-focused system of child welfare that promotes broader, preventative safeguarding agendas is by no means complete worldwide, either in policy or in practice within or beyond sport. Indeed, as the chapters in this book indicate, the extent to which countries have adopted a proactive safeguarding approach within sport and the extent to which proactive approaches to safeguarding children in sport are implemented vary considerably, even among countries within family service or child-focused orientated welfare systems such as Denmark and Germany (see Chapters 2 and 5).

International developments in safeguarding in sport

Much of the legislative, policy and practice change in children's welfare in recent years has been prompted by growing understandings of, and a willingness to engage with, children's rights (Gilbert et al. 2011). Indeed, awareness and commitment for children's welfare has progressed globally since the establishment of the UNCRC (United Nations General Assembly 1989), particularly among academics and policy-makers, if not always among sports organizations. The UNCRC contains 54 articles, most of which set out how children should be treated. These rights are often grouped into four themes – survival rights, development rights, protection rights, and participation rights – and many have implications for sport and its responsibility to safeguard children (see David 2005 for further details). Sport, however, has been slow to respond to the impact of the UNCRC and, as the chapters in this book illustrate, in many countries measures to promote children's rights and welfare in sport were prompted not by international law or moral imperatives but by high-profile cases of abuse, usually sexual abuse, covered by domestic media.

Other international organizations within and outside sport have also begun to recognize sport's responsibility to safeguard and protect children and promote children's rights. The world's largest children's charity, UNICEF, which has a history of violence- and abuse-prevention work *through* children's sport, recently acknowledged that children can be exploited and abused *in* sport. In 2010, UNICEF published a landmark report on violence to children in sport (Brackenridge et al. 2010), and the United Nations Office on Sport for Development and Peace

(UNOSDP) has identified child protection as an area of strategic priority (UNOSDP International Working Group 2009).

Similarly, the world's most influential sports organization, the International Olympic Committee (IOC), has begun to raise awareness of, and set out its commitment to, safeguarding and protecting children in sport. It has adopted consensus statements on sexual harassment and abuse in sport (IOC 2007), on training the elite child athlete (IOC 2005), on evaluating the health of elite athletes (IOC 2009) and on the health and fitness of young people through physical activity and sport (Mountjoy et al. 2011). In the Olympic year 2012, the IOC also published audio-visual online education resources to raise awareness of children's rights and welfare issues in sport.

On a European level, the Lanzarote Convention (Council of Europe 2005) provides a framework for EU countries to meet their obligations to safeguard and protect children. The guidelines, known formerly as the Council of Europe Convention on the Protection of Children against Sexual Exploitation and Sexual Abuse, came into force in 2010 and while its focus is on preventing and managing the sexual exploitation of children, it is underpinned by a children's rights discourse that foregrounds the best interests of the child. While such developments should, rightly, be viewed positively, their influence on sports practice remains unknown.

Organization of this book

This book is divided into two parts. Part I critically analyses current safeguarding and child protection policy and practice in sport across a variety of countries to provide a picture of the context in sport worldwide. This represents one of the most comprehensive reviews to date of the global landscape of safeguarding and child protection in sport and provides a starting point for critical international comparisons. This said, and notwithstanding the acknowledgement that no book could effectively cover all countries or even regions of the world, we recognize several important omissions in the countries represented in this book. Developments in sport in the Global South, such as the regions of South America, the Indian subcontinent, the Caribbean and much of sub-Saharan Africa and South East Asia, are under-represented. We know of important and exciting developments in some of these areas, often initiated and supported by national and international children's charities, but to the best of our knowledge academic work on safeguarding and child protection in sport in these regions is limited.

Equally, we are aware of the differences in terminology used in the different chapters that comprise Part I. As others who have worked in an international context have found, it is 'a challenge to understand the different linguistic and cultural terms, definitions, meanings and the measures used in different countries – terms [such as] child protection and safeguarding, and definitions of abuse and policy interventions sometimes vary in their meaning and implications between countries' (Parton 2010). Each of the countries represented in Part I have adopted language, laws, policies and practices that reflect the history of their child welfare systems, and consequently the language used differs accordingly.

Part II of the book explores a range of issues related to safeguarding and child protection in sport, including many that receive less media coverage, generate less public concern, remain under-researched and are consequently not covered in previous texts on child welfare in sport. In this sense, the topics covered in this section represent safeguarding issues that, to date, have been marginalized in sport, where the focus of most policy developments has been driven by concerns about child abuse, particularly sexual abuse (Brackenridge 2001). They represent the broader, more holistic face of safeguarding in sport and a new frontier for policymakers, legislators, researchers and practitioners.

References

Alexander, K., Stafford, A. and Lewis, R. (2011) *The Experiences of Children Participating in Organized Sport in the UK*, Edinburgh: University of Edinburgh/ NSPCC.

American Academy of Paediatrics (2000) 'Intensive training and sports specialization in young athletes', *Pediatrics*, 106: 154–7.

Brackenridge, C. H. (1997) 'He owned me basically: women's experience of sexual abuse in sport', *International Review for the Sociology of Sport*, 32: 115–30.

— (2001) *Spoilsports: understanding and preventing sexual exploitation in sport*, London: Routledge.

Brackenridge, C. and Kirby, S. (1997) 'Playing safe? Assessing the risk of sexual abuse to elite child athletes', *International Review of the Sociology of Sport*, 32: 407–18.

Brackenridge, C., Kay, T. and Rhind, D. (2012) *Sport, Children's Rights and Violence Prevention: a sourcebook on global issues and local programmes*. Online. Available HTTP: <www.brunel.ac.uk/__data/assets/pdf_file/0009/259344/UNICEF-book-whole-text-6–12–12.pdf> (accessed 25 October 2013).

Brackenridge, C., Fasting, K., Kirby, S. and Leahy, T. (2010) *Protecting Children from Violence in Sport: a review with a focus on industrialized countries*, Florence: Innocenti Publications.

Chief Secretary to the Treasury (2003) *Every Child Matters*, London: The Stationary Office.

Council of Europe (2005) *Council of Europe Convention on the Protection of Children against Sexual Exploitation and Sexual Abuse*. Online. Available HTTP: <www.coe. int/t/dghl/standardsetting/children/default_en.asp> (accessed 15 November 2013).

David, P. (1999) 'Children's rights and sports: young athletes and competitive sports – exploit and exploitation', *The International Journal of Children's Rights*, 7: 53–81.

— (2005) *Human Rights in Youth Sport: a critical review of children's rights in competitive sports*, New York: Routledge.

Department for Children, Schools and Families (2009) *Working Together to Safeguard Children Consultation Document: guide to inter-agency working to safeguard and promote the welfare of children*, London: Department for Children, Schools and Families.

Department for Culture, Media and Sport (2012) *Creating a Sporting Habit for Life: a new youth sport strategy*, London: Department for Culture, Media and Sport. Online. Available HTTP: <www.gov.uk/government/uploads/system/uploads/attachment_data/file/78318/creating_a_sporting_habit_for_life.pdf> (accessed 25 October 2013).

Department for Education (2013) *Working Together to Safeguard Children: a guide to inter-agency working to safeguard and promote the welfare of children*. Online. Available

HTTP: <http://media.education.gov.uk/assets/files/pdf/w/working%20together.pdf> (accessed 10 October 2013).

Department of Health (1995) *Child Protection: clarification of arrangements between the NHS and other agencies*, London: Department of Health.

Department of Health, Physical Activity, Health Improvement and Protection (2011) *Start Active, Stay Active: a report on physical activity for health from the four home countries' Chief Medical Officers*, London: Department of Health, Physical Activity, Health Improvement and Protection. Online. Available HTTP: <www.gov.uk/government/uploads/system/uploads/attachment_data/file/216370/dh_128210.pdf> (accessed 25 October 2013).

Donnelly, P. (1993) 'Problems associated with youth involvement in high-performance sport', in B. R. Cahill and A. J. Pearl (eds) *Intensive Participation in Children's Sports*, Champaign, IL: Human Kinetics.

— (1997) 'Child labour, sport labour: applying child labour laws to sport', *International Review for the Sociology of Sport*, 32: 389–406.

— (1999) 'Who's fair game? Sport, sexual harassment and abuse', in P. White and K. Young (eds) *Sport and Gender in Canada*, Oxford: Oxford University Press.

Gilbert, N. (ed.) (1997) *Combating Child Abuse: international perspectives and trends*, Oxford: Oxford University Press.

Gilbert, N., Parton, N. and Skivenes, M. (2011) *Child Protection Systems: international trends and orientations*, New York: Open University Press.

International Olympic Committee (2005) *IOC Consensus Statement on Training the Elite Child Athlete*. Online. Available HTTP: <www.olympic.org/Documents/Reports/EN/en_report_1016.pdf> (accessed 15 November 2013).

— (2007) *IOC Consensus Statement on Sexual Harassment and Abuse in Sport*. Online. Available HTTP: <www.olympic.org/Documents/Reports/EN/en_report_1125.pdf> (accessed 15 November 2013).

— (2009) *IOC Consensus Statement on Periodic Health Evaluation of Elite Athletes*. Online. Available HTTP: www.olympic.org/Documents/Reports/EN/en_report_1448.pdf (accessed 15 November 2013).

International Safeguarding Children in Sport Working Group (2013) *Draft International Standards for Safeguarding and Protecting Children in Sport*. Online. Available HTTP: <http://assets.sportanddev.org/downloads/international_sports_safeguarding_children_standards_draft.pdf> (accessed 15 November 2013).

Kerr, G. A., Berman, E. and De Souza, M. J. (2006) 'Disordered eating in women's gymnastics: perspectives of athletes, coaches, parents, and judges', *Journal of Applied Sport Psychology*, 18: 28–43.

Laird, S. E. (2013) *Child Protection: managing conflict, hostility and aggression*, Bristol: Polity Press.

Lonne, B., Parton, N., Thomson, J. and Harries, M. (2009) *Reforming Child Protection*, Oxon: Routledge.

Melton, G. B. (2009) 'Foreword,' in B. Lonne, N. Parton, J. Thomson and M. Harries (eds) *Reforming Child Protection*, Oxon: Routledge.

Micheli, L., Mountjoy, M., Engebretsen, L., Hardman, K., Kahlmeier, S., Lambesrt, E., Ljungqvist, A., Matsudo, V., McKay, H. and Sundberg, C. J. (2011) 'Fitness and health of children through sport: the context for action', *British Journal of Sports Medicine*, 45: 931–6.

Mountjoy, M. et al. (2011) 'International Olympic Committee consensus statement on the health and fitness of young people through physical activity and sport', *British Journal of Sport Medicine*, 45: 839–48.

Munro, E. and Calder, M. (2005) 'Where has child protection gone?', *The Political Quarterly*, 76: 439–45.

Munro, E. and Parton, N. (2007) 'How far is England in the process of introducing a mandatory reporting system?', *Child Abuse Review*, 16 :5–16.

Parton, N. (2005) *Safeguarding Childhood: early intervention and surveillance in late modern society*, Basingstoke: Palgrave MacMillan.

— (2008) 'The Change for Children programme in England: towards the preventive-surveillance state', *Journal of Law and Society*, 35: 166–87.

— (2010) '*International comparison of child protection systems*', paper presented at the SFI conference, Copenhagen, Denmark, September 2010.

— (2011) 'Child protection and safeguarding in England: changing and competing conceptions of risk and their implications for social work', *British Journal of Social Work*, 41: 854–75.

Part I
Global perspectives

1 Safeguarding and child protection in sport in England

Melanie Lang and Mike Hartill

When British Olympic swimming coach Paul Hickson was convicted in 1995 of the rape and sexual assault of young athletes under his care, the Amateur Swimming Association, like most other English sports organizations, had no strategy for safeguarding and protecting athletes from abuse. The Hickson case drew national attention to sexual abuse in sport, although sports organizations initially denied such abuse was widespread and branded Hickson 'a bad apple', an aberration that had nothing to do with the culture of sport. Further revelations of child sexual abuse in British sport surfaced in the late 1990s, resulting in intense media scrutiny and an emerging 'moral panic' around child sexual abuse in sport that arguably continues to shape safeguarding policies to this day. In the 20 years since Hickson's conviction, British sport has been positioned as a world leader in athlete welfare, with developments from within and outside sport shaping the governance and practice of sport. This chapter highlights the background to these developments and discusses current strategies in place to safeguard and protect children and young people in sport in England.

Safeguarding, child protection and athlete welfare

Legislation forms the framework for children's welfare in the United Kingdom (UK). However, because the laws and structure in each of the home nations of the UK varies, this chapter focuses on the situation in sport in England, where a child is defined as under age 18 (Department for Children, School and Families 2010). The child welfare system in England is a product of its history, with developments predominantly emerging in reaction to high-profile cases of abuse, often sexual abuse, and there is no single piece of legislation that covers child welfare in England. The framework for the current system was established with The Children Act 1989 (Department of Health 1989) and its related guidance, particularly Working Together to Safeguard Children (Department for Children, School and Families 2010; Department for Education 2013; Department of Health and Social Security 1998). These set out how children should be protected from 'significant harm', defined as ill-treatment, including sexual abuse and non-physical forms of ill-treatment, or the impairment of physical or mental health, or of physical, intellectual, emotional, social or behavioural development (Department for Children, School and Families

2010). Importantly, the Act applies only to local authorities and the courts; all other organizations, including sport, are exempt from its requirements.

The requirements of the Children Act 1989 encapsulate the term 'child protection' (Parton 2001), which is used to collectively represent 'the activity that is undertaken to protect specific children who are suffering, or are likely to suffer, significant harm' (Department for Children, School and Families 2010: 35). The focus of child protection is specifically on protecting children from 'significant harm', in other words providing predominantly reactive services to protect children from abuse; the four sub-categories of child abuse are: sexual, physical and emotional abuse plus neglect (Department of Health and Social Security 1988).

In 2000 there was a shift towards more preventative services for all children, signalled in the document Every Child Matters (Chief Secretary to the Treasury 2003) and its related legislation the Children Act 2004 (Department for Education and Skills 2004), by the term 'safeguarding', meaning:

> ... the process of protecting children from abuse or neglect, preventing impairment of their health and development, and ensuring they are growing up in circumstances consistent with the provision of safe and effective care that enables children to have optimum life chances and enter adulthood successfully.
> (Department for Children, School and Families 2010: 27)

Rather than focusing only on protecting children from abuse, this new safeguarding agenda is more holistic and broad-ranging in its remit. It covers all issues that have the potential to disrupt a child's health and development, regardless of their cause, leading to criticisms that the role of the state is becoming broader, more interventionist and regulatory, resulting in the emergence of a 'preventive-surveillance state' (Parton 2008: 166).

The Children Act 2004 also made clear that all sectors of society, including sport, are responsible for safeguarding children. For example, sports organizations are urged to follow 'appropriate codes of practice for staff, particularly sports coaches' (Department for Children, School and Families 2010: 49), including creating child protection officers and establishing procedures for reporting child welfare concerns. Indeed, the most recent guidance reiterates that voluntary and private sector organizations, including those in sport, should have a range of safeguarding measures in place and that staff must be aware of how to report concerns (Department for Education 2013).

Nevertheless, while recent government policies have tended to be framed around 'safeguarding children' (Parton 2006), recent high-profile cases of child abuse in England – the physical abuse case involving Baby P,[1] the sex abuse scandal involving the Catholic Church,[2] historic sexual abuse allegations against celebrity Sir Jimmy Savile[3] and allegations of sexual abuse in some of the country's most successful music schools[4] – have again put the term 'child protection' at the core of governmental concerns. Currently, then, the terms 'safeguarding' and 'child protection' are often used alongside one another, and while there is an acknowledged interest in proactively promoting children's welfare and positive development (safeguarding), the central tenet of legislation remains on protecting children from harm caused by abuse, predominantly sexual abuse (child protection) (Parton 2012).

A further important development in child welfare came in an amendment to the Sexual Offences Act 2003, which introduced the offence of abuse of trust. While the age of consent for sexual relations in England is 16, this Act made it a criminal offence 'for a person aged 18 or over to engage in sexual activity with, or directed towards, a person under that age if he is in a position of trust in relation to that person' (Home Office 1999). The law defines specific roles and settings where even apparently consensual sexual activity between a young person aged 16 or 17 and those in positions of trust, responsibility or authority constitutes a criminal offence. Crucially for sport, while settings such as educational institutions, residential care homes, hospitals and youth offender institutions are all named, the definition of 'position of trust' excludes roles and settings in sport, although coaches would be covered by this legislation if they were employed by and working within a school (CPSU 2011). However, as there is currently no offence of abuse of trust legislation specifically relating to sport, the only way sports governing bodies can deal with this issue is as a poor practice disciplinary matter.

Safeguarding and child protection developments in sport

Until the late 1990s, sports organizations in England were excluded from child welfare legislation, in part because the traditional autonomy of the sports sector made the government reluctant to intervene (Houlihan 1997). This has resulted in 'a legacy of traditionalism and resistance to change' (Brackenridge 2001: 10), including making sport slower than other institutions to adopt social reforms for child welfare. The Hickson case was a wake-up call for sport. The case cost the Amateur Swimming Association (ASA) around £1 million in lost sponsorship (Bringer 2002) and prompted a 'moral panic' (Cohen 1972) around child sexual abuse in sport that drove national governing bodies (NGBs) and external sports agencies to act. There was considerable resistance from inside sport, however, with NGBs initially denying abuse in sport was a significant issue (Boocock 2012). Rather than understanding abuse as facilitated and hidden by the cultural norms of sport (Brackenridge 2001), officials insisted it was caused by the incursion into sport by predatory paedophiles intent on gaining access to children. Tellingly, this is despite Hickson himself not matching this profile – Hickson was a former competitive swimmer, had moved into coaching when his swimming career ended and was a well-qualified and respected coach with a wife and child (Williams 2003).

Following Hickson's arrest, a series of other cases of child athletes being sexually abused by their coaches emerged in football, gymnastics, karate, diving and horse riding. In response, and following pressure from some sport stakeholders – sports development officers, athletes' parents, researchers – in 2000 Sport England, the agency responsible for funding affiliated NGBs, teamed up with the UK's largest children's charity, the National Society for the Prevention of Cruelty to Children

(NSPCC), to convene a Child Protection in Sport Task Force. The group produced an action plan for child protection in sport and led to the creation in 2001 of the Child Protection in Sport Unit (CPSU), the first government-backed agency with responsibility for safeguarding and child protection in sport. The CPSU began implementing the action plan through the development of sports-related resources and offering NGBs advice, training and support on welfare issues from child protection procedures to whistleblowing, codes of conduct and inclusion. The same year a Sport England audit revealed serious gaps in NGBs' systems for dealing with abuse cases (CPSU 2010). To address this, Sport England began linking NGB funding to the implementation of child protection policies and by 2002 all state-funded NGBs had such a policy in place (Boocock 2002). This is clearly a positive step for protecting children in sport and research in football, rugby league and swimming suggests most members welcome the introduction of such policies although there is some doubt about the impact in practice (Hartill and Prescott 2007; Independent Football Commission 2005; Lang 2009). Importantly, however, these requirements are only for NGBs funded by Sport England, of which there are currently around 125 (Sport England 2013b); for other NGBs there are no such requirements and it is unknown what, if any, measures they have in place to safeguard the welfare of their young participants.

The Standards

In 2003 the CPSU introduced a set of standards for child protection for NGBs to work towards as a condition of funding, called the Standards for Safeguarding and Protecting Children in Sport (CPSU 2003, 2006a), and shortly after published a national strategy for safeguarding and child protection in sport (CPSU 2006b). The Standards, which reflect requirements in the Children Acts 1989 and 2004, focus on protecting children from, and managing cases of, abuse, but they also cover broader safeguarding concerns, for example encouraging strategies to promote equity (CPSU 2006a). Crucially, the efficacy of this development has yet to be explored. According to the CPSU, 85 of 95 publicly funded sports agencies have achieved the Advanced Level of the Standards. However, some NGBs are thought to have closed their junior sections or opted to forgo funding rather than comply (Brackenridge 2008).

Amongst other things, the Standards require NGBs to have designated staff in charge of safeguarding and child protection. Clubs have a Club Welfare Officer (CWO) (sometimes known as the Club Protection Officer) and NGBs have a national safeguarding lead officer (LO), who champions safeguarding and child protection and manages cases of abuse referred to them from clubs. Those in these roles are crucial to children's welfare in sport, yet many lack expertise in child welfare issues, and some have multiple responsibilities, acting as CWO or LO while also having other duties. To support NGBs in managing safeguarding and child protection concerns, in 2013 an independent National Safeguarding Panel for Sport (NSP) was established. The NSP, which includes solicitors and professionals from social work and the police, conducts safeguarding and abuse investigations for NGBs and acts as an arbitrator in serious safeguarding disciplinary cases (CPSU 2013).

While Sport England has provided the CPSU with £1 million in funding over two years to develop and embed safeguarding and child protection in sport (Sport England 2013a), NGBs are not required to set aside a minimum amount for this in the way they do for other operating costs, such as coaching. Consequently, NGBs have different budgets for safeguarding and child protection, dependent on their size and, in some cases, the value attributed to the area by senior management. Many LOs and CWOs, especially those in smaller NGBs, are volunteers, which raises questions about the efficacy of the roles and the value placed on safeguarding among NGB senior staff. Meanwhile, CWOs say other staff do not take their role seriously and that safeguarding and child protection is not prioritized in clubs and, in some instances, not publicized to club members (Hartill and Prescott 2007; Lang 2009). In addition, some NGBs struggle to find people to take on CWO and LO roles, perhaps due to the specialist nature of the role and the workload involved.

The Standards also introduced criminal background checks for individuals working with children in sport, bringing sport in line with the Police Act 1997 which required criminal history checks on anyone working with vulnerable groups, including children. Checks are processed through the Disclosure and Barring Service (DBS) (introduced in 2013 to replace the Criminal Records Bureau) and search the applicant's spent and unspent convictions as well as serious cautions, reprimands and final warnings. Whilst the DBS is very new, background checking in one form or another has been in place since 2002, despite criticisms that it fails to identify first-time offenders and does not prevent future offending; a DBS check, for example, would not have flagged Paul Hickson as a potential abuser. There is also anecdotal evidence that some sports clubs are not vetting staff as required (see for example Margeson 2012) and concern that background vetting deters volunteers and puts financial and resource pressure on sports clubs (Kay et al. 2008).

Education forms another key strand of the CPSU Standards. All sports staff must undergo safeguarding and child protection awareness training every three years. The CPSU, some NGBs and sports coaching organizations (such as sports coach UK) offer their own face-to-face safeguarding and protecting children workshops, with refresher courses often taking place online. However, there is a trend for some NGBs to move such training online to cut costs, in some cases for all members (as with, for example, the British Canoe Union) and in other cases only for members who do not have close contact with children (as with, for example, Badminton England and England Hockey). While some coaches complain attendance at such courses is both expensive and time consuming, especially for volunteers not wanting a career in coaching (Lang 2009), education is recognized as the most efficient way of enacting change. The concern about moving safeguarding and child protection training wholly online is that this approach is less engaging (Schmeeckle 2003) and may make it easier for stereotypical views about child abuse and child abusers to go unchallenged.

The post-Standards framework

For NGBs who have achieved the Standards, the CPSU introduced the Sports Safeguarding Framework (CPSU 2012) in 2012 to further develop and embed NGBs' safeguarding and child protection strategies. The Framework, which like the Standards is linked to receiving funding, requires NGBs to audit their current position against four stages – forming, developing, embedding or continually improving – and create an action plan of how to improve. In addition, most recently the CPSU devised a set of International Standards for Safeguarding and Protecting Children in Sport in conjunction with international children's charities and sport for development organizations (Ruuska 2013). These International Standards are being piloted in several sports organizations worldwide in 2013–14 ahead of being rolled out internationally.

Research

In the decades since Hickson's imprisonment, research has failed to keep pace with the considerable developments in the law, policy and practice of safeguarding and child protection in sport. Around 88 per cent of 5–15-year-olds take part in sport (Department for Culture, Media and Sport 2013) yet there is currently no data on the prevalence of abuse and neglect in sport in England. The information is difficult to come by as neither Sport England nor the CPSU require NGBs to keep records, and NGBs are reluctant to release the information due to concerns about reputational damage and the financial cost of potential litigation. The most relevant information to date comes from a study of university students reflecting on their experiences in sport as children (Alexander et al. 2011). While participating in sport was a positive experience for most, 75 per cent of young people reported experiencing emotionally harmful treatment, 24 per cent reported experiencing physical harm, 29 per cent reported experiencing sexual harassment and 3 per cent reported experiencing sexual harm, including rape. The figures were similar for male and females. Fellow athletes were the most common perpetrators, followed by coaches.

As with policy developments, sexual abuse has tended to be the focus of other research in England. Studies have developed our understanding of which athletes are most vulnerable to sexual abuse, with Brackenridge (1997) suggesting that those at or just before puberty and who have low self-esteem, friendship difficulties, a poor family bond and who look up to their coaches as role models are most at risk. Research by Hartill (2011) has attempted to develop Brackenridge's theoretical arguments on sexual abuse in sport through an application of Pierre Bourdieu's sociological concepts to the experiences of sexually abused boys in sport.

But while concerns over abuse in sport and wider society have resulted in improved legislative and policy protections for children in England, an unintended consequence of such developments has been increased public anxiety about false accusations of abuse. Studies suggest coaches and other adults working with children in sport are afraid of being accused of abuse and are consequently distancing themselves from athletes (Lang 2010, 2014). This is a worrying development given that coaches, like all adults, have a responsibility for safeguarding athletes and are well placed to spot physical and emotional symptoms of abuse.

Researchers in England have also been among the first to consider emotional abuse in sport. Gervis and Dunn (2004) found that of 12 elite child athletes across six sports, all had experienced emotional abuse or behaviour from coaches that had threatened their emotional well-being. Similarly, a study of professional youth footballers found that intimidation and abuse, both verbal and physical, is used by managers to exert control over players, socializing them into 'what is often an abusive and violent workplace' (Kelly and Waddington 2006: 149).

Other research has begun to investigate the culture of modern sport and its implications for the safeguarding of young athletes more broadly. For example, questions have been raised about training methods in swimming and football, where early specialization and intensive training place young athletes at risk of injury, mental and physical 'burnout' and emotional harm (Lang and Light 2010; Green 2007). Similarly, studies have identified how normalized coaching practices serve to control athletes, rendering them more vulnerable to abuse and to accepting training regimes that risk their physical and emotional health (Lang 2010). Such behaviours, while normalized in sport, would not be tolerated in other realms and suggest that children's welfare is a secondary concern to the production of successful performers. For this reason, studies have suggested the culture and structure of modern sport is not conducive to implementing child welfare initiatives (Tomlinson and Yorganci 1997).

Conclusion and future directions

England has undoubtedly been at the centre of events in the field of safeguarding and child protection in sport, both in research and policy development. It is also clear that similar debates have been conducted within other countries, such as the Netherlands and Germany (see Chapters 4 and 5), within a similar period. What is missing, particularly from the English approach, is a robust evaluation of the policies which have been implemented and the impact they have had (see Chapter 19). Early research into the implementation of child protection policy indicated some resistance to its imposition upon sport: a 'sledgehammer to crack a nut' (Hartill and Prescott 2007: 244). Arguably, safeguarding is far from embedded within much of English sport and resistance to its tenets within sports governance, as well as the coaching fraternity, continues (Piper et al. 2013). As the new safeguarding framework is implemented, it will be interesting to see how these tensions are addressed and to what extent they can be resolved.

Notes

1   Seventeen-month-old baby Peter Connelly died in London after suffering more than 50 injuries over an eight-month period, during which he was repeatedly seen by welfare

professionals. The child's mother, her boyfriend and a third man were convicted in 2009 of causing or allowing the death of a child. The case, which came to be known as the Baby P case, gained notoriety and led to a review of child protection services.

2 In the late 2000s, allegations surfaced of widespread sexual abuse by members of the Roman Catholic Church in the UK, Ireland and elsewhere in Europe and North America.

3 Sir Jimmy Savile was a well-known TV presenter, charity fundraiser and celebrity, and is now considered 'one of the UK's most prolific known sexual offenders' (Gray and Watt 2013: 24). In 2012, one year after his death, police began investigating historic abuse by the star following allegations of sexual abuse and rape by Savile in the 1970s. He is suspected of numerous offences against some 450 children and adults, predominantly sexual in nature, between 1955 and 2009.

4 In 2013, the former director of the Cheetham School of Music in Manchester, north west England, was convicted of indecently assaulting a pupil more than 30 years earlier. Other staff at the school have also been arrested and the police are investigating what lawyers called 'habitual indecent assault' at the school (BBC 2013).

References

Alexander, K., Stafford, A. and Lewis, R. (2011) *The Experiences of Children Participating in Organized Sport in the UK*, Edinburgh: University of Edinburgh/ NSPCC.

Brackenridge, C. H. (1997) 'He owned me basically: women's experience of sexual abuse in sport', *International Review for the Sociology of Sport,* 32: 115–30.

— (2001) Spoilsports: understanding and preventing sexual exploitation in sport, London: Routledge.

Brackenridge, C. (2008) *'Coach-swimmer interaction: traps, pitfalls and how to avoid them'*, paper presented at the 16th FINA World Sports Medicine Congress, Manchester, Apri.

Boocock, S. (2002) The Child Protection in Sport Unit, in C. H. Brackenridge and K. Fasting (eds) *Sexual Harassment and Abuse in Sport: international research and policy perspectives*, London: Whiting and Birch.

— (2012) The United Kingdom's Child Protection in Sport Unit, in C. Brackenridge, T. Kay and D. Rhind (eds) *Sport, Children's Rights and Violence Prevention: a sourcebook on global issues and local programmes*, London: Brunel University Press.

Bringer, J. (2002) *'Swimming coaches' perceptions and the development of role conflict and role ambiguity'*, unpublished PhD thesis, Cheltenham and Gloucester College of Higher Education.

British Broadcasting Corporation (2013) *Cheetham School of Music: more sex abuse claims*. Online. Available HTTP: <www.bbc.co.uk/news/uk-england-manchester-21411241> (accessed 1 July 2013).

Chief Secretary to the Treasury (2003) *Every Child Matters*, London: Chief Secretary to the Treasury.

Child Protection in Sport Unit (2003) *Standards for Safeguarding and Protecting Children in Sport*, 1st edn, Leicester: CPSU.

— (2006a) *Standards for Safeguarding Children in Sport*, 2nd edn, Leicester: CPSU.

— (2006b) *Strategy for Safeguarding Children and Young People in Sport*. Online. Available HTTP: <www.thanet.gov.uk/pdf/The%20Safeguarding%20Children%20 in%20Sport%20Strategy%202006–2012.pdf> (accessed 19 July 2013).

— (2010) *'The Child Protection in Sport Unit'*, paper presented at the European Sport for Development and Peace International Working Group, Brussels, Belgium, December.

— (2011) *CPSU Briefing: abuse of positions of trust within sport.* Online. Available HTTP: <www.wru.co.uk/downloads/Abuse_of_positions_of_trust_within_sport_wdf81074. pdf> (accessed 1 July 2013).

— (2012) *The Framework for Maintaining and Embedding Safeguarding for Children in and Through Sport.* Online. Available HTTP: <thecpsu.org.uk/resource-library/2013/ the-framework-for-maintaining-and-embedding-safeguarding-for-children-in-and-through-sport> (accessed 12 July 2013).

Child Protection in Sport Unit (Spring 2013) *Relay: the Child Protection in Sport Unit newsletter.* Online. Available HTTP: <www.thecpsu.org.uk/resource-library/2013/ relay-issue-23/> (accessed 17 July 2013).

Cohen, S. (1972) *Folk Devils and Moral Panics*, London: MacGibbon and Kee.

Department for Children, School and Families (2010) *Working Together to Safeguard Children: a guide to inter-agency working to safeguard and promote the welfare of children*, London: Department for Children, School and Families.

Department for Culture, Media and Sport (2013) *Taking Part October 2011 to September 2012: supplementary child report.* Online. Available HTTP: <www.gov.uk/government/ publications/taking-part-october-2011–to-september-2012–supplementary-child-report--2> (accessed 28 June 2013).

Department for Education (2013) *Working Together to Safeguard Children: a guide to inter-agency working to safeguard and promote the welfare of children*, London: Department for Education.

Department for Education and Skills (2004) *The Children Act 2004*, London: Department for Education and Skills.

Department of Health (1989) *The Children Act 1989*, London: Department of Health.

Department of Health and Social Security (1988) *Working Together: a guide for inter-agency co-operation for the protection of children*, London: Department of Health and Social Security.

Gervis, M. and Dunn, N. (2004) 'The emotional abuse of elite child athletes by their coaches', *Child Abuse Review*, 13: 215–23.

Gray, D. and Watt, P. (2013) *Giving Victims a Voice: joint report into sexual allegations made against Jimmy Savile*, London: Metropolitan Police Service/NSPCC.

Green, C. (2007) *Football Clubs Stand Accused.* Online. Available HTTP: <www.bbc. co.uk/programmes/b007l0dk> (accessed 18 July 2013).

Hartill, M. (2011) *'The sexual subjection of boys in organized male sport'*, unpublished PhD thesis, Edge Hill University.

Hartill, M. and Prescott, P. (2007) 'Serious business or 'any other business? Safeguarding and child protection policy in British rugby league', *Child Abuse Review*, 16: 237–51.

Home Office (1999) *Caring for Young People and the Vulnerable? Guidance for preventing abuse of trust*, London: Home Office.

Houlihan, B. (1997) *Sport, Policy and Politics: a comparative analysis*, London: Routledge.

Independent Football Commission (2005) *Report on Child Protection in Football*, Stockton-on-Tees: Independent Football Commission.

Kay, T., Armour, K., Cushion, C., Thorpe, R. and Pielichaty, H. (2008) *Are We Missing the Coach for 2012?* Online. Available HTTP: <www.thelssa.co.uk/lssa/sportnation/ AreWeMissingTheCoachFor2012.pdf> (accessed 18 June 2008).

Kelly, S. and Waddington, I. (2006) 'Abuse, intimidation and violence as aspects of managerial control in professional soccer in Britain and Ireland', *International Review for the Sociology of Sport*, 41: 147–64.

Lang, M. (2009) '*Swimming in the Panopticon: an ethnographic exploration of good practice and child protection in competitive youth swimming*', unpublished PhD thesis, Leeds Metropolitan University.

— (2010) 'Surveillance and conformity in competitive youth swimming', *Sport, Education and Society*, 12: 19–37.

Lang, M. (2014) 'Touchy subject: A Foucauldian analysis of coaches' perceptions of adult-child touch in youth swimming', *Sociology of Sport Journal*.

Lang, M. and Light, R. (2010) 'Interpreting and implementing the Long Term Athlete Development Model English swimming coaches' views on the (swimming) LTAD in practice', *International Journal of Sports Science and Coaching*, 5: 388–402.

Margeson, A. (2012) *Cheshire Cricket Club: club welfare officer's newsletter October 2012*. Online. Available HTTP: <www.cheshirecricketboard.co.uk/County%20Welfare%20 Officer's%20Newsletter.pdf> (accessed 22 July 2013).

Parton, N. (1991) *Governing the Family: child care, child protection and the state*, London: Macmillan.

Parton, N (2001) 'Risk and professional judgement', in L. Cull and J. Roche (eds) The Law and Social Work, Basingstoke: Palgrave Macmillan.

Parton, N. (2006) *Safeguarding Childhood: early intervention and surveillance in a late modern society*, Basingstoke: Palgrave Macmillan.

— (2008) 'The "Change for Children" programme in England: towards the preventive-surveillance state', *Journal of Law and Society*, 35: 166–87.

— (2012) 'The Munro review of child protection: an appraisal', *Children and Society*, 26: 150–62.

Piper, H., Garratt, D. and Taylor, B. (2013) 'Child abuse, child protection, and defensive "touch" in PE teaching and sports coaching', *Sport, Education and Society*, 18: 583–98.

Ruuska, M. (4 June 2013) *Move to Protect Children in Sport*. Online. Available HTTP: <www.sportanddev.org/en/connect/myinfo.cfm?5705/Move-to-protect-children-in-sport> (accessed 15 July 2013).

Schmeeckle, J. M. (2003) 'Online training: an evaluation of the effectiveness and efficiency of training law enforcement personnel over the internet', *Journal of Science Education and Technology*, 12: 205–60.

Sport England (10 January 2013) *Sport England Boosts Funding to Allow More Young People to Enjoy Sport in a Safe Environment*. Online. Available HTTP: <www. sportengland.org/media-centre/news/2013/january/10/sport-england-boosts-funding-to-help-more-young-people-enjoy-sport-in-a-safe-environment> (accessed 15 July 2013).

Sport England (4 June 2013) *Sporting Activities and Governing Bodies Recognized by the Sports Councils*. Online. Available HTTP: <www.sportengland.org/our-work/national-work/national-governing-bodies/sports-that-we-recognise> (accessed 15 July 2013).

Tomlinson, A. and Yorganci, I. (1997) 'Male coach-female athlete relations: gender and power relations in competitive sport', *Journal of Sport and Social Issues*, 21: 134–55.

Williams, Y. (2003) 'Government-sponsored professional sports coaches and the need for better child protection', *Entertainment Law*, 2: 55–84.

2 Safeguarding children and young people in Danish sport

Jan Toftegaard-Støckel

Almost two decades after media revelations about child sexual abuse in Danish sport first appeared, measures to safeguard and protect children and young people in sport remain underdeveloped and terms such as 'child protection' and 'safeguarding' are still not an active part of the vocabulary of organized sport in the country. Meanwhile, what limited political and legislative progress has been made in this area has tended to be driven by concerns about child sexual abuse; other forms of abuse and wider issues relating to safeguarding athletes and promoting children's rights have yet to be addressed. This chapter charts how sport and the government in Denmark were first alerted to concerns about children's welfare in sport, and how sport has moved from initial denial to begrudging acceptance of the problem. It discusses specific regulations enacted to protect athletes from abuse both in and beyond sport, primarily to safeguard against sexual abuse, and highlights the limitations of such approaches before touching on potential signs of change in the culture of Danish sport.

Early revelations of abuse in sport

In 1995, a broadcast journalist called Charlotte Melin lifted the lid on child sexual abuse in Danish sport in a TV documentary that revealed coaches from various sports had been convicted for sexually abusing child athletes (TV2 Sporten 1995). The documentary also featured an interview with then-chief executive officer (CEO) of the National Olympic Committee and National Sport Confederation of Denmark (NOC*DIF), the largest sports organization in the country with 61 affiliated sports federations and more than 9,000 clubs (NOC*DIF 2012). During the interview, the CEO Kai Holm was asked the age at which it was legal for an athlete to engage in sexual relations with a coach, and his view on sports' responsibility for preventing child sexual abuse. Holm's response was indicative of the ignorance about child abuse in sport at the time and of the organizational denial that would plague sport for a further decade – he argued that sexual abuse was not widespread in Danish sport and that coach-athlete sexual relations were acceptable so long as the athlete was 15 years old, the age of consent in the country. In fact, as Melin pointed out, Danish law states that, 'Anyone who has sexual intercourse with a person under the age of 18 years old and who is the responsible caretaker or educator of that person is punishable by up to four years in prison' (penal code §223).

At the time of the documentary, previous attention had focused almost entirely on familial abuse and there were no policies on children's welfare or child protection in Danish sport, no research on the extent of the problem and no formal system for managing or recording allegations. Yet despite the documentary highlighting the welfare of children and young people in sport for the first time, sports authorities remained reluctant to act.

In the years following the documentary, researchers also began to show an interest in sexual abuse in sport. Studies by Nielsen (Nielsen 1998b) of student athletes and of elite youth coaches estimated that 2 per cent and 5 per cent of respondents, respectively, had experienced such abuse. When these findings were presented at a meeting of representatives from NOC*DIF, the response was, again, anger, disbelief and denial; the figures, the representatives argued, were low, *only* between 2 and 5 per cent. There was a similar response at a second meeting of more than 50 attendees from various sport associations – a CEO from the karate association even stormed out when martial arts were mentioned as a discipline in which multiple allegations of sexual abuse had been made (Nielsen 1998a). Meanwhile, research into how sport organizations managed allegations of child abuse in these early days found most cases were handled informally and behind closed doors so as to avoid negative publicity (Nielsen 2004).

Then in 1999, I began working with two broadcast journalists on another more in-depth documentary on sexual abuse in sport. The documentary, titled *The Dangerous Volunteers*, was broadcast in early 2000 (DR TV 1 2000) and centred on how the culture of sport at the time – with no restrictions on who could coach and no knowledge about child protection at sports clubs – allowed coaches convicted of sexual abuse to continue to offend against athletes. It also identified how members of a group calling itself the Danish Paedophile Association openly discussed gaining access to children through sport clubs. The documentary provoked intense public and political debate and sparked calls for the sports authorities to stop convicted sex offenders from entering sport. Meanwhile, the Danish Paedophile Association was disbanded following a Ministry of Justice investigation into its activities. It has, however, since re-emerged online.

The emergence of policy change

At the grass-roots level, sports clubs found it difficult to accept the findings from the *Dangerous Volunteers* documentary. At the time, most clubs had little understanding or experience of child abuse or its prevention and found it difficult to acknowledge that, in the cosy environment of their club, where everyone knew everyone else, they could be harbouring a sex offender. However, key sport stakeholders started to take note. In response to the *Dangerous Volunteers* documentary, in early 2001 NOC*DIF began recommending their affiliated members check the criminal history of coaches at the recruitment stage, although this remained only a recommendation. DGI, however, argued that criminal background checks did not offer sufficient protection for young athletes and called for clubs to devise their own course of action instead. In addition, both organizations suggested affiliated clubs begin debating the kinds of behaviour they deemed acceptable, although no further information on how to structure these discussions was provided and there were no checks to see if clubs followed this advice.

As recently as the early 2000s, then, Denmark's two largest sports organizations were only willing to go as far as *recommend* rather than *require* action to prevent known sex offenders from entering sport. This is particularly surprising given that Denmark has signed up to several international resolutions aimed at safeguarding children's welfare in sport and beyond. For example, Denmark ratified the United Nation's Convention on the Rights of the Child (UNCRC) (United Nations General Assembly 1989) in 1991, and signed up to the Council of Europe's (CoE) Resolution on the Prevention of Sexual Harassment and Abuse of Women, Young People and Children in Sport (CoE 2000), both of which make it clear that concrete action rather than recommendations are needed to protect children from abuse. The CoE's resolution states that governments should develop a national prevention policy with an associated action plan for implementation of the resolution recommendations (CoE 2000), while the UNCRC requires the implementation of child protection prevention strategies and mechanisms to identify, report, refer, treat and follow-up violations against children' (United Nations General Assembly 1989).

To date, the protections offered by these frameworks remain unfulfilled. For example, none of the CoE's requirements, including the development of national policies against abuse in sport and the creation of clear ethical guidelines for coaches, trainers and managers, have yet been implemented by national sport organizations in Denmark. Equally, the government did not create a national plan of action as required under the UNCRC until 2003, and even then the plan contained no fixed deadlines for the implementation of measures within it. Similarly, although the International Olympic Committee (IOC) issued a statement on sexual harassment and abuse in sport in 1997 (IOC 2007), neither NOC*DIF nor DGI have ever officially acknowledged this.

In the year following the *Dangerous Volunteers* documentary, NOC*DIF produced a brochure with the title 'The unheard abuse' (Bundgaard et al. 2000) advising sports federations and clubs on sexual abuse prevention and how to implement procedures for managing allegations of abuse. DGI followed suit, producing guidelines for coaches on good practice when working with youth athletes. However while well intentioned, many of the 10 guidelines seem to be more concerned with protecting coaches from allegations of abuse than with protecting athletes and are based on traditional heterosexist understandings of abuse as perpetrated by males on female victims. For example, guideline five tells coaches never to enter the changing rooms of athletes of the opposite sex, while guideline eight states that coaches, to avoid rumours and wrongful allegations, should self-report to a club member if they have behaved in a way that could be misinterpreted.

The next major landmark came in 2007, when the elite sport organization Team Denmark published a code of ethics for competitive sports in cooperation with NOC*DIF (DIF-TeamDenmark 2006). The code, which has separate sections for coaches, athletes and spectators, provides a baseline for acceptable behaviour in sport but also notes that due to cultural differences between sports, organizations and clubs also need to develop specific ethical 'norms' applicable to their discipline. However, the code is not without its problems. For example, in the section on athlete behaviour, it says athletes should avoid intimate contact with their coach, a suggestion that places the burden of responsibility on the athlete rather than the more powerful coach. It also fails to recognize that most sexual abuse appears, on the surface, consensual as it takes place following an often lengthy period of grooming during which the perpetrator gains the victim's trust and, ultimately, their apparent complicity in the abuse (Brackenridge 2001).

The children certificate background checks

In early 2001, following the broadcast of the *Dangerous Volunteers* documentary, NOC*DIF began recommending their affiliated members complete criminal record background checks on new coaches. Since then background checks have been a highly contested issue, debated in the Danish parliament and within voluntary organizations. Discussions have focused on two main concerns: (1) that criminal history background checks create a false sense of security for organizations using them as they only identify coaches with previous convictions for sexual offences, and (2) that because they contain information about all convictions, not just those related to sexual crimes, their content is often irrelevant for child protection purposes and may breach an individuals' right to privacy (Bindslev 2003; Ritzau 2005).

In response to these concerns, a new law was enacted in June 2005 to create a so-called Children's Certificate (Ministry of Culture 2005). The Children's Certificate differs from the traditional criminal record background check in two ways. First, it only records an individual's convictions for sexual offenses against children under the age of 15, which is the age of consent in Denmark. Second, it continues to display this information until individuals reach 80 years old, even after such convictions are spent. Children's Certificate checks apply to anyone working with children under 15 years old for more than three months or on at least three occasions during a three-month period, or for coaches, instructors, team leaders or teachers who work with children for more than two weeks continuously. Individuals apply through the organization they are working for and the service is free. Following a Children's Certificate check, it is up to the organization to decide whether an individual should be permitted to work with children, and organizations can be held liable for neglect of duty if they fail to carry out a Children's Certificate check or permit someone with a conviction for a sexual offence against a child under the age of 15 to work with children (Ministry of Culture 2005).

DIF*NOC estimates that more than 90 per cent of sport clubs comply with the requirements about obtaining mandatory Children's Certificates (Rasmussen and Dam 2008). As of 2013, a total of 59 Children's Certificate checks or approximately 0.1 per cent of all checks returned have been positive, that is, they have shown a conviction for a sexual crime against a child under the age of 15. Despite this low number, the former minister of cultural affairs with responsibility for sports, Brian Mikkelsen, spoke out in favour of the checks in 2008, arguing that, 'the law has proved its worth. Think of the 59 [positive records], even though these people knew they were going to be checked. Imagine how many this has deterred. We've saved a lot of children' (Rasmussen and Dam 2008).

Children's Certificate checks have several limitations, however. First, individuals working with young people between 15 and 17 years old are not required to undertake the checks. In other words, an individual applying to work as a coach with 15–17–year-olds could have been convicted of a sexual offense against a child under the age of 15 but no one would know because they are not required to undertake a check. This contradicts other areas of Danish law such as penal codes §§ 223–4, which acknowledge the rights of young people up to 18 years old to be protected. It also leaves young people under the age of 18 vulnerable to abuse by people in positions of authority over them. All young people are vulnerable to abuse by people in positions of power over them, such as coaches, teachers, etc. (Brackenridge 2001). In a hearing held by the Parliament Committee of Culture (2004), the association of boarding school teachers suggested the age limit on Children's Certificates be raised to 18 years old. However, the ministry did not make reference to this point in its summary of the hearing so the issue was not raised again.

In addition, the checks do not record convictions for sexual crimes against young people aged 16 and 17 years old; only traditional criminal history background checks, which are still required for other positions with children, such as before becoming a teacher or a foster parent, record this information. Moreover, Children's Certificate checks only apply to new staff; individuals currently working with children under the age of 15 are exempt. DIF*NOC and others expressed concern about this exemption during discussions about the new law and argued the requirement should apply to all staff. However, the employer's association the Confederation of Danish Employers opposed this suggestion, arguing it would interfere with existing employment contracts and DIF*NOC's concerns were overruled (Folketinget 2004).

Finally, there is concern that although Children's Certificate checks are now a requirement, some clubs are still not using them while others rely on them too much, treating them as the *only* prevention measure available rather than one of many tools. There is, for example, anecdotal evidence that some club members are in denial that abuse could occur in their club; a sports magazine reported in 2005 that a club leader at a small gymnastics club argued Children's Certificate checks were unnecessary as, 'it [abuse] could not happen in the club because everybody knows each other well and they would definitely notice if something was wrong' (Wachs 2005). Meanwhile, one empirical study of 2,000 Danish youth sport clubs affiliated to either DIF*NOC or DGI found that only 2 per cent of clubs would ask for a Children's Certificate check when recruiting someone they knew well to a coaching post, while only 5 per cent said they would ask for such checks if employing a coach from a different club (Toftegaard-Støckel 2012).

Aside from the introduction of Children's Certificates, other developments also have implications for sport. In 2003 the Ministry of Social Affairs issued a national action plan for the prevention of sexual abuse and exploitation (Ministry of Social Affairs 2003). The plan comprised somewhat vague recommendations for raising awareness of sexual abuse among the public and in schools, and for developing more coordinated procedures for managing sexual abuse within municipal social service departments. There were, however, no fixed deadlines for achieving these recommendations, and the ministry acknowledged that legislative change was required to ensure the establishment of coherent policies and procedures. To this end, the following year an amendment was made to the Danish Law on Social Services and the Law on Legal Protection and Administration in Social Matters. It stated that:

> Municipalities must develop a coherent [child protection] policy for children that aims to ensure coherence between general [abuse] prevention work and activities targeted at children and young people in need of special support. The policy must be in writing, cohesive and adopted by the municipal council and published.
>
> (Folketinget 2004)

Yet despite this change and the opportunity it presents to offer protection to children, an evaluation in 2011 found that only two out of three municipalities had met these new requirements (SISO 2011). There remains, then, little evidence that these plans have become integrated with child protection measures at local level.

Concluding thoughts

Since revelations about child sexual abuse in sport emerged in the mid-1990s, Danish sports organizations have moved from initial denial of the problem to general acceptance that sexual abuse can and does occur in sport. In doing so, sports organizations have argued they are meeting their obligations and deflected media criticism of corporate negligence.

However almost two decades on, the terms 'safeguarding' and 'child protection' are still not an active part of the vocabulary of organized sport in Denmark, and sport's own guidelines and advice have done little to raise awareness of the issue. Sport still refuses to acknowledge the extent of the problem and instead continues to argue that the sexual abuse of athletes in sport is a relatively rare occurrence and that the scale of sport's response should reflect this. Consequently, neither of Denmark's major sports organizations has mandated that its members implement strategies to protect children and young people, and implementing codes of ethics for coaches, athletes and parents remains optional. In addition, sports organizations have yet to fulfil their international obligations under the UNCRC (United Nations General Assembly 1989) or the CoE (2000), and neither DIF*NOC nor DGI have ever officially acknowledged the IOC's Consensus Statement on Sexual Harassment and Abuse in Sport.

There are myriad reasons why sports organizations are so reluctant to engage in prevention work, and it is too simplistic to argue they are simply ignorant or afraid of engaging with the issue. From my experience, the two Danish national sport organizations have an interest in preventing sexual and other forms of abuse in sport, but they are afraid implementing child protection measures would deter volunteers, as it has been suggested occurs elsewhere (Nichols and Taylor 2010).

There are signs organizational change may be on its way, however. While the age of consent for sex is 15 years old in Denmark, penal code §223 raises this to 18 years old in relationships of unequal power, for example where a coach is in a position of authority over an athlete. In 2012 50–year-old Niels Thomassen, a well-respected karate coach and president of his local club, was prosecuted under this law for abusing a 17–year-old athlete in his club and was sentenced to 60 days in prison (Vestesen 2012). After the verdict NOC*DIF banned Thomassen from youth coaching for ten years (Jespersen 2013). After serving his sentence, Thomassen returned to the club to resume his position as club president. On several occasions in early 2013, the club board was challenged by newspaper journalists about the controversial decision of having a convicted sex abuser within the club. The club board argued this was acceptable because the board was acting within the NOC*DIF rules and because Thomassen was not coaching, although as he was the only club member qualified to instruct to black belt level, concerns were raised whether this was genuinely the case. The athlete Thomassen had abused spoke out at her anger at her abuser being allowed to return to the club, saying she no longer felt able to train there and arguing the decision to allow Thomassen to return constituted a further violation of her rights, this time by the system. The case caused a media storm and prompted the karate association to exclude Thomassen's club from the national karate association. The case in karate marked a new more athlete-centered approach to athlete welfare and offers some hope that sport organizations are beginning to accept their responsibility for safeguarding young people in sport.

References

Bindslev, M. W. (2003) 'Criminal background checks are no guarantee for avoiding perpetrators', *Politiken*, Copenhagen: 28 August.

Brackenridge, C. (2001) *Spoilsports: understanding and preventing sexual exploitation in sport*, London: Routledge.

Bundgaard, T., Darfeldt, J., Carlsen, H., Skotte, A. and Juhl, K. (2000) *The Unheard Abuse*, Copenhagen: NOC and National Sports Confederation of Denmark.

Council of Europe (2000) *Resolution on the Prevention of Sexual Harassment and Abuse of Women, Young People and Children in Sport (3/2000)*. Online. Available HTTP: <www.coe.int/t/dg4/sport/resources/texts/spres00.3_en.asp> (accessed 1 June 2013).

Culture Committee (2004) *Hearing and Commented Overview of Hearing Statements from the Minister of Culture*. Online. Available HTTP: <www.folketinget.dk> (accessed 1 June 2013).

DIF/Team Denmark (2006) *Ethical Codes for Competitive Sport in Denmark*. Online. Available HTTP: <www.vark.dk/pdf/diverse/etisk_kodeks.pdf> (accessed 13 May 2013).

DR TV 1 (2000) *The Dangerous Volunteers*. Online. Available HTTP: <www.dr.dk/Bonanza/serie/Dokumentar/dokumentar.htm> (accessed 30 September 2013).

Folketinget (2004) *Law about Change to the Law on Social Service and the Law on Legal Rights and Public Administration of Social Services*. Online. Available HTTP: <www.retsinformation.dk/forms/r0710.aspx?id=132411> (accessed 1 June 2013).

IOC (International Olympic Committee) (2007) *Consensus Statement on Sexual Harassment and Abuse in Sport*, Lausanne: International Olympic Committee.

Jespersen, L. (2013) 'Convicted karate coach: my path is clean', *Ekstra Bladet*, 19–20.

Ministry of Culture (2005) *Law on the Acquisition of Criminal Records for Hiring Personnel*. Online. Available HTTP: <www.retsinformation.dk/Forms/r0710.aspx?id=11961> (accessed 11 November 2013).

Ministry of Social Affairs (2003) *Plan of Action for the Fight Against Child Sexual Abuse*, Copenhagen: Ministry of Social Affairs.

National Olympic Committee and National Sport Confederation of Denmark (2012) *Member Statistics*. Online. Available HTTP: <www.dif.dk> (accessed 28 October 2013).

Nichols, G. and Taylor, P. (2010) 'The balance of benefit and burden? The impact of child protection legislation on volunteers in Scottish sports clubs', *European Sport Management Quarterly*, 1, 31–47.

Nielsen, J. T. (1998a) '*Secrets of the coach*', unpublished thesis, University of Copenhagen.

—— (1998b) *Sexual Abuse in Sport: data presentation at the House of Sport for the National Olympic Committee and National Sport Confederation of Denmark*, unpublished note, December 1998.

—— (2004) '*The Illusion of sport intimacy*', unpublished thesis, University of Copenhagen.

Rasmussen, H. and Dam, C. (2008) 'Law on paedophilia has passed its test', *DR Sporten*. Online. Available HTTP: <www.dr.dk/Sporten/Oevrig_sport/2008/01/16/202420.htm> (accessed 16 January 2008).

Ritzau (2005) 'Disagreement in the party Venstre about children's certificates', *Berlingske*. Online. Available HTTP: <www.b.dk/danmark/uenighed-i-venstre-om-boerneattester> (accessed 11 November 2013).

SISO (2011) 'Local districts plans and procedures on the prevention of child sexual abuse', *Servicestyrelsen*. Online. Available HTTP:<www.google.com/url?sa=t&rct=j&q=&e src=s&frm=1&source=web&cd=2&ved=0CCsQFjAB&url=http%3A%2F%2Fwww.ocialstyrelsen.dk%2Fsiso%2Ffiler%2FKommunernesberedskaberSISOkortlgning.pdf&ei=5SOGUqmJMomOtQbGxoGICw&usg=AFQjCNHGmPNdRfpbTzivG58sdvj rM9TlBw> (accessed 1 June 2013).

Sports Confederation of Denmark (2012) *Organization of Sports*. Online. Available HTTP: <www.dif.dk/en/om_dif/oranisation-s-of-s-sports#content-top> (accessed 30 September 2013).

Toftegaard-Støckel, J. (2012) 'The risk of sexual abuse in the Danish club system', in C. Brackenridge (ed.) *Sport, Children's Rights and Violence Prevention: a sourcebook on global issues and local programmes*, London: UNICEF.

TV2 Sporten (1995) *Sport Special*, TV documentary directed by Melin, C.

United Nations General Assembly (1989) *The United Nations Convention on the Rights of the Child*, Geneva: United Nations.

Vestesen, B. (2012) *Punishment: Coach Sentenced to Jail for Sex with 17 Year Old*. Online. Available HTTP: <www.fyens.dk/article/20281:Odense--Straf--Traener-faar-faengsel-for-sex-med-17–aarig-elev 17–02– 2013> (accessed 11 November 2013).

Wachs, J. (2005) 'Children's certificates – what do we do now?', *Udspil DGI*. Online. Available HTTP: <www.e-pages.dk/dgi/54/30> (assessed 16 November 2013).

3   Preventing child maltreatment and transgressive behaviour in Flemish sport

Tine Vertommen, Jan Tolleneer, Guillaume Maebe and Kristine De Martelaer

In 2004 Marc Dutroux was convicted of kidnapping, torturing and sexually abusing six girls aged 8 to 19 years old, four of whom died (British Broadcasting Corporation 2004). The case sent shockwaves across Belgium and led to a reorganization of the country's law enforcement agencies. While the Dutroux case raised the public and political profile of sexual abuse in Belgium, at the time it had no impact on sport. It took disclosures in 2010 of widespread sexual abuse in the Catholic Church for pressure to mount to such an extent that sport began to act.

Child maltreatment and transgressive behaviour

Belgium is a federal state comprising three regions each with their own legal jurisdiction – the Brussels-Capital Region, the Flemish Region and the Walloon Region. The two largest regions are the Dutch-speaking region of Flanders in the north and the French-speaking region of Wallonia in the south. Sports federations are commonly split into a Flemish and a French-speaking section, each of which sits under a federal-level umbrella organization. Because sport is organized separately within each language community, policies can differ across communities. This chapter focuses on developments in child welfare in the Flanders region, which is home to approximately 60 per cent of the country's 11 million citizens.

A child is defined in Belgium as anyone under the age of 18, while the age of sexual consent is 16 years old. In children's services in Belgium, the term 'child maltreatment' is used. This is understood as incorporating five forms of maltreatment: physical abuse, physical neglect, sexual abuse, emotional abuse and emotional neglect. However, although the term 'child abuse' is central to this definition, it is not defined in the Belgian Penal Code. Rather, examples of behaviours constituting child abuse are provided within the Belgian Penal Code, such as the Act of 28 November (Ministry of Justice 2001), which legislates against: the rape and indecent assault of minors under the age of 16, juvenile prostitution of anyone below the age of 18, child pornography, sexual/genital mutilation, coercing indecent sexual behaviour, abduction, family abandonment, inflicting physical injury and deliberately withholding food and care (Vermeulen 2001). Notably, emotional abuse and neglect are not covered in this or other elements of the Belgian Penal Code, although these are recognized as child maltreatment within children's services.

In practice, then, understandings of child maltreatment among welfare practitioners are broader than strict legal definitions in the country and are more aligned with international definitions from the World Health Organization and the International Society for the Prevention of Child Abuse and Neglect, which defines child maltreatment as including:

> all forms of physical and/or emotional ill-treatment, sexual abuse, neglect, negligence and commercial or other exploitation, which results in actual or potential harm to the child's health, survival, development or dignity in the context of a relationship of responsibility, trust or power.
>
> (Butchart et al. 2006: 9)

The term 'transgressive behaviour' has also become popular recently among child welfare practitioners and policymakers. The term is useful as it incorporates a wide variety of maltreatment especially that not within a relationship of unequal power, and is therefore useful for classifying a wider range of behaviour, such as peer-on-peer violence. Sensoa, the Flemish Expertise Centre for Sexual Health, identifies sexual abuse as the most extreme form of transgressive behaviour, defined as 'intentional or unintentional, whereby no consent is given, and/or that is coerced, and/or whereby the victim is much younger or in a dependent relation to the perpetrator' (Frans and Franck 2010: 27).

Empirical research

Official statistics and scientific data on the number of child maltreatment cases are scarce in Belgium. Based on information from the public prosecutor, between 2008 and 2012 there were 54,001 prosecutions for physical child maltreatment, including child maltreatment and child abandonment – an average of 10,800 per year (Statistical Analysts of the Public Prosecutor 2013). The most recent figures incorporating sexual abuse date from 2004–2009 and show that an average of 9,401 prosecutions for 'sexual abuse and paedophilia' are brought each year in Belgium (Belgian Chamber of Representatives 2011), although more than half do not result in a conviction, mostly because of a lack of evidence or because the perpetrator is unknown. Criminal convictions for the sexual assault and rape of minors are significantly lower. Between 2008 and 2011, an average of 429 offenders per year were convicted of child rape (Service for Criminal Policy 2013), although these figures do not represent the number of sexually abused children as one perpetrator may have multiple victims.

In Flanders, Confidential Centres for Child Abuse and Neglect are responsible for managing allegations of child maltreatment. In 2005 some 6,534 children were referred to centres in the Flanders region for suspected maltreatment, while in 2012 the figure was 7,368 children, or approximately 5.6 children per 1,000 minors (Child and Family 2012). This increase can be attributed to growing vigilance over child maltreatment following high-profile sexual abuse awareness campaigns (Akers et al. 2011). Of course, these numbers only represent cases and children referred to an official agency, and some cases will not make it to such services.

One of the earliest studies into child maltreatment in Flanders explored the experiences of physical violence in the family among young people aged 10–18 years old in the region. It found that 1.3 per cent reported being beaten 'often' or 'almost always' by their mother, 1.4 per cent by their father and 0.6 per cent by both parents (Van den Bergh et al. 2003). These figures were probably an under estimate, however, as the study defined child maltreatment only in terms of physical abuse by a parent, only surveyed one child per family and only studied children within a limited age range.

Sexual maltreatment has received more empirical attention in Belgium. Bal and colleagues (2003) explored reports of sexual abuse among Belgian children aged 11–19. The results indicated that 10 per cent had experienced sexual abuse. Meanwhile, a 2010 study of 2,014 Belgian adults asked about experiences of unwanted sexual touching and sexual abuse as a child. In total, 9 per cent of women and 3 per cent of men said they had experienced these behaviour before they reached 18 years old (Pieters et al. 2010). A large-scale study of sexual health in Flanders, known as the Sexpert study, explored sexually transgressive behaviour in 1,731 respondents and found that 22 per cent of females and 11 per cent of males reported having experienced sexually transgressive behaviour ranging from unwanted sexual touching, being forced to watch pornographic content, and rape and attempted rape when they were children (Buysse et al. 2013).

There have also been studies on child maltreatment in sport, although the focus has been on sexually transgressive behaviours at the expense of other forms of maltreatment. Vanden Auweele et al. (2008) studied the experiences of unwanted sexual behaviours in sport among first-year female students at two Flemish universities between 2005 and 2007. Between 2 and 14 per cent of respondents reported what was defined as 'very serious unacceptable behaviour' from coaches, such as indecent exposure, being asked for sex in exchange for a reward or being touched sexually without their consent. Meanwhile, between 17 and 50 per cent of respondents reported experiencing what was termed 'serious unacceptable behaviour' from coaches, such as having their breasts or buttocks stared at or experiencing sexual comments. Although there were limitations with the study – there were significant differences in the response rate at the two universities, the study focused only on male coach behaviours towards female athletes, and the sample was not representative of the Flemish sport population – the results suggest female student athletes' experiences of unwanted sexual behaviour from coaches is common.

Research on this topic with children is limited due to the methodological and ethical challenges. One exception is a 2011 study by the Flemish Office of the Children's Rights Commissioner, a consultative body of the Flemish Parliament that handles complaints and provides advice to ensure compliance with children's rights regulation in Flanders. The study surveyed 1,925 Flemish students between

10–18 years old about their experiences of sexually transgressive behaviour at home, school and in their leisure activities, including sport. Of the 356 children who responded about experiences in sport, 10 per cent said they had experienced sexually transgressive behaviour at least once (Flemish Office of the Children's Rights Commissioner 2011) compared with 33 per cent and 3 per cent who experienced such behaviour at school and within youth organizations such as the Boy Scouts, respectively. Most reported peers as perpetrators.

Promoting ethics in sport

Until the mid-2000s, Belgian sport had paid little attention to children's welfare. This began to change in 2004. Experts from seven European countries worked with the Flemish branch of Panathlon International to draft the Panathlon Declaration on Ethics in Youth Sport (Panathlon International 2004). Panathlon International was founded in 1951 to promote positive values in youth sport and is now recognized by the International Olympic Committee (IOC) and the United Nations Children's Fund (Panathlon International 2012). The Panathlon Declaration on Ethics in Youth Sport is a charter that sports organizations can sign to show their commitment to upholding ethical values in youth sport (Panathlon International 2012). The declaration, which has been signed by hundreds of national and international sports organizations, emphasizes equity, fair play and ethics but does not explicitly mention child maltreatment, child abuse or other transgressive behaviour. This omission is intentional; because the declaration's focus was on accentuating the positive values of sport, its authors deliberately avoided mentioning child maltreatment to avoid deterring children and young people, their parents and sport sponsors from sport (Vanden Auweele 2004).

The Flanders government endorsed the Panathlon declaration in 2006 following a symposium organized by the Flemish Sports Federation and the Flemish branch of Panathlon International. Now around 55 per cent of Flemish youth sports clubs have a code of ethics, of which between 33 and 40 per cent endorse the Panathlon declaration (De Waegeneer and Willem 2013; Seghers et al. 2012). However, while the declaration marks a positive starting point for policy development on ethics in youth sport, there has been no evaluation of its impact and whether, and the extent to which, it influences practice remains unknown.

The theme of sports ethics promulgated by the Panathlon Declaration also influenced Flemish government legislation. The Medically and Ethically Justified Sports Practice Decree came into force in 2007 and was amended the following year. It promoted so-called 'ethically justified sports practice', which the Decree defined as 'the body of positive values and the relating preventative and curative measures, provisions and recommendations which everybody is to take into account to safeguard and promote the ethical dimension in sports' (Council of Europe 2009: 2). The Decree required sports federations to implement guidelines around at least one of six themes relating to ethical sports practice. Unsurprisingly, federations are more likely to select less sensitive thematic areas (Seghers et al. 2012). In 2011–2012 for example, 29 per cent of federations selected the theme of fair play, 28 per cent selected children's rights, 20 per cent solidarity, 9 per cent inclusion, 9 per cent physical and psychological integrity and 3 per cent respect for diversity (Vandenhoudt 2013).

Although these requirements have the potential to force sports organizations to take action on unethical behaviours, arguably the Decree does not go far enough. For example, it allows sports federations to select only one theme so they may ignore other ethical issues. Additionally, federations' compliance with the Decree is judged on their apparent commitment to implementing guidelines on their chosen theme rather than on concrete developments such as specific actions or actual achievements (Hendrickx 2007; Government of Flanders 2008). These limitations weaken the Decree's impact. To help federations meet the Decree's requirements, in 2009 the Flemish government funded the International Centre Ethics in Sports (ICES), an independent association of experts in sport ethics and physical education, to advise federations and, with the Flemish Sports Federation, develop workshops on ethical issues in sport (ICES 2010). However, funding was withdrawn the following year and federations were left to work towards meeting their legal requirements on their own.

Addressing child maltreatment in sport

While the topic of ethics in sport drove policy developments in the mid-2000s, concerns about child maltreatment in sport did not emerge for several more years. The issue came to prominence when in 2010 an inquiry was launched into allegations of widespread sexual abuse by members of the Roman Catholic clergy in Belgium (Belgian Chamber of Representatives 2011). During hearings at the Special Commission into the affair in 2011, the Belgian Olympic and Interfederal Committee (BOIC) and other sports organizations acknowledged they had no mechanisms in place for reporting or managing allegations of child maltreatment, despite having a legal responsibility to protect children. This caused outrage among the representatives and resulted in Flemish sport authorities being publically shamed for their inaction. Consequently, later that year BOIC organized a symposium on sexual abuse in sport, which led to a series of recommendations: (1) the creation of a central 'reporting point' for cases of maltreatment and abuse in and beyond sport; (2) the appointment of welfare officers in sport federations and clubs; (3) increased investment in coach education, specifically to help coaches understand how to manage allegations of maltreatment and abuse; and (4) developing a campaign to raise awareness of maltreatment and abuse among all stakeholders in sport (BOIC 2011). However, the recommendations stopped short of mandating criminal background checks for all adults in sport out of concern this would deter volunteers and would be too difficult to implement (BOIC 2011).

The Flemish Sports Council, the advisory body to the Flemish minister of sport, made similar recommendations. It suggested current routes for reporting alleged maltreatment be reorganized to create a central reporting point, with referrals of maltreatment in sport dealt with by experts with knowledge of the sports context (Flemish Sports Council 2011). The Flemish Sports Council also suggested the adoption of a zero-tolerance policy on all forms of transgressive behaviour in sport as well as the funding of research and a resource centre on maltreatment and transgressive behaviour in sport. Some of these recommendations, such as the development of a general helpline, an awareness raising campaign and the creation of a resource centre, were subsequently implemented. The Flemish government also commissioned ICES to manage a two-year project to 'provide expertise related to ethically justified sports practice, including issues of integrity, sexual abuse and violence' (Claus 2012: 1). The project involves four Flemish universities conducting research, the findings of which ICES translates into practical advice for policymakers and practitioners. ICES also supports sport federations by helping them develop policies and providing training on maltreatment and transgressive behaviour in sport.

In 2012, after the Parliamentary Commission's recommendations following disclosures of sexual abuse in the Catholic Church, a telephone helpline was established across the Flemish region where current and past victims of violence, abuse and maltreatment in all settings can report their experiences (Government of Flanders 2012). The helpline, which has the number 1712, refers callers to the appropriate services, be that the police, counselling or advocacy groups, welfare services or the judicial system. It also collates reports of the cases it receives, providing a valuable resource for future research. Flemish sport authorities refer those seeking advice to the helpline.

Around the same time, two organizations working in preventing sexually transgressive behaviour created a framework to fill a perceived gap in policy relating to educating young people about sexuality and sexual development (Frans and De Bruycker 2012a). Sensoa, the Flemish Expertise Centre for Sexual Health, and Child Focus, an organization that campaigns against child sexual exploitation, devised the Sexuality and Policy Framework to promote children's physical and sexual integrity, improve prevention and management policies and provide resources for organizations working with children on developing positive understandings of sexuality and sexual development. The framework was adapted for a sports context in 2012 (Frans and De Bruycker 2012b) and developed into a manual for sports clubs by ICES and the Flemish Sports Federation (Vandevivere et al. 2013).

The manual helps clubs implement policies to promote children's physical and sexual integrity and contains six tools to assist with this. One of the key tools is what is known as the flag system. The flag system has received praise from professionals in other youth settings for its usefulness in assessing sexual behaviour by, and involving, children (Frans and Franck 2010). It features 30 scenarios involving athletes, coaches and other sports leaders engaging in a variety of behaviours. Users assess each of the 30 scenarios according to six criteria: (1) consent, (2) equality, (3) free will, (4) age appropriateness, (5) context appropriateness and (6) self-respect. For each scenario, they present a coloured flag – from green for the least serious to black for the most serious. The aim is to raise awareness of physically or sexually transgressive behaviour and empower athletes to speak out about their experiences of such behaviour. An evaluation of the system is planned by the end of 2013 (Vertommen et al. 2013).

Concluding comments

Crucially, while the flag system and other developments discussed here represent important steps towards sport accepting responsibility for children's welfare, there is currently no evidence of the effectiveness of such initiatives. It is possible that sport stakeholders, many of whom are volunteers, will either be unaware of such initiatives or reluctant to take on the additional work required to implement them. Some in sport have already questioned whether it is sport's responsibility to educate young people on sexuality and sexual development or to 'solve other social problems' (Seghers et al. 2012: 86). It is the task of regional and national sports federations to stimulate support for such initiatives, and the success of this remains to be seen.

Robust evaluations of the initiatives mentioned here are now required. ICES is planning an evaluation of the measures it has helped develop, and it is crucial the outcomes of this and other research are publicized, including in education courses for sports professionals such as undergraduate and postgraduate degrees in Physical Education, to ensure they reach the widest possible sports audience.

Continued collaboration is also required between ICES and sport stakeholders, academics and child welfare experts. This should involve research on child maltreatment and transgressive behaviour in sport, the findings of which should be translated into advice for practitioners to ensure their practice is informed by evidence. While child sexual abuse created an impetus for recent policy actions, Flemish policymakers should not overlook other types of child maltreatment, such as peer-on-peer harassment or the unrealistic pressure often placed on youth athletes to perform. Finally, and importantly, in all future developments, the experiences and voices of children and young people themselves should be included.

We have found sport administrators keen to break the silence on maltreatment and transgressive behaviour in sport. That developments in this area were not prompted by high-profile cases of child abuse in sport in Belgium, as was the case in England and elsewhere (see Chapter 2), may be an advantage in this regard – it means policymakers had the opportunity to deliberately and proactively introduce protection and prevention measures that were developed in consultation with stakeholders, rather than as a result of intense public scrutiny.

References

Akers, A. Y., Holland, C. L. and Bost, J. (2011) 'Interventions to improve parental communication about sex: a systematic review', *Pediatrics*, 127: 494–510.

Bal, S., Van Oost, P., De Bourdeaudhuij, I. and Combrez, G. (2003) Avoidant coping as a mediator between self-reported sexual abuse and stress-related symptoms in adolescents, *Child Abuse and Neglect*, 27: 883–97.

Belgian Chamber of Representatives (2011) *Report Special Commission on the Handling of Sexual Abuse and Facts of Paedophilia in a Relationship of Authority in Particular Within the Church*. Online. Available HTTP: <www.dekamer.be/FLWB/PDF/53/0520/53K0520002.pdf> (accessed 3 September 2013).

Belgian Olympic and Interfederal Committee (BOIC) (2011) *Report Colloquium Sexual Abuse in Sport*. Online. Available HTTP: <www.olympic.be/Home/tabid/38/ctl/Details/mid/568/ItemID/1691/language/nl-NL/Default.aspx> (accessed 3 September 2013).

British Broadcasting Corporation (2004) *Profile: Marc Dutroux*. Online. Available HTTP: <www.news.bbc.co.uk/2/hi/europe/3522367.stm> (accessed 15 October 2013).

Butchart, A., Phinney Harvey, A. and Fürniss, T. (2006) *Preventing Child Maltreatment: a guide to taking action and generating evidence*, Geneva: World Health Organization.

Buysse, A., Caen, M., Dewaele, A., Enzlin, P., Lievens, J., T-Sjoen, G., Van Houtte, M. and Vermeersch, H. (eds) (2013) *Sexpert: sexual health in Flanders*, Gent: Academia Press.

Child and Family (2012) *The Child in Flanders*, Brussel: Kind en Gezin.

Claus, C. (2012) *General Call: providing expertise in the field of ethically justified sports practice, including the issues of integrity, sexual abuse and violence*, Brussels, unpublished document.

Council of Europe (2009) *13 July 2007 Flemish Parliament Act on Medically and Ethically Justified Sports Practice*. Online. Available HTTP: <www.coe.int/t/dg4/sport/doping/antidoping_database/Reports/2009/leg/LEG1–BEL-FLA_EN.pdf> (accessed 10 October 2013).

De Waegeneer, E. and Willem, A. (2013) *Codes of Ethics in Flemish Sport Clubs and the Role of the Coach*. Online. Available HTTP: <www.bloso.be/vlaamsetrainersschool/Pages/VTSredactioneel.aspx> (accessed 3 September 2013).

Flemish Office of the Children's Rights Commissioner (2011) *Violence Reported and Counted: recommendations for the prevention of violence towards children and youth*, Brussels: Kinderrechtencommissariaat.

Flemish Sports Council (2011) *Child Abuse in Sport: advice of the Flemish Sports Council*. Online. Available HTTP: <www.cjsm.vlaanderen.be/raadcjsm/SR_sport/> (accessed 15 October 2013).

Frans, E. and De Bruycker, A. (2012a) *Framework on Physical and Sexual Integrity and Policy in Sport: quality, prevention and reaction in your organization*. Online. Available HTTP: <www.cjsm.be/gezondsporten/nieuws/raamwerk-lichamelijke-en-seksuele-integriteit> (accessed 3 September 2013).

—— (2012b) *Framework on Sexuality and Policy: quality, prevention and reaction in your organization*. Available HTTP: <www.childfocus.be/uploads/Preventie/RaamwerkSeksualiteit.pdf> (accessed 3 September 2013).

Frans, E. and Franck, T. (2010) *The Flag System: talking to children and youths about sex and sexually transgressive behaviour*, Antwerp: Garant.

Government of Flanders (2008) *Decision of the Flemish Government Amending the Decision of the Government of Flanders of 31 May 2002 on the Recognition and Funding Conditions of the Flemish Sports Federations, the Umbrella Organization and the Organizations for Leisure Sports and the Decision of the Government of Flanders of 20 June 2008 Implementing the Decree of 13 July 2007 on Medically Justified Sports Practice*. Online. Available HTTP: <www.ejustice.just.fgov.be/cgi_loi/change_lg.pl?language=nl&la=N&cn=2008121942&table_name=wet> (accessed 3 September 2013).

—— (2012) *One Central Reporting Point for Violence and Abuse*. Online. Available HTTP: http://www4wvg.vlaanderen.be/wvg/welzijnensamenleving/1712/Paginas/default.aspx (accessed 15 October 2013).

Hendrickx, F. (2007) *Ethically Justified Sports: a starting note for policy*, KU Leuven, unpublished note.

International Centre Ethics in Sports (ICES) (2010) *Past Activities*. Online. Available HTTP:<www.ethicsandsport.com/nl/c/archivecalendar/voorbije-activiteiten>(accessed 15 October 2013).

Ministry of Justice (2001) *Act of 28 November 2000 on the Criminal Protection of Minors*. Online. Available HTTP: <www.ejustice.just.fgov.be/cgi_loi/change_lg.pl?language=n l&la=N&cn=2000112835&table_name=wet> (accessed 15 October 2013).

Panathlon International (2004) *Panathlon Declaration on Ethics in Youth Sport*. Online. Available HTTP: <www.panathlon.net> (accessed 3 September 2013).

Panathlon International (2012) *Panathlon International Mission*. Online. Available HTTP: <www.panathlon.net/organizzazione_leggi.asp?lingua=inglese&tabellaMenuOrizzont ale=filosofia&id_menuorizzontale=4&id_sottomenuorizzontale=0&id=1> (accessed 9 October 2013).

Pieters, J., Italiano, P., Offermans, A. M. and Hellemans, S. (2010) *The Experiences of Women and Men with Psychological, Physical and Sexual Violence*, Brussels: Institute for the Equality of Women and Men.

Seghers, J., Scheerder, J., Boen, F., Thibaut, E. and Meganck, J. (2012) *Medically and Ethically Justified Sport: promoting physical, psychological and social wellbeing among youths in Flemish sports clubs*, Leuven: KU Leuven.

Service for Criminal Policy (2013) '*Conviction Statistics Concerning Sexual Abuse of Minors',* unpublished document.

Statistical Analysts of the Public Prosecutor (2013) '*Number of Child Maltreatment Affairs Referred to the Public Prosecutor in 2008–2012',* unpublished document.

Van den Bergh, B., Ackaert, L. and De Rycke, L. (eds) (2003) *Youth: communication, child rearing and welfare in context – 10–18–year-olds, parents and teachers questioned*, Antwerp and Apeldoorn: Garant.

Vanden Auweele, Y. (ed.) (2004) *Ethics in Youth Sport: analyses and recommendations*, Tielt: Lannoo Campus.

Vanden Auweele, Y., Opdenacker, J., Vertommen, T., Boen, F., Van Niekerk, L., De Martelaer, K. and De Cuyper, B. (2008) 'Unwanted sexual experiences in sport: perceptions and reported prevalence among Flemish female student-athletes', *International Journal of Sport and Exercise Psychology*, 6: 354–65.

Vandenhoudt, J. (2013) '*Overview of the Themes and Guidelines on Ethically Responsible Sport Submitted by the Recognized Sport Federations',* unpublished document.

Vandevivere, L., Cools, S., Vandenhoudt, J., Frans, E., Vertommen, T., De Martelaer, K., Geenen, M. and De Bruycker, A. (2013) *Physical and Sexual Integrity: a manual for sport clubs*. Online. Available HTTP: <www.ethicsandsport.com/nl/x/432/handleiding> (accessed 3 September 2013).

Vermeulen, G. (ed.) (2001) *Criminal Protection of Minors*, Antwerpen and Apeldoorn: Maklu.

Vertommen, T., De Martelaer, K. and Vandevivere, L. (2013) '*Towards a prevention policy against sexual harassment and abuse in Flemish sport*', paper presented at the European Sociological Association, Turin, August.

4 (Sexual) intimidation in sport in the Netherlands

Nicolette Schipper-van Veldhoven, Tine Vertommen and Lieke Vloet

The Netherlands Olympic Committee and Netherlands Sport Confederation (NOC*NSF) is the umbrella body for organized sports in the Netherlands and includes 76 national sport federations which incorporate around 26,000 sport clubs with 4.8 million members (almost one-third of the population). In total, 65 per cent of 12–17-year-olds in the Netherlands are members of a sports club; for children between 6 and 11 years old, as many as 66 per cent are members and one-third of Dutch people are in some way involved in organized sport (Tiessen-Raaphorst et al. 2010).

In 1996 a group of three female Olympians officially accused their former elite judo coach, Peter Ooms, of sexual abuse between 1987 and 1993. Whilst similar cases had previously been brought to public attention, the status of those involved generated high-profile media coverage. In addition to being fired and suspended for three years by the disciplinary commission of the Netherlands Judo Union, Ooms was found guilty by a criminal court. He was given a four-month suspended sentence (Trouw 1997). Some witnesses claimed that the judo organization had known about Ooms' inappropriate behaviour for years. The response of the sport world was unprecedented. Not only were the coach's actions publicly rejected but there were also calls for measures to prevent further sexual intimidation. This resulted in the development of a *specific* policy to prevent sexual intimidation within sport, called 'Project Seksuele Intimidatie' (NOC*NSF 1996).

Whilst much of the concern in the Netherlands has been about children and young people's welfare in sport, the main focus of attention – sexual intimidation – means that the discussion is not confined only to children. NOC*NSF refers to 'sexual intimidation' as a collective term that includes sexual harassment and abuse.

Sexual intimidation in sport: the Dutch response

Prior to the Ooms case, attempts by Dutch sport federations to create a policy to prevent sexual intimidation for their particular sport had failed due to a lack of support within the general assembly of NOC*NSF. Some federations did not accept that sexual intimidation occurred within their organization whilst others expressed concerns that raising the issue would create the impression that there was a particular problem with their sport or club. However, in November 1996, following the Ooms case, the NOC*NSF 'Policy to prevent and combat sexual intimidation in sport' was adopted at the general assembly (in which all sport federations are represented) (NOC*NSF 1996).

One of the first steps was to develop a code of conduct for all coaches in sport (NOC*NSF 1997). This code derives from the International Olympic Committee's Code of Ethics (see IOC 2013) and was developed in discussion with more than 100 representatives from Dutch sport organizations. A key feature of the code was the formulation of an operational definition of 'seksuele intimidatie' (sexual intimidation/sexual violence): 'any form of sexual behaviour or sexual advances, in a verbal, nonverbal or physical sense, intentional or unintentional, experienced by the person as unwanted or forced' (Weber et al. 2006: 1). In this definition, the NOC*NSF uses the term 'sexual intimidation' as a collective term that includes sexual harassment and sexual abuse. The final code of conduct for coaches was accepted by the Dutch general assembly on 4 November 1997, and from this point sport federations committed themselves to taking appropriate measures to prevent and manage cases of sexual intimidation in sport. Since January 2013, all federations have been obliged to include the code of conduct for coaches in their regulations, including stating the penalties for non-compliance and the procedure for judging penalties.

A research-based approach

Supported by the (development of the) 1996 code of conduct for coaches, simultaneously the NOC*NSF began a nationwide programme against sexual intimidation in sport. The programme had two main goals: first, to develop a structure that assists sport federations in dealing with an incident of sexual intimidation; and second, to develop a prevention programme for eliminating the permissive, bystander culture within sport that came to light in the judo case (Moget and Weber 2008).

To create a strong foundation for this new policy, the NOC*NSF commissioned research into the risk factors for sexual intimidation in sport (Cense 1997) and used the findings from this study to underpin its policy development. Drawing on the theory of international expert David Finkelhor (1986), the researchers identified clusters of risk factors associated with (1) the coach, (2) the sport context, and (3) the athlete (Cense and Brackenridge 2001). Based on this risk-factor model, the NOC*NSF and sport federations formulated a series of preventative policy instruments (discussed in the next section). The study also provided direction for the formulation of several general strategies to prevent sexual intimidation in sport based around reducing risk, changing the *laissez-faire* culture and empowering athletes.

Policy implementation

A range of resources were also developed to assist the federations in establishing both prevention measures (to reduce the likelihood of abuse occurring) and repressive (or responsive) measures (so they are able to respond appropriately when it does). Resources have been established in three areas (Weber et al. 2006):

Communication and education

Discussing sexual intimidation is not common in Dutch society in general but perhaps even less so in sport. There remains a great deal of reluctance around confronting these issues in sport, especially within sport organizations that rely heavily on volunteers. To open up communication channels, the NOC*NSF offers sport federations different tools: a) freely available (digital and printed) brochures for different target groups to raise awareness about ways of preventing sexual intimidation and approaches to handling incidents or allegations; b) a website exclusively dedicated to the topic of sexual intimidation (NOC*NSF 2012a) that includes a biographical documentary featuring two athlete 'survivors' of severe sexual intimidation perpetrated by their coaches; and c) coach education films that feature a particular ethical dilemma relevant to sport.

Handling allegations

In 1997, the NOC*NSF telephone helpline for sexual intimidation in sport (Hulplijn voor seksuele intimidatie in de sport) was established. This emergency telephone service serves as a point of contact for reporting incidents of sexual intimidation in sport and provides advice and support for victims, their parents and those accused of sexual intimidation. In addition, the helpline offers advice to sport organizations facing an incident of sexual intimidation. When it was first set up, the helpline was hosted by two national general helpline organizations (SOS Telephonic Hotline and Child Line) but it soon became apparent that a more sport-specific approach was required to encourage reporting and ensure incidents were adequately followed up. Consequently, since 2002 the helpline has been independently hosted by the NOC*NSF, and at the time of writing the helpline employs 18 counsellors. The helpline refers callers to a pool of specially trained counsellors or 'national confidential agents' for advice and support, and there are specific counselling teams for victims and also for the accused.

Furthermore, in 2005 a special court of arbitration for sport called the Instituut Sportrechtspraak (Institute for Sports Law) which includes separate divisions for doping and sexual intimidation was founded to handle allegations of sexual intimidation on behalf of sport federations. Since January 2013, NOC*NSF has also provided a standard protocol for each federation that is unaffiliated to the national institute for disciplinary law in sport. This protocol makes the inclusion of the code of conduct for coaches, mentioned above, mandatory and, since

November 2011, each federation has also had to have at least one named individual who can be contacted in confidence about concerns over sexual intimidation.

Prevention: Policy implementation

Guidelines on how to implement the prevention policy have also been created by the NOC*NSF in cooperation with the lobby group the Netherlands Organization for Volunteers (Vereniging Nederlandse Organisaties Vrijwilligerswerk, NOV). These require organizations to adhere to seven steps in relation to sexual intimidation. In summary, organizations must: (1) highlight the issue; (2) evaluate/audit their own situation; (3 and 4) endorse and implement relevant policies and codes; (5) appoint and train local officers to lead on the issue and to serve as a first point of contact; (6) pay special attention to their recruitment processes and guidelines; and (7) inform and involve all stakeholders on the policy. A digital toolkit for sport clubs is available to help them establish their own prevention policy with specific information about all seven steps and supplemented with an incident protocol (see NOC*NSF 2012b).

In addition, the general assembly decided on 13 May 2008 to consider supplementing the prevention policy on sexual intimidation with two additional measures: a criminal background check for sport leaders; and the establishment of a 'black list' or registration system for people convicted of sexual intimidation by a sport federation's disciplinary committee. The registration system was approved by the general assembly in 2011 and came into effect at the beginning of 2013. The automated system, approved by the Data Protection Authority and funded by the Ministry of Health, Welfare and Sport, registers offenders after a legal or disciplinary conviction in sport for the duration of the penalty.

Most sports clubs are run by volunteers in 'close-knit' environments where there is little perceived need for criminal record checks. To stimulate action, a pilot project was started across three sectors, including sport. Since 2012 a criminal record check can now be requested by administrators of a sports club for sport volunteers, without charge, from the Ministry of Justice. It can also be requested free of charge outside sport, by voluntary sector organizations working with young people (below 20 years of age) and for those working with people with learning difficulties and disabilities.

The sport sector was also represented in a national prevention project called 'In Safe Hands' (NOV 2010) which is made available to all volunteers in the Netherlands, including organizations working in the mental health care, Scouting and children's camps sector. This project consists of: a toolkit called 'Sexual Intimidation: A Training Module for Social Safety Advisers'; the development of a national registration system for offenders, based on the one used in sport and with the hope of integrating both systems; and the development of disciplinary law for volunteers (NOC*NSF 2012b). For coaches, there is also a coach education module called 'Etiquette for Coaches' that is delivered through online and face-to-face workshops and aims to help club coaches recognize, prevent and manage sexual intimidation (NOC*NSF 2012c).

Support

The support any prevention programme receives from affiliated federations is essential to its effectiveness, as is the degree to which sport federations are willing to drive the programme forward at the local level. Although sport federations initially expressed concerns about sexual intimidation, after a decade of prevention policy the NOC*NSF were concerned that instead of being proactive owners of the policy and its associated resources, the sports federations were merely passive consumers, in most cases accessing it only after an incident had occurred (Weber et al. 2006). To ensure the policy's effective use, strategic action was taken by communicating directly with local sport clubs and the tools originally devised for sport federations were rewritten to make them more accessible for local sport clubs.

Research on sexual intimidation in sport

Although the sexual intimidation programme started with a study on risk factors, the focus of the NOC*NSF and sport federations was on developing and implementing policy. Research on the prevalence of sexual intimidation and research into the use of sexual intimidation policy instruments in sport emerged years later. As elsewhere, the focus for sport federations and the NOC*NSF was the prevention of sexual intimidation through the development and implementation of policy. Yet initially the incidence of sexual intimidation in sport remained unknown, leading the NOC*NSF to begin collecting some data in 2005 through the first quantitative study of its kind in the country. Unfortunately, this study failed to attract sufficient respondents. However, using incident registration forms from the database established through the NOC*NSF 'helpline', the NOC*NSF commissioned research on the available data from the database between 2001 and 2010 (see Vertommen 2011; Vertommen et al. 2013). The study found that incidents reported to the helpline came from 46 different sports and that victims were most often children and young people, while the identified perpetrators were most often adult coaches. In 68 per cent of incidents, sexually harassing behaviour occurred over a long period of time.

A more recent study (Serkei et al. 2012) into the sexual intimidation prevention tools implemented by the NOC*NSF, found that only 11 per cent of the 382 sport clubs surveyed were familiar with the helpline and only 3 per cent had used the helpline, mainly for policy advice rather than for support relating to actual incidents. In addition, almost 70 per cent per cent of clubs had no policy to prevent sexual harassment and 66 per cent had no policy to deal with complaints. The main reason given for the lack of policy on sexual intimidation was the assumption that it does not occur in their particular environment. For example: 'we never had an incident. Worrying parents is not our intention so we don't need a policy', 'there is no risk because we are a small club', 'we have other concerns such as maintaining our members' (Serkei et al. 2012: 24).

While the best known elements of the strategy were the code of conduct (27 per cent) and the confidential agents (22 per cent), in total three-quarters of all the respondents were unfamiliar with the NOC*NSF policy instruments, although the elements that respondents were aware of were considered effective and meaningful. This suggests it is important to regularly remind stakeholders about existing policy instruments. After more than a decade of reactive and proactive prevention policy, only a small part of the Dutch sporting family is aware of, and familiar with, the instruments.

(Un)wanted behaviour in Dutch sport

After considering developments in relation to sexual intimidation in more depth, we now set out the broader political and policy context in the Netherlands in relation to ethical issues in sport.

In 2006, in response to media attention regarding verbal and physical aggression against soccer referees, and a study which showed that six out of ten referees in amateur soccer were confronted with aggression (Hetterscheid 2006), the Dutch Ministry of Health, Welfare and Sport commissioned a meta-review of available data on popular sport[1] (Tiessen-Raaphorst and Breedveld 2007). In addition 12 sports organizations/experts were interviewed. The study found that *inter alia* 12 per cent of sport participants report that they have witnessed physical aggression in sport during the past three years, and one in eight referees reported that they 'sometimes' or 'frequently' felt unsafe whilst refereeing matches. Sport was given a figurative 'yellow card'.

Such developments perhaps indicate a reduced public tolerance for unethical conduct within sport. A follow-up study (Tiessen-Raaphorst et al. 2008) on amateur sport wanted to know whether undesirable practices in sport occur more often or are more serious than in other sectors of society. The study administered questionnaires to 2357 sports participants aged 12 years and older and 589 sports club administrators. Findings revealed that one in five Dutch citizens aged 12 years or over had experienced undesirable behaviour in sport, either as a victim or witness. Of these, 11 per cent were themselves victims, which is equivalent to 2 per cent of the Dutch population as a whole. Witnesses and victims most often report verbal aggression (12 per cent), physical aggression (6 per cent) and sexual harassment (1 per cent). Men and young people (12–19 years of age) experience one or more forms of undesirable behaviour more often than women and older people (aged 65+). Footballers (43 per cent) and participants in other team sports (29 per cent) experience undesirable behaviour more often than participants in other sports (19 per cent).

Furthermore, half the directors of sport clubs have received complaints of unwanted behaviour, usually relating to verbal aggression (27 per cent), vandalism (22 per cent) and theft (18 per cent) (Tiessen-Raaphorst et al. 2008). In more than half the cases, those responsible for the behaviour were spoken to, given a warning or the police were notified. For 13 per cent of the victims and witnesses, the experience was sufficiently serious to lead them to quit sport (Tiessen-

Raaphorst et al. 2008). Overall, the study found that 26 per cent of the sample had experienced unwanted behaviour in sport (aged 12 years and older) (Tiessen-Raaphorst et al. 2008). However, they also experienced undesirable behaviour in *all* sectors of Dutch society such as in school (23 per cent); on public transport (23 per cent); at work (30 per cent); within the night-time economy (53 per cent); and on the streets (73 per cent). As the Dutch sport environment is not experienced as more unsafe compared to other sectors, 'the yellow card' awarded in the earlier research (Tiessen-Raaphorst and Breedveld 2007) was withdrawn. However, the research revealed much about sport in the Netherlands and has led to significant policy changes.

Based on the recommendations made by the Social and Cultural Planning Office (an interdepartmental scientific institute) (Tiessen-Raaphorst et al. 2008), the NOC*NSF and 11 sport federations funded by the Dutch Ministry of Health, Welfare and Sport initiated a programme called Together for Sportsmanship and Respect. The aim was to improve behaviour on and around sport fields through campaigns directed at: (1) highlighting wanted behaviour within sport clubs; (2) creating action plans for participating sport federations; (3) analysing rules within the game and codes of conduct; and (4) improving public perception of the importance of promoting respectful behaviour in sport. The programme was monitored between 2009 and 2011 and the results revealed that, despite the campaigns, unwanted behaviour in sport did not decrease and incident rates remained unchanged from those in 2007. However, it was found that within the clubs participating in the programme, board members were more aware of ethical issues in sport and were more active in addressing them (Lucassen and van Kalmthout 2012).

An integrated programme

In 2011 the policy 'A Safe Sport Environment: 2011–2016' was published (Ministry of Health, Welfare and Sport 2011). This new policy, developed by the NOC*NSF, adopts a zero-tolerance approach to harassment, abuse and other forms of unethical conduct across all sports. This policy is based on the previous programmes 'Sexual Intimidation' and 'Together for Sportsmanship and Respect'. However, on 4 December 2012, during the first year of the programme, an assistant referee, Richard van de Nieuwenhuizen, was beaten to death by teenage boys at an amateur football game. In response to the public outcry that followed, the new policy was scaled-up and further investment made in this initiative with greater involvement from central government. Crucially, this integrated programme will be monitored and evaluated by NOC*NSF, the sport federations and a research institute. Outcomes will be reported annually to the Minister of Sport so that impact can be gauged.

Concluding comments

Moral outrage and indignation often prompts social change. However, long-term change requires stakeholders to believe in and take ownership of policy. Perhaps the first step in this regard is to conquer the taboo around (sexual) intimidation in sport. Sport federations and sport clubs in the Netherlands are, arguably, yet to fully acknowledge the fact that (sexual) intimidation and other undesirable behaviour does happen within *their* organizations. Whilst the NOC*NSF is pleased and proud to lead on this issue, more pro-active engagement by the wider sports community in the Netherlands is now required.

Note

1 The term 'popular sport' is used here to mean recreational sport in both organized and non-organized forms, including competitive sport. The term does not include professional and elite sport.

References

Cense, M. (1997) *Red Card or Carte Blanche: risk factors for sexual harassment and abuse in sport*, Arnhem: Transact and NOC*NSF.
Cense, M. and Brackenridge, C. H. (2001) 'Temporal and developmental risk factors for sexual harassment and abuse in sport', *European Physical Education Review*, 7: 61–79.
Finkelhor, D. (ed.) (1986) *A Sourcebook on Child Sexual Abuse*, London: Sage.
Hetterscheid, E. (2006) *Violence Against Referees in the Amateur Branch of the Soccer Federation*, Apeldoorn: Stichting Sto(m)p.
International Olympic Committee (2013) *Ethics*. Online. Available HTTP: <www.olympic.org/Documents/Commissions_PDFfiles/Ethics/code-ethique-interactif_en_2013.pdf> (accessed 16 September 2013).
Lucassen, J. and Kalmthout, J. van (2012) *You Can Only See It, If You Know It: final results monitoring programme 'Together for Sportsmanship and Respect'*, Utrecht: Mulier Instituut.
Ministry of Health, Welfare and Sport (2011) *Towards a Safer Sport Climate*. Online. Available HTTP: <www.rijksoverheid.nl/nieuws/2011/04/22/schippers-komt-met-breed-gedragen-actieplan-voor-veiliger-sportklimaat.html> (accessed 9 May 2013).
Moget, P. and Weber, M. (2006) 'NOC*NSF project sexual harassment in sport in the Netherlands: 1996–2006', *Tijdschrift voor Lichamelijke Opvoeding* (Journal of Physical Education), 3: 14–26.
— (2008) *Vulnerabilities, Pitfalls and Chances in Sports: a decade of social security policies in Dutch sports*, CD-Rom Panathlon International.
Moget, P., Weber, M. and Veldhoven, N. van (2012) 'Sexual harassment and abuse in Dutch sports: a short review of early research and policy by the NOC*NSF', in C. H. Brackenridge, T. Kay and D. Rhind (eds) *Sport, Children's Rights and Violence Prevention: a sourcebook on global issues and local programmes*, Uxbridge: Brunel University Press.
Netherlands Olympic Committee*Netherlands Sports Confederations (1996) *Sexual Intimidation*. Online. Available HTTP: <http://nocnsf.nl/nocnsf.nl/olympische-droom/

sport-en-maatschappij/seksuele-intimidatie/seksuele-intimidatie> (accessed 9 May 2013).

— (1997) *Code of Conduct for the Prevention of Sexual Harassment in Sport*, Arnhem: NOC*NSF.

— (2012a) *Sexual Intimidation*. Online. Available HTTP: <www.watisjouwgrens.nl> (accessed 9 May 2013).

— (2012b) *Sexual Intimidation: information for administrators of sports clubs*. Online. Available HTTP: <http://nocnsf.nl/cms/showpage.aspx?id=12243> (accessed 16 September 2013).

— (2012c) *Sexual Intimidation: information for coaches*. Online. Available HTTP: <http://nocnsf.nl/cms/showpage.aspx?id=1504> (accessed 16 September 2013).

NOV-Vereniging Nederlandse Organisaties Vrijwilligerswerk (2010) *In Safe Hands*. Online. Available HTTP: <www.inveiligehanden.nl> (accessed 9 May 2013).

Serkei, B., Goes, A. and de Groot, N. (2012) *From Blind Confidence to Responsible Policy: usefulness and effectiveness of NOC*NSF policy instruments sexual harassment*, Utrecht: MOVISIE.

Tiessen-Raaphorst, A. and Breedveld, K. (2007) *A Yellow Card for Sport: a quick scan of desirable and undesirable practices in and around grassroot sports*. Den Haag: Sociaal Cultureel Planbureau.

Tiessen-Raaphorst, A., Lucassen, J., Dool, R. van den and Kalmthout, J. van (2008) *Little Crossed the Line: a study on unwanted behaviour in sport for all*, Den Haag: Sociaal Cultureel Planbureau.

Tiessen-Raaphorst, A., Verbeek, D., de Haan, J. en K. Breedveld (2010) *Sport for Life: report on sport 2010*, Den Haag: Sociaal en Cultureel Planbureau.

Trouw (1997) *Judo Knew of Ooms Sexual Abuse and Harassment for Years*. Online. Available HTTP: <www.trouw.nl/tr/nl/5009/Archief/archief/article/detail/2578288/1996/11/11/Judobond-wist-al-jaren-van-machtsmisbruik-en-seksuele-intimidatie-Ooms.dhtml> (accessed 9 May 2013).

Vertommen, T. (2011) *Analysis of the Helpline for Sexual Harassment in Sport*, Arnhem: NOC*NSF.

Vertommen, T., Schipper-van Veldhoven, N., Hartill, M. J. and Eede, F. Van Den (2013) 'Sexual harassment and abuse in sport: the NOC*NSF Helpline', *International Review for the Sociology of Sport* (OnlineFirst).

Weber, M., Bruin, A. P. de and Moget, P. (2006). *The Dutch Programme Against Sexual Harassment in Sports, 1996–2006*, Arnhem: NOC*NSF.

5 Child protection in German sport

Bettina Rulofs

Club sport represents a cherished social institution in Germany. The German Olympic Sports Confederation (Deutscher Olympischer Sportbund or DOSB) records 27.8 million memberships in over 91,000 sports clubs. Affiliated to the DOSB are 16 sport federations responsible for organizing sport in their respective states; 62 national governing bodies (NGBs); and 20 sport federations with specific remits (e.g. Special Olympics Germany) (e.g. German Olympic Sports Confederation 2013). Organized sport is, then, both a complex and powerful force in German society.

The DOSB is responsible for both the development of elite athletes and community sport. In its mission to promote humanistic values through sport, it challenges unethical conduct such as doping or other forms of manipulation (German Olympic Sports Confederation 2013). There are 7.8 million members of German sports clubs that are under the age of 18 and the support of young athletes – whether by fostering their personality development or by protecting them from violence and manipulation – represents a particular challenge for the DOSB. For example, in the midst of the 2012 Olympic Games, the German media reported that a coach of the German Olympic Swimming Team faced charges in an ongoing legal investigation concerning the sexual abuse of an underage female athlete. Most striking was that neither the DOSB nor the German Swimming Federation was aware of the case against the coach; on the contrary he was nominated to travel to the Olympics as a coach and athlete caretaker (Die Welt 2012; Die Tageszeitung 2012).

Such incidents have highlighted the extent to which the protection of children is sufficiently embedded within the frameworks, policies and procedures of German sports organizations and how prepared they are to respond to the issue of child abuse in sport. This chapter considers these issues beginning with a consideration of the German debate around child protection in sport. It then examines current German research on this issue and concludes with a description of, and critical reflection on, current policy measures.

Historical background and development of the issue

Ethical issues in children's elite sport have been a long-standing concern in Germany (Meinberg 1984). Empricial studies have focused on the pressures and risks for adolescents performing at the elite level (Bette et al. 2002; Frei et al. 2000; Richartz and Brettschneider 1996) prompting policy measures such as developing coach-education. Interestingly, the terms 'safeguarding children' or 'child protection' – as they are used explicitly in the Anglo-American settings – are not common in Germany. The concept of 'safeguarding children in sports' with its broad perspective of including the prevention of emotional, phyisical and sexual abuse currently has no equivalent in German sport. Lately, the term 'child protection' has emerged on the sport-political agenda, but the term is strongly connected to activities concerning the prevention of *sexual* harassment and abuse. Inevitably, then, this chapter reflects this focus.

In Germany, the term 'sexualized violence' (SV) has gained currency within scientific and professional discourse; it encompasses a wide range of behaviours (physical and non-physical) based on the execution of power, subjection and humiliation by means of sexual behaviour. The focus of this term is on the demonstration of power via sexual violence (Bundschuh 2010; Klein and Palzkill 1998; Rulofs 2006). SV in sport first entered German public discourse in 1995. The media reported that Karel Fajfr, an internationally acclaimed figure skating coach, was found guilty of 11 cases of sexual abuse and two cases of bodily harm. In all instances the victims were young, elite, female athletes. Despite the seriousness of the charges, a parents' initiative campaigned publicly in support of Fajfr, pointing out that he had guided many athletes to successes. Fajfr was punished with a two-year suspended sentence and a fine of 25,000 Deutsche Mark (around £10,600). He was also banned from coaching for three years. Two other officials also received a fine of 9,000 Deutsche Mark (around £3,800) each because they had concealed the abuse (Hettrich 1995).

Following this event, the Regional Ministry for Women's Politics in North-Rhine-Westphalia (one of the 16 German federal states) commissioned the academics Birgit Palzkill and Michael Klein to conduct a study of violence against women and girls in sport (Klein and Palzkill 1998). The study revealed, for the first time, sexual harassment and abuse in German sport and argued that sport-specific structures might facilitate the development of SV. The findings were generally received with ambivalence and some organizations expressed opposition to their public dissemination fearing reputational damage. The study's authors were even blamed for egregiously dragging sports organizations through the mud. Eventual publication was largely due to the persistence of Ilse Ridder-Melchers, former Minister for Women's Politics in North-Rhine-Westphalia (today she is vice-president of the DOSB).

A small number of sport organizations did respond by developing prevention campaigns but the majority of clubs and federations quickly returned to business as usual. For many years the leading organization in the prevention of sexualized violence in German sport was the Regional Sports Federation of North-Rhine-Westphalia (Landessportbund Nordrhein-Westfalen or LSB NRW). In 1997 the LSB NRW started to develop an extensive prevention campaign called 'Silence protects the transgressors' ('Schweigen schuetzt die Falschen', see below). Over the past 10 to 15 years, several cases of sexual harassment and abuse in the realm of sport have become public. For example in 2009, a national athletics coach was sentenced to eight years imprisonment for the sexual abuse of eight young male athletes over a period of several years (Spiegel Online 2009).

Nevertheless, it was not until 2010 that stakeholders finally accepted that the prevention of sexualized violence in German sport required a thorough prevention campaign. Public outcry over reports of large-scale sexual abuse in churches and boarding schools prompted the German federal government to initiate several measures. One of these measures was the creation of a national helpline which registered 4,725 telephone calls and 1,575 letters from victims or other persons for the period May 2010 to August 2011 (Fegert et al. 2011). This further prompted the government to establish a national round table with all relevant stakeholders in the field of childcare and youth work (including the DOSB as the largest youth organization in Germany). Standards of child protection were agreed for all sectors working with children and adolescents and a number of campaigns against sexualized violence were initiated, including within the sports system.

German research

Klein and Palzkill's (1998) study was the first to deal with the topic of sexual violence in German sport. The study is based on qualitative interviews with victims of sexual harassment and abuse (SHA) and with other key stakeholders e.g. head of the Olympic training centre, policymakers, leaders of sport organizations, coaches, physical education teachers, etc. The interviews were conducted at various levels of sport, including elite, recreational and school sport. In addition to highlighting the substantial taboo around SV, the authors identified particular facilitating structures in the realm of sport. Among these facilitating structures are gendered hierarchies, relationships of dependency between coaches and athletes, and an intense focus on the body and success (Klein and Palzkill 1998). Of note is that this seminal study of sexualized violence in German sport focused chiefly on violence against girls and women, but excluded the experiences of boys and men.

Prior to and following this study, research on this topic remained remarkably quiet in Germany, with a few small exceptions focused on analysis of secondary literature and offering few new empirical insights (Engelfried 1997). There is, then, currently no data on the prevalence or incidence of sexualized violence in German sport. Official police crime data do not distinguish amongst cases of abuse by setting and victim-surveys of unreported abuse similarly do not distinguish sport from other child and youth activities (Mueller 2007). Nevertheless, sexual harassment and abuse in sport remain an issue today. Public sensitivity has developed alongside an increasing number of media reports, including incidents in the field of sport.

In 2011, for example, one of Germany's most important TV channels, the ARD, broadcast a documentary called 'The Coach was the Perpetrator' which told the story of a 25–year-old man, 'Heiko', who was sexually abused by his coach in a sports club setting when he was 12 years old. It took many years until 'Heiko' was able to talk about his abuse and to report the case to the police. It was eventually revealed that a total of 30 young boys were abused by this coach. In the German sports context this documentary has become an important reference for illustrating the suffering of young victims and the circumstances under which SV might develop in sports.

As mentioned, the German federal government established a nationwide telephone helpline from May 2010 to August 2011. A systematic review of the hotline's data shows 1,094 calls from people alleging sexual abuse in institutions (e.g. schools, churches, clubs, children's homes). Among these cases were 64 instances in which callers pinpointed clubs – 26 specifically identified as sports clubs – as the scene of abuse (Fegert et al. 2012: 118).

Despite the lack of research on SV in German sport, a recent study commissioned by the Deutsche Sporthilfe (German Sport Aid) offers valuable insight into the welfare of German athletes. In a large-scale survey of elite athletes (n=1,154), 11 per cent of respondents admitted to suffering from burnout; 9 per cent complained of depression; and 41 per cent admitted to knowingly taking health risks in the name of their sporting careers (Breuer and Hallmann 2013). Amongst the causes listed by respondents for these behaviours are the immense pressure to succeed (89 per cent), the environmental pressure (the environment of the athlete and his/her entourage) (80 per cent), the pursuit of recognition (70 per cent), and existential fear (58 per cent) (Breuer and Hallmann 2013: 81). These recent findings have provoked critical discussion amongst the media and sports leadership alike concerning the state of Germany's elite athletes and the need to provide them with better support. Following these results, it has to be asked whether elite sport provides a safe and healthy environment within which children and young people can develop. Given that the literature identifies pressures to succeed, fear of de-selection, and relationships of dependency as significant environmental obstacles for child protection and the prevention of SV, the sporting environment, in which all are present, requires a particularly decisive and systematic plan of action (Brackenridge 2001; Klein and Palzkill 1998).

Child protection and prevention policies in sport

The club sport system in Germany is a complex structure with manifold subdivisions and responsibilities. Consequently, the following discussion of current policies for child protection and prevention of sexualized violence at the different levels of German sport (national, regional, local) represents only a brief and illustrative overview.

National measures

Since 2010, following the disclosure of numerous cases of sexual abuse in institutions, the federal government has organized regular round table conferences on the topic of child sexual abuse to develop common prevention and intervention standards. Moreover, a national 'Independent Commissioner concerning Questions of Child Sexual Abuse' (UBSKM) was established. This Independent

Commissioner now serves to support, monitor and evaluate the progress of German organizations in implementing prevention and intervention policies. Having had a presence at the round table discussions, the DOSB, together with the German Sport Youth ('Deutsche Sportjugend' or DSJ), is subsequently required to develop its own prevention and intervention policies.

The first major step towards removing the taboo surrounding sexualized violence in German sport was the adoption of the Munich Declaration at the 2010 DOSB general assembly. The DOSB and its subsidiary bodies explicitly committed themselves to the task of preventing sexualized violence. It is important to note that this declaration and its following activities are focused on the prevention of sexual abuse and harassment, not addressing the broader perspective of child protection including other forms of abuse (emotional, physical) (German Olympic Sports Confederation 2010a). The overall goal of this project was further solidified in a DOSB position paper published in 2010. The aim of this paper is to develop a sports culture sensitive to SV. These goals are specified by a five-step programme (German Olympic Sports Confederation 2010b):

1   Each case of abuse is one too many. We will contribute to the investigation of each case.
2   We request our member organizations and clubs, to implement specific measures to prevent SV in sport.
3   On the basis of existing experiences in our member organizations, DOSB and DSJ will develop a modular package of activities designed to develop and implement individual action plans against SV within each member organization in sport.
4   We are going to clarify how information on convicted offenders can be shared among sport organizations.
5   DOSB and DSJ provide continuous exchange concerning the topic with and among member organizations in sport.

In connection with this five-step programme the DSJ assembled a working group of experts, which has met regularly since 2010 to advise its executive committee on prevention and intervention strategy. The DSJ and its panel of experts (including the author) have since been the driving force behind the development and implementation of a series of national-level prevention policies. Examples are the launching and expanding of a sport-specific internet platform for child protection; developing and publishing an annotated guideline for sports clubs (cf. Rulofs 2011); and creating an education curriculum on the prevention of SV.

The DSJ further asked each of its 98 member organizations to appoint a child protection officer and in 2010 introduced annual symposia for the purpose of professional exchange among the child protection officers. All in all, these activities seem to be very important steps in the field of child protection in sport. For the first time, sport federations and clubs in Germany can rely on information and measures that are provided by the national umbrella organization. The guidelines for sport clubs and the regular symposia offered by the DSJ seem to have been well received.

Yet controversy surrounds the question of whether, and to what extent, child protection should be required and regulated by strict standards. Particularly disputed is the question of whether volunteers and temporary employees at sports clubs should have to produce official certificates of good conduct in order to, for example, serve as coaches or youth leaders. Currently national child protection laws only require full-time employees to do so. Given that a large portion of German sport is run on a volunteer-basis – 8.8 million volunteers are presently active in sports clubs (cf. DOSB 2013) – stakeholders in sports organizations fear that stricter standards – such as requiring police record checks and the corresponding regulations – will discourage volunteers (cf. Rulofs and Emberger 2011). The child protection literature, however, argues that transparency of staff activities and background checks on workers represent crucial criteria for effective child protection (Brackenridge 2001; Youth Work North Rhine-Westphalia and the German Child Protection Agency 2010). Individual sports federations (e.g. the Berlin Sports Youth and the Regional Sports Federation of North-Rhine Westphalia) have meanwhile made significant strides, demanding, or at least strongly recommending, that member organizations request police record checks.

The imposition of obligatory regulations in relation to adult involvement in youth sport are highly contested and evoke strong feelings in Germany. This is perhaps to be expected given the still very young tradition of child protection in sport. Beyond sport (e.g. education) obligatory measures in child protection (such as police record checks) have long been established and are well accepted in Germany.

Given the short lifespan of the national prevention campaign and the methodological challenges of evaluating social policy, there exist few concrete conclusions regarding the impact of current prevention policies. However, in 2012 the 'Independent Commissioner concerning Questions of Child Sexual Abuse' conducted a questionnaire survey to assess the progress of German child and youth-work institutions, including the 98 member federations of the DOSB. Findings revealed that all state-level sports federations demonstrated having incorporated the issue into their educational system, but only 47 per cent of NGBs and 17 per cent of sports federations with specific tasks had done so (Independent Commissioner for Issues of Child Sexual Abuse 2012). Given that NGBs are responsible for the wellbeing of junior high-performance athletes, considerable improvements are required.

Furthermore, policies and procedures for responding to abuse allegations are far less developed. Only 64 per cent of state-level federations, 48 per cent of NGBs and 57 per cent of federations with specific tasks possess well-defined policies for dealing with allegations of child sexual abuse (Independent Commissioner for Issues of Child Sexual Abuse 2012). In other words, in 2012, between 40–50 per cent of the umbrella sports organizations still did not have policies for handling suspicions or allegations of SV. These findings are particularly alarming given that children and youth affected by sexual abuse must often address adults more than once before action is taken. This delay owes in no small part to the reality that institutions are not adequately prepared to deal professionally and consistently with this problem.

Regional and local activities

As noted above, the State Sports Federation of North Rhine-Westphalia (NRW) can certainly be considered a trailblazer in the area of child protection in sport. With 17.8 million citizens, NRW is the most populous German state; moreover, with its 20,000 sports clubs with over 5 million members, it is a 'sport intensive' state. To date many activities are related to the NRW campaign 'Silence protects the transgressors': posters and brochures for raising awareness on this issue within NRW's sports clubs, education and training materials, and quality standards for clubs.

One of the campaign's overarching standards are regular evaluation studies, two of which, in 2003/2004 and 2010, have already taken place. Using qualitative interviews with stakeholders in NRW sports club, the studies focus on the extent of acceptance of the campaign (Rulofs 2007; Rulofs and Emberger 2011). The findings show a general buy-in to the campaign and an emerging sensitization. Moreover, attitudes about the responsibility of sport in relation to child protection have improved over the years. Unlike in 2003/2004, interviewees in 2010 believed that child protection represented an important and explicit responsibility of sports organizations and stated they were more inclined to break the silence around SV in sport. However, there still existed considerable uncertainty in handling sexual abuse allegations. Interviewees particularly desired the creation of a professional sports clearing house or sport-specific telephone 'hotline'. They further complained that existing policies and materials focused too heavily on women and girls, neglecting boys and men. A need to strengthen local networks of child protection in cities and communities also emerged.

Some of the suggestions garnered from these studies, such as the development of information brochures for boys, have already been implemented in NRW. Others are in planning, such as a pilot project aimed at strengthening local prevention networks of child protection agencies, the local police and sports facilities.

Conclusion

Germany has witnessed a great deal of activity in the areas of child protection and the prevention of sexualized violence over the past three years, including within sport. The effectiveness of the steps taken has largely gone unrecognized, despite one of the most important advances being a long-overdue end to the general societal, as well as sports-specific, silence surrounding sexual harassment and abuse. The role of the media in this development cannot be overstated; critical and sustained media reporting of cases of abuse were the necessary catalyst behind the emerging societal expectation that leadership in childcare and youth work appropriately handle past instances of abuse as well as work to prevent future cases. The complex German sports system now faces the unique challenge of transferring policies developed by national-level organizations to the more than 91,000 local-level sports clubs.

References

Bette, K.-H., Schimank, U., Wahlig, D. and Weber, U. (2002) *Biographical Dynamics in Competitive Sports: possibilities of doping prevention in adolescence*, Cologne: Sport & Buch Strauß.

Brackenridge, C. (2001) *Spoilsports: understanding and preventing sexual exploitation in sport*, London: Routledge.

Breuer, C. and Hallmann, K. (2013) *Dysfunctions of Elite Sport: doping, match-fixing and health risks as seen from the perspective of population and athletes*, Bonn: Federal Institute for Sport Science.

Bundschuh, C. (2010) 'Child sexual abuse', in S. Seidenstücker and B. Mutke (eds) *Practical Guide for the Care and Guidance of Children and Adolescents Volume 1*, Merching: Forum Verlag.

German Olympic Sports Confederation (2010a) *Position Paper – Preventing and Combatting Sexual Violence and Abuse of Children and Young People in Sport*. Online. Available HTTP: <http://www.dsj.de/fileadmin/user_upload/Dokumente/Handlungsfelder/Praevention/sexualisierte_Gewalt/Positionspapier_DOSB-Praesidium_2010_php.pdf> (accessed 27 May 2013).

— (2010b) *Protection from Sexual Violence in Sport*. Online. Available HTTP: <http://www.dosb.de/fileadmin/fm-dosb/downloads/Sexualisierte_Gewalt/Sexualisierte_Gewalt_Schutz_Praevention_DOSB_Erklaerung.pdf> (accessed 27 May 2013).

— (2013) *Short Profile of the German Olympic Sports Confederation*. Online. Available HTTP: <http://www.dosb.de/de/organisation/philosophie/kurzportraet-des-dosb/> (accessed 27 May 2013).

Die Tageszeitung (2012) *Abuse Scandal in the Swimming Association: again, no-one knew anything*. Online. Available HTTP: <www.taz.de/Missbrauchsaffaere-beim-Schwimm-Verband/!99425/> (accessed 27 May 2013).

Die Welt (2012) *Sexual Abuse – swimming coach in court*. Online. Available HTTP: <www.welt.de/sport/olympia/article108610312/Sexueller-Missbrauch-Schwimmtrainer-vor-Gericht.html> (accessed 27 May 2013).

Engelfried, C. (eds) (1997) *Time Out: sexuality, violence and interdependencies in sport*, Frankfurt: Campus.

Fegert, J. M., Rassenhofer, M., Schneider T., Seitz, A., König, L. and Spröber, N. (2011) *Final Report on the Scientific Research of the Independent Commisioner for the Clearing of Child Sexual Abuse*. Online. Available HTTP: <www.uniklinik-ulm.de/fileadmin/Kliniken/Kinder_Jugendpsychiatrie/Dokumente/Endbericht_Mittelfassung17112011_A4.pdf> (accessed 29 July 2013).

— (2012) 'Listening to victims: results of the scientific research on the helpline of the independent commissioner for the clearing of child sexual abuse and the discussion of a research agenda', in S. Andresen and W. Heitmeyer (eds) *Destructive Processes: disrespect and sexual violence against children and adolescents in institutions*, Weinheim, Basel: Beltz Juventa.

Frei, P., Lüsebrink, I., Rottländer, D. and Thiele, J. (2000) *Pressures and Risks in Female Gymnastics: part 2 – insider views, educational perspectives and consequences*, Schorndorf: Hofmann.

Hettrich, A. (1995) *Faijfr Guilty: figure skating coach received two years suspended sentence*. Online. Available HTTP: <www.welt.de/print-welt/article664514/Fajfr-schuldig-gesprochen.html> (accessed 24 July 2013).

Independent Commissioner for Issues of Child Sexual Abuse (2012) *Monitoring the State of Implementation of the Recommendations Delivered by the Round Table 'Child Sexual Abuse' (2012–2013): status report of the first wave of data collection*. Online. Available HTTP: <http://beauftragter-missbrauch.de/course/view.php?id=31> (accessed 27 May 2013).

Klein, M. and Palzkill, B. (1998) *Violence Against Girls and Women in Sport*, Düsseldorf: Ministry of Women, Youth, Family and Health, North Rhine-Westphalia.

Meinberg, E. (1984) *Children's High-Performance Sport: heteronomy or self-development. Educational, anthropological and ethical orientation*, Cologne: Strauß.

Mueller, U. (2007) 'Sexual violence and abuse – a topic for sport? ', in B. Rulofs (ed.) *Silence Protects the Wrong People: sexualized violence in sport – situation analysis and opportunities for action*, Düsseldorf: Ministry of the Interior of North Rhine-Westphalia.

Richartz, A. and Brettschneider, W.-D. (1996) *Becoming World Champion and Mastering School: the double burden of school and high performance training*, Schorndorf: Hofmann.

Rulofs, B. (2006) 'Violence in sport from the perspective of gender studies', in I. Hartmann-Tews and B. Rulofs (eds) *Handbook of Sport and Gender*, Schorndorf: Hoffmann-Verlag.

— (2007) 'Prevention of sexualized violence in sport – an analysis of the preliminary measures in North Rhine-Westphalia', in B. Rulofs (ed.) *Silence Protects the Wrong People: sexualized violence in sport – situation analysis and opportunities for action*, Düsseldorf: Ministry of the Interior of North Rhine-Westphalia.

Rulofs, B. and Emberger, D. (2011) *Prevention of Sexual Violence in Sport – between voluntarism and commitment? Analysis of the perception and acceptance of specific prevention measures of the sports federation in North Rhine-Westphalia from the perspective of functionaries in sport*, unpublished report to the Ministry for Sport North Rhine-Westphalia.

Rulofs, B. in collaboration with: H. Brandi, G. Busch, K. Gramkow, J. Hunz, M. Korn, N. Rittgasser, D. Sahle and K. Witte (2011) *Against Sexual Violence in Sport – annotated guidelines for sports clubs to protect children and adolescents*, Frankfurt: German Sport Youth and the German Olympic Sports Confederation.

Scherler, K. (1989) 'Children's high performance sport and sports policy consequences: once again it's time to break the silence', *Sportpädagogik*, 2: 2–5.

Spiegel Online (2009) *Bavaria: German national coach confesses to hundredfold child abuse*. Online. Available HTTP: <www.spiegel.de/panorama/justiz/bayern-bundestrainer-gesteht-hundertfachen-kindesmissbrauch-a-643530.html> (accessed 01 April 2012).

Youth Work North Rhine-Westphalia and the German Child Protection Agency (2010) *A Guide to Criminal Record Checks in Public Children's and Youth Work and in the Work of the Child Protection Agency*, Wuppertal: Eigenverlag.

6 Safeguarding and child protection in sport in two Southern European countries

Greece and the Republic of Cyprus

Stiliani 'Ani' Chroni and Maria Papaefstathiou

The sexual exploitation of youth athletes has recently received significant media attention in Greece and the Republic of Cyprus. However, in both countries there is a lack of policy and guidance for protecting children from violence and misconduct in sports contexts. Neither country has developed codes of conduct for people working for and with children in sport, nor do they have any recognizable system of child protection in sport. These two countries on the Mediterranean basin display some common socio-cultural features. Nonetheless, country-specific historical, societal and institutional elements have played key roles in how they organize and govern children's sport. In this chapter we discuss the systems in place to protect children, the structure of sport and the landscape of child welfare in sport.

Greece

Greece is in the midst of a process of modernization, becoming more individualistic and diverse (Chroni et al. 2013). Nevertheless, traditional values, such as the centrality of the traditional family unit and Greek Orthodox religion, remain strong (Katrougalos and Lazaridis 2003). Consequently, issues related to child abuse, particularly in relation to sexual violence, are taboo and are thought best handled in the private sphere of the family. So while laws and organizations exist to reactively manage child abuse, and cases of sexual abuse have been prosecuted by Greek courts, Greece has no national strategy for proactively safeguarding children.

Competitive sports in Greece, at recreational, amateur and professional level, are overseen by the General Secretariat of Sport (GSS). This government office functions as an independent body but is funded by the state and lies within the jurisdiction of the Sub-ministry of Sport, which currently operates within the Ministry of Education, Religious Culture and Sport. The sub-minister of sport took over responsibility for decision-making within the GSS from the GSS general-secretary in 2012, when the sub-ministry was established. This lack of stability within the leadership of sport in Greece makes it difficult to establish consistent actions and decisions on any topic. Additionally, while the GSS has overall management control of sport, at amateur level sport takes place in extra-curricular clubs and is funded by athletes' families and the sport federations, which are funded by the GSS. This family involvement in young people's sport has a long history and has become increasingly important as state funding is reduced under austerity measures imposed following the financial crisis in 2010. It also serves to reinforce cultural understandings of the family as responsible for children's welfare in sport, as in wider society.

Legislation on child abuse

The proactive term 'safeguarding' is not embedded in Greek society. Instead the term 'child abuse' is used to refer to sexual, physical and emotional abuse and neglect. Much of the regulatory framework to protect children from abuse in Greece has focused on sexual abuse and exploitation. Most organizations, excepting the Greek Ombudsman for Children's Rights, deal reactively with child abuse and punishing offenders rather than proactively safeguarding children. In 2003, the Children's Ombudsman was founded to defend and promote the rights of children, defined under Greek law as individuals under the age of 18. It argued for the implementation of a National Plan of Action for Children's Rights in its 2003–11 report but this has yet to materialize. The report also noted the need for ministerial support for the creation of a national referral centre to monitor child abuse as such statistics are not currently gathered in or beyond sport – a fact that has contributed to a lack of understanding about the scale of child abuse in Greece (Tsirigoti et al. 2010).

Greece has signed up to the Council of Europe (CoE) Convention on the Protection of Children against Sexual Exploitation and Sexual Abuse (CoE 2012), which it ratified in 2009. However, the Children's Ombudsman (Greek Ombudsman Department of Children's Rights 2012) noted that no framework has been issued in Greece for the implementation of key measures in the Convention. For example, Article 5 paragraph 3 obliges individuals in regular contact with children to undergo criminal background screening but provisions have yet to be put in place to mandate this in Greece. The failure to implement strategies for protecting children is a common theme in the country; the National Observatory for the Rights of Children was established in 2001 to prepare and monitor policies to promote children's rights, but it is still not fully operational and its role has not been fully clarified for reasons that have not been disclosed.

Some laws are specifically relevant to sport. Article 31 of law 2725/1999 provides the framework for coaches convicted of a sexual crime to have their coaching licence revoked, while article 130 of the same law permits coaches to be banned for life from sport for inappropriate behaviour. Meanwhile law 3727/2008 bans individuals from working with children if they have been prosecuted for or convicted of sexual crimes. Law 3727/2008 provides a clear framework for preventing child abuse, punishing perpetrators and establishing international cooperation on child sexual abuse, although as the Children's Ombudsman has noted many aspects of the legislation have yet to be implemented.

The GSS also has procedures to protect children in sport. Coaches applying for a license to practise must undergo a criminal record check. Once a license is granted, however, there is no requirement for further checks. Criminal record checks are only reliable the day they are issued and are not a predictor of future behaviour (Brackenridge 2001). In recent years it has been suggested that sports clubs are increasingly requiring follow-up checks before recruiting new coaches, although there can be no certainty of this until it is mandated by the GSS. Moreover, many coaches in Greece are not formally qualified and, as such, work without a licence and without any background checks.

As it stands, then, while some laws and policies exist to protect children from abuse in sport, progress has been slow; the legislative and policy framework in this area remains limited, training on abuse is almost non-existent and statistics on abuse are not gathered.

Research on abuse

What little is known about child abuse in and beyond sport comes from studies mainly conducted within the Institute of Child Health (ICH), which was founded to provide specialized health prevention services and develop educational resources on child health. Most focus on child sexual abuse. One study from the ICH (Nikolaidis et al. 2008) found that children experienced verbal and physical abuse within the family and in school and that 4.7 per cent of respondents had experienced sexual touching.

Studies have also looked at sexual harassment, which is part of a continuum of sexual violence which, at its extreme, includes abuse (Fitzgerald et al. 1988). Of 209 women studying in higher education sport departments in Greece, Fasting et al. (2012) found that 32 per cent of respondents reported being sexually harassed by a male athlete and 16 per cent by a male coach. A similar study of female sport students found 40 per cent had experienced sexual harassment by males and 18 per cent by females (Fasting et al. 2011). Meanwhile, Chroni and Fasting (2009) found that Greek female athletes reported experiencing more sexual harassment from men outside sport, such as male teachers, students, family members or other males (64 per cent) than from men inside sport, such as coaches, athletes and members of the management team (42 per cent).

Meanwhile, there is only limited data about sexual abuse and harassment specifically in a sports environment, and there is currently no data on boys and men's experiences of abuse or harassment. While the media reports anecdotal cases of male abuse and harassment in Greek sports, the magnitude and characteristics of the problem remain unknown.

Waking up to abuse in sport

Sport has been slow to accept that abuse occurs within its ranks and there is not yet a recognizable child protection system in Greek sport. When in 2012 a male coach was arrested for sexually abusing several male athletes, the first author of this chapter jointly wrote an article for an online Greek sports newspaper that highlighted the existence and consequences of sexual abuse in sport and called on survivors of such abuse to come forward (Sarris with Chroni 2012). The article received little public reaction, attesting to the magnitude of the societal taboo around sexual abuse.

The high-profile case of basketball coach Nikos Sirigakis on the island of Crete provoked some response from the authorities in 2011. The 47–year-old Sirigakis was charged with sexually abusing 53 players aged 12–17 years old under his care. Sirigakis claimed he abused the boys to 'make men' out of them and prime them for success; it was, he said, not about sex but about making his athletes 'Spartans' (TLife 11 December 2011). Sirigakis was convicted in 2013 and sentenced to 220 years in prison.

Following Sirigakis' arrest, the parent's association from local schools organized a series of lectures on sexual abuse in sport, and the local football association held a forum to raise awareness of sexual abuse among parents and coaches. The GSS's general secretary for sport, Panagiotis Bitsaxis, attended the forum and condemned sexual abuse (for a review see Chroni 2012) – the first and only time the GSS has publicly acknowledged the existence of sexual abuse in sport.

Following the case, the GSS introduced a policy that allowed the licence of coaches charged with a sexual crime against an athlete to be recalled, even if the coach was later found not guilty. By spring 2013, the GSS had recalled the licences of five coaches – two in basketball, one in cricket, one in fencing and one in taekwondo (Chroni 2013). In addition, the Committee of Sportsman Spirit, which is part of the Hellenic Olympic Committee, introduced life bans for coaches who have lost their licence. At the time of writing, four of the five coaches to have their licences revoked have also been banned by the Committee of Sportsman Spirit; the case relating to the fifth coach is pending. However, these regulations are not always upheld. One of the four coaches is still working as a coach because local governmental agencies have refused to endorse the punishments (Chroni 2013) suggesting Greece has some way to go before abuse in sport is taken seriously by everyone. The GSS has a significant role to play in this respect; it has only once, in 2012, publicly acknowledged the existence of sexual abuse in sport. Without the GSS taking a more open and proactive stance, raising awareness of sexual abuse in sport is likely to be slow.

The future

Research on the prevalence and incidence of abuse is needed to establish the extent of the problem in Greek sport. Additionally, a strategy for protecting young people in sport is required, including a system to report suspicions of sexual, physical and emotional abuse and neglect; codes of conduct for coaches, athletes and other sports personnel; and child protection training for stakeholders. To facilitate change, in January 2012 and May 2013 the first author of this chapter proposed a workshop on preventing sexual abuse and harassment in sport to the GSS Office of Sport and Fitness Clubs, which is responsible for coach licensing. No response was received.

The Republic of Cyprus

Cyprus has until recently constituted a hierarchically structured society in which women and children have been marginalized and children were largely considered the 'property' of their parents (Angelides et al. 2009). Consequently, child abuse has been considered taboo and 'a family affair'. These traditional cultural attitudes mean the government has made only basic legal provisions for children's welfare, resulting for many years in a system that reflected 'the familistic nature of the southern European welfare model' (Katrougalos and Lazaridis 2003: 83). This traditional approach to abuse and children's welfare needs to be understood in the context of the country's political and historical background. The island has a turbulent history: it only gained independence from Britain in 1960, was invaded by Turkey in 1974 and was hit hard by the recent European economic crisis. These and other challenges have meant child welfare is marginalized, resulting in minimal intervention and support from the state.

Since Cyprus joined the European Union (EU) in 2004, the government's role in child welfare issues and the position of children in Cypriot society have begun to change. In 2007 the national Office for the Commissioner of Children's Rights (OCCR) was established to monitor and raise awareness of children's rights. Since then, it has ratified two National Action Plans and set priorities for children's rights, positioning children as autonomous actors in decisions relating to their lives (see OCCR 2013). Consequently, the OCCR (2011: 8) argues that 'Cyprus may be classified among the countries where children generally enjoy a high level of respect of their rights'. However, the OCCR only operates throughout the geographic area under the control of the Republic of Cyprus since the country's de facto division following the Turkish invasion in 1974. Consequently, the protections offered by the OCCR do not apply to children in areas outside the government's control (OCCR 2011). In addition, austerity measures placed on the country following the financial crisis in 2012 may yet impinge on the OCCR's plan to further develop children's rights provision.

Legislative framework to protect children

In relation to children's welfare, the OCCR uses the term 'child protection' and it makes clear that children have the right to be protected from abuse, including sexual harassment, bullying and sexual, physical and emotional abuse. Meanwhile, the Cyprus Department of Social Welfare (CDSW) refers to 'child abuse', including sexual, physical and emotional abuse (Georgiades 2009). While there is no national system for collecting statistics on child abuse in Cyprus, growing awareness of the issue has prompted an increase in research (for example Hope for Children 2013). One of the few national studies on the prevalence of child abuse found that of 1,000 people aged 16 and over, 47 per cent of men and 53 per cent of women had been abused as children (UNCRD 2000). Of this, 34 per cent said they had experienced physical and emotional abuse, 28 per cent had experienced emotional abuse, 26 per cent physical abuse and 5 per cent sexual abuse. Another study found 20 per cent of participants aged 12 to 18 had experienced physical abuse and 10 per cent had been sexually abused (Advisory Committee for the Prevention and Combating of Violence in the Family (ACPCVF) 2004). The same study revealed that in contrast to sexual abuse, which was perceived to be unacceptable, participants normalized emotional and physical abuse.

While the OCCR and the CDSW recognize multiple forms of abuse, tackling child sexual abuse has been the government's focus and, as such, has driven recent policy developments. This is in part following pressure from non-governmental organizations and the high-profile media coverage of child sexual abuse cases, leading to suggestions that child sexual abuse is 'probably the worst and most monstrous form' of abuse (Koursoumba 2013: 2). In privileging child sexual abuse, other forms of abuse – some of which may be more common – have become marginalized and potentially normalized. This approach can also increase concerns about false allegations (Lang forthcoming) and results in more paternalistic attitudes towards children.

Interestingly, most Cypriot media coverage of sexual abuse in sport has been of cases from Greece, particularly cases involving male coaches abusing male athletes, such as the arrest of a cricket coach in Corfu for paying a 17–year-old male athlete for sex (Ant1News 12 May 2013). In such stories the abuser is commonly portrayed as a pathological 'monster', drawing attention away from the extent to which the culture of sport is to blame for such abuse (Fasting 2012) and implying that such abuse does not happen in Cypriot sport.

Cyprus' entry into the EU, and consequently to European child abuse prevention treaties, awakened political and cultural interest in child abuse. Cyprus signed the CoE's Convention on the Protection of Children against Sexual Exploitation and Sexual Abuse in 2007. The Convention mandates that signatories adopt legislation against sexual violence, including sexual abuse, and take measures to prevent and protect children and to prosecute offenders. However, Cyprus has yet to ratify the Convention (CoE 2013), so there has been no legislative reform to align domestic laws with the Convention. To address this, the government signed up to the CoE's One in Five campaign, so called because it is estimated that one in five young people are victims of sexual violence (Kleinsorge 2011). The campaign raises awareness of sexual violence against children and pushes for the ratification of the Convention. It has received significant publicity in Cyprus, further compounding the profile of child sexual abuse in the country.

Meanwhile, preventing other forms of abuse, particularly physical abuse, is stymied by disparities in legislation. For example, while physical abuse is prohibited under the 1956 Children's Law, corporal punishment by a parent, teacher or other adult working in loco parentis is exempt (OCCR 2011). Consequently, no parent, teacher or other adult in charge of children has been prosecuted in the country for physical abuse carried out under the guise of corporeal punishment. The law also only applies to young people up to the age of 16, despite Cyprus ratifying the UN Convention on the Rights of the Child (UNCRC) in 1991, which defines a child as under 18 (UN General Assembly 1989). To rectify these issues, the Commissioner has called for the Children's Law to be updated in line with international standards, but no action has yet been taken.

Overall, then, while Cyprus has ratified the UNCRC and European treaties on preventing child abuse, progress has been slow, and co-ordination between services involved in managing abuse, including the police, social services and health departments, is inefficient (Cyprus Mail 2012).

Developments in sport

While awareness is growing that child protection is an issue for sport, developments to protect youth athletes have been minimal. Policies and procedures on child protection in sport are rare, as are codes of conduct for coaches. There is little evidence of systematic coach education on child protection and children's rights or on identifying the signs of abuse and the mechanisms to report it, even though professionals working for the ministries of health, labour and social insurance and education, among others, are obliged to report such concerns (ACPCVF 2002). Moreover, national policies relating to child athletes are commonly underpinned by a bio-scientific discourse that draws on scientific, technical and psychological knowledge and places little value on athlete's broader social and emotional development (Lang 2009). It is perhaps not surprising then that the Cyprus Sport Organization (CSO), which is funded by the government and runs sport through its affiliated national governing bodies, has yet to address the issue of abuse in its ranks. For example, in a report detailing the CSO's ideas for managing and professionalizing sport in the country (CSO 2011), no reference was made to preventing child abuse.

One positive development in raising awareness of abuse and harassment in sport occurred at a conference organized by the CSO's Women and Sport Committee in 2013 (Cyprus Olympic Committee 2013). Two presentations at the conference touched on abuse and harassment – one announced reflections of the presenter-member of Women and Sport Committee from participating at a European Conference on preventing sexualized violence in sport, while in the other the second author of this chapter presented empirical data on sexual harassment and abuse from around the world and announced the results of a European project on preventing sexualized violence in sport (Chroni et al. 2012). The presentations sparked animated discussions among attendees at the conference, which included policymakers, athletes and academics. It can only be hoped that this represents a turning point for the issue of abuse and harassment in youth sport.

Conclusion

Neither Greece nor Cyprus currently has a national-level strategy to protect athletes from abuse or promote their rights in sport. Such a strategy is urgently needed in each country but must be underpinned by rigorous sport-specific research that takes into account the historical, political and socio-cultural characteristics of the country at hand. The current awareness of, and sensitivity to, children's rights that is evident in both countries provides a positive starting point from which to develop a framework for athlete and child protection in sport. As a minimum, this framework should include training on recognizing and reporting abuse, for coaches, athletes and other sport stakeholders. Finally, as Greece and Cyprus are both members of the EU they are well positioned to learn about best practice in child protection from other member states with a longer history of involvement in this area.

However, developments in this area are contingent on everyone involved in sport, and particularly those in leadership positions, acknowledging that child abuse happens in sport and that sport has a responsibility to act to protect its members and to allow athletes a say in their own sporting lives.

References

Advisory Committee for the Prevention and Combating of Violence in the Family (2002) Manual of Departmental Procedures on Handling Incidences of Family Violence, Nicosia: Consulting Committee.

— (2004) Prevalence and Types of Violence against Children in the Cypriot Family. Online. Available HTTP: <www.familyviolence.gov.cy/upload/research/erevna_2004.pdf> (accessed 8 October 2013).

Angelides, P., Papanastasiou, E., Papanastasiou, K., Mavroides, Y. and Panaou, P. (2009) Level of Information and Views of among Cypriot Society about Children's Rights, Nicosia: OCCR.

Ant1News (2013) Cricket Coach Arrested for Molesting Minor in Corfu. Online. Available HTTP: <www.ant1iwo.com/ellada/2013/05/12/proponhths-omadas-kriket-sthn-kerkyra-sy/> (accessed 1 June 2013).

Brackenridge, C. H. (2001) Spoilsports: understanding and preventing sexual exploitation in sport, London: Routledge.

Chroni, S. (2012) 'Breaking the cycle of child sexual abuse (Greece)', in S. Chroni, K. Fasting, M. J. Hartill, N. Knorre, M. Martin Harcajo, M. Papaefstathiou, D. Rhind, B. Rulofs, J. Toftegaard Støckel, T. Vertommen and J. Zurc (eds) Prevention of Sexual and Gender Harassment and Abuse in Sports: initiatives in Europe and beyond, Frankfurt: Deutsche Sportjugend.

Chroni, S. (2013) Personal Communication with the Office of Sport and Fitness Clubs of the General Secretariat of Sports, Athens, Greece, May 25.

Chroni, S. and Fasting, K. (2009) 'Prevalence of male sexual harassment among female sport participants in Greece', Inquiries in Physical Education and Sport, 3: 288–96. Online. Available HTTP: <www.hape.gr/emag.asp> (accessed 2 January 2013).

Chroni, S., Diakaki, E. and Papaioannou, A. (2013) 'Athletes' careers in Greece: towards a culturally infused future', in N. Stambulova and T. Ryba (eds) *Athletes' Careers Across Cultures*, London: Routledge.

Chroni, S., Fasting, K., Hartill, M. J., Knorre, N., Martin Harcajo, M., Papaefstathiou, M., Rhind, D., Rulofs, B., Toftegaard Støckel, J., Vertommen, T. and Zurc, J. (2012) *Prevention of Sexual and Gender Harassment and Abuse in Sports: initiatives in Europe and beyond*, Frankfurt: Deutsche Sportjugend.

Council of Europe (2012) Protection of Children against Sexual Exploitation and Sexual Abuse. Online. Available HTTP: <www.coe.int/t/dghl/standardsetting/children/Introduction_Convention_en.asp> (accessed 1 June 2013).

— (2013) Convention on the Protection of Children against Sexual Exploitation and Sexual Abuse. Online. Available HTTP: <conventions.coe.int/Treaty/Commun/ChercheSig.asp?NT=201&CM=&DF=&CL=ENG> (accessed 1 June 2013).

Cyprus Mail (2012) Cyprus Lags on Child Rights. Online. Available HTTP: <www.cyprus-mail.com/childrens-rights/cyprus-lags-child-rights/20120207> (accessed 7 February 2012).

Cyprus Olympic Committee (2013) Women in Society and Sport. Online. Available HTTP: <www.olympic.org.cy/media/attachments/olympic_rythm/EOAK_-_H_Gineka_stin_Koinonia_kai_ton_Athlitismo_-_Olympic_Rythms_Vol_1_2013.pdf> (accessed 1 June 2013).

Cyprus Sport Organization (2011) CSO Strategy 2020: right to exercise – citizens in action. Online. Available HTTP: <www.cyprussports.org/2020.html> (accessed 1 June 2013).

Fasting, K. (2012) 'What do we know about sexual harassment and abuse in sport in Europe?', paper presented at The Safer, Better, Stronger! Prevention of Sexual Harassment and Abuse in Sport conference, Berlin, November.

Fasting, K., Chroni, S. and Knorre, N. (2012) 'The experiences of sexual harassment in sport and education among European female sports science students', Sport, Education and Society, 1–16.

Fasting, K., Chroni, S., Hervik, S. E. and Knorre, N. (2011) 'Sexual harassment in sport toward females in three European countries', International Review for the Sociology of Sport, 46: 76–89.

Fitzgerald, L. Shullman, S., Bailey, N., Richards, M., Swecker, J., Gold, Y., Omerod, M. and Weitzman, L. (1988) 'The incidence and dimensions of sexual harassment in academia and the workplace', Journal of Vocational Behaviour, 32: 152–75.

Georgiades, S. D. (2009) 'Child abuse and neglect in Cyprus: an exploratory study of perceptions and experiences', Child Abuse Review, 18: 60–71.

Greek Ombudsman Department of Children's Rights (2012). P*arallel Report to the UN Committee on the Rights of the Child*, Athens: The Greek Ombusdman.

Hope for Children (HFC) (2013) Beat Bullying Campaign. Online. Available HTTP: <www.hfcbeatbullying.info/en> (accessed 1 June 2013).

Katrougalos, G. and Lazaridis, G. (2003) Southern European Welfare States: problems, challenges and prospects, Hampshire: Palgrave Macmillan.

Kleinsorge, T. (2011) Legal Protection of Children from Sexual Exploitation: the 'Lanzarote Convention' and the One in Five Campaign. Online. Available HTTP: <srsg.violenceagainstchildren.org/sites/default/files/consultations/law_reform/presentations/tanja_klainsorge_legal_protection_of_children_from_sexual_exploitation.pdf> (accessed 1 June 2013).

Koursoumba, L. (2013) 'The role of Children's Ombudsman in establishing national inter-sectoral collaboration', paper presented at the Meeting on the Network of Contact Parliamentarians to Stop Sexual Violence against Children, Berlin, March.

Lang, M. (2009) 'Swimming in the Panopticon: an ethnographic exploration of good practice and child protection in competitive youth swimming', unpublished Ph.D thesis, Leeds Metropolitan University.

— (forthcoming) 'Touchy subject: A Foucauldian analysis of coaches' perceptions of adult-child touch in youth swimming', Sociology of Sport Journal.

Nikolaidis, G., Petroulaki, K., Tsirigoti, A., Fatsea, E., Milioni, F. and Skiadopoulos, K. (2008) Study on the Development of Epidemiological Tools for Continuous Surveillance of the Incidence of Child Abuse and Neglect, Athens: Institute of Child Health.

Office for the Commissioner of Children's Rights (2011) Report of the Commissioner for Children's Rights in Cyprus to the UN Committee on the Rights of the Child. Online. Available HTTP: <www.childcom.org.cy/ccr/ccr.nsf/All/C860 5F7BFB72C6B5C2257 9D000336E35?OpenDocument> (accessed 13 January 2012).

— (2013) Action Plans: priority areas. Online. Available HTTP: <www.childcom.org.cy/ccr/ccr.nsf/DMLplan_gr/DMLplan_gr?OpenDocument> (accessed 3 August 2013).

Sarris, T. with Chroni, S. (2012) 'Sexualized violence, taboo and sport', Gazzetta.gr. Online. Available HTTP: <www.gazzetta.gr/podosfairo/article/item/280428–seksoyaliki-bia-tampoy-kai-athlitismos> (accessed 30 July 2013).

TLife (11 December 2011) Challenges of the Paedophile of Rethymnon: 'this way i would make them spartans'. Online. Available HTTP: <www.tlife.gr/Article/NEWS/0–9–25053.html> (accessed 20 August 2013).

Tsirigoti, Petroulaki and Nikolaidis (2010) Current Situation Concerning Child Abuse and Neglect in Greece, Athens: Institute of Child Health.

UNCRD (2000) 'Results of the "Violence in the Cypriot Family" study', cited in S.D. Georgiades, (2009) 'Child abuse and neglect in Cyprus: an exploratory study of perceptions and experiences', *Child Abuse Review*, 18: 60.

United Nations General Assembly (1989) The United Nations Convention on the Rights of the Child, Geneva: United Nations.

University of Nicosia Centre for Research and Development (2000) Violence in the Cypriot Family. Online. Available HTTP: <www.familyviolence.gov.cy/upload/research/erevna_2000.pdf> (accessed 29 October 2013).

7   Child protection and welfare in Spanish sport

Montserrat Martin

Spain does not yet have any official policy or protocol in relation to the protection of children from maltreatment and abuse in sport settings. Within Spanish culture, sport is considered a sacrosanct space and an ideal instrument through which to instil values and discipline within children and young people. However, in the past 12 months, several cases of child sexual abuse (CSA) in competitive sport have presented a serious challenge to sports authorities in Spain.

In particular, the high-profile trial of karate coach, Fernando Torres Baena, for the sexual abuse of more than 50 children enrolled in his elite karate school over a period of 20 years shocked Spanish society (Ayala and Ayala 2013). Further, in 2013 the highly acclaimed coach, Jesús Carballo, was accused of having sexually abused one of his gymnasts, Olympian Gloria Viseras, in the late 1970s 'when she was a minor under his tutelage' (Iríbar 9 July 2013). A police investigation concluded that Viseras' accusation was entirely credible. This was accepted by the Spanish High Sports Council (Consejo Superior de Deportes, or CSD) (Iríbar 2013a, 2013b). However, the statute of limitations under Spanish Law on CSA offences currently prevents a legal case being brought against Carballo.

Spanish society, then, has only just begun to acknowledge that child abuse also happens in sport. To this extent, there is not a great deal to report in terms of action taken by governing agencies, nevertheless, it is important to document the current environment in Spain. This chapter attempts to capture the broad context as well as recent events and intends to provide a point of departure in what will hopefully be the start of a long journey for Spanish sport as it begins to address the issues of child maltreatment, child protection and safeguarding.

Spanish context

For a Western European country, Spain is a relative latecomer regarding the public acknowledgement and prevention of CSA. However, important studies have been conducted (López 1994; López et al. 1995; Cantón and Cortés 2000) and increased attention from the mass media has raised awareness of CSA in Spain considerably (Pereda et al. 2007).

Media coverage of this issue began in 1991 (*La Nueva España*, 1991) when José Luis Magaña-Chueca, a football coach, was sentenced to 15 years in prison for 20 offenses of sexually abusing at least 15 male children, 10–11 years old, between 1987 and 1989 in a Spanish town called Soria. However, he absconded. Magaña-Chueca was not located until 2003, in the United Kingdom, where he was arrested but could not be extradited (Hervada 2003). He apparently then 'started a new life in Peckham [London], running a youth football team ... after passing Football Association background checks' (Widdup 2009). A second case came to light in 1993 in the Premiership football club Rayo Vallecano. In this case de las Heras, the under 12s coach, was found guilty of sexually abusing 14 of the children, 10–11 years old, in his team. He was sentenced to four years in prison, prohibited from working as a coach for ten years and ordered to pay 9,000 Euros (approximately £7,500) to each victim (El País 1995).

Echeburúa and Guerricaechevarría (2011) argue that for a country which underwent 40 years of dictatorship in the twentieth century and where democracy is relatively young, there is a 'natural tendency' for CSA to be ignored by collectives and institutions in Spanish society. It will doubtless come as no surprise to readers to hear that sport is one of the public institutions which failed to acknowledge the problem. It is interesting to note, then, in response to the arrest of Fernando Torres Baena in February 2010, the first statement of the Karate Canary Island Federation, by José Pérez, was to emphasize apparent public confidence in the sport, stating 'licences to compete in karate have increased by 17 per cent' (Televisión Canaria Dos 2010). Whilst he promised that 'the surveillance is going to be *exquisite*, especially in the programmes for high profile children's karate' (Televisión Canaria Dos 24 March 2010), no reference was made to any specific measure to protect children from abuse. He also implied that Torres Baena's sexual abuse of children was unrelated to the context in which it occurred: 'people know that one person does not represent the whole collective...this is not what identifies karate.' The 'one bad apple doesn't spoil a barrel' response serves to distance the organization from its responsibilities in safeguarding children's welfare. Such defensive responses have been heavily criticized for failing to prioritize children's needs and for failing to take the abuse of children in sport contexts seriously (Brackenridge 2001).

Child sexual abuse in Spain

Prevalence research

The results of the most recent international epidemiology of CSA shows that 7.4 per cent of boys have undergone some kind of sexual abuse in comparison to 19.2 per cent of girls (Pereda et al. 2009b). There is no systematic data collection on CSA in Spain, however, a Ministry of Health study (López 1994) found that prevalence rates of CSA in Spain – 18.9 per cent (15.2 per cent for males and 22.5 per cent for females) – are comparable to that of other Western countries. This study also found that 12 per cent of 'perpetrators' are under 20 years old:

66 per cent of whom are male and 33 per cent female (López et al.1995). A study in the Basque country produced somewhat different findings with rates of CSA at 10 per cent for adult men and 15 per cent for adult women (De Paúl et al. 1995). Another study carried out with Barcelona University students confirms these results (Pereda and Forns 2007; Pereda et al. 2009a). Therefore, research confirms that CSA has enough presence in Spanish society to be considered as a social problem which needs attention and the investment of public resources.

Spanish law

The Spanish Constitution 1978 introduced the protection of children as an institutional obligation in the article 39.4. Spain ratified the United Nation's Convention on the Rights of the Child (UN General Assembly 1989) on the 6 December 1990. Whilst it has developed domestic policies that oppose the sexual exploitation of children (Aguilar-Cárceles 2009) the extent to which these policies have been implemented has been strongly criticized by Save the Children who warn of the 'serious deficiencies' in the Spanish judicial system in cases of child sexual abuse. For instance, the report states that 'given the difficulty of proving the facts, the Administration of Justice tends to file the cases without proper investigation of the causes, leaving the victims in serious situations of vulnerability and risk' (Save the Children 2012: 8).

This report evidences that Spanish Justice is not following the European directives regarding child protection, which made the Spanish Government create a 'New Plan of Childhood and Adolescence 2013–2016' (Government of Spain 2013). This Plan aims to review the age of sexual consent in Spain, which currently stands at 13, the second lowest in Europe, after the Vatican, which is 12. The plan strongly advocates increasing the age of marriage and consent from 14 and 13 respectively, to 16 years of age.

Furthermore, some inconsistencies have been identified within Spanish Law regarding sexual activity with children. A 13–year-old child can legally consent to have sexual relations with any other person, including adults; is entitled to get married at 14 and yet requires parental consent until the age of 16 to have an abortion. Furthermore, Aguilar-Cárceles (2009: 216) points out that for 'child pornography offenses, children are considered all those under 18 years', yet in sexual abuse offenses children are considered those under 13 years old.

Interestingly, a law on child protection passed in January 1996 provided the concept of mandatory reporting of children at risk – something quite forward-thinking for that time. Article 13 states: 'Anyone or any person in authority, and especially those who for their profession or function detect a risk situation of a minor, must communicate it to the authorities without prejudice to provide the immediate necessary assistance.' Despite this, according to Aguilar-Cárceles (2009) and Pereda et al (2007), many professional bodies, such as psychologists, social workers and medical staff, are not aware of this legal obligation. It can only be assumed that those involved in sport are even less aware of this obligation.

Guillén-Sádaba et al. (2002) identified four areas of weakness for protecting children under Spanish law: (1) the slow speed with which CSA cases progress through the judicial system (particularly troubling as in most cases victims have to co-exist with their perpetrators while the investigation/case is taking place); (2) the lack of specialization of the personnel dealing with CSA cases; (3) the lack of efficient and adequate protocols to identify when a child has been sexually abused; and (4) the lack of co-ordination and transparency between the various organizations dealing with CSA. In summary, the Spanish system of child protection is failing to meet the needs of abused children.

The Save the Children (2012) report, referenced above, confirmed these system shortages, also pointing out the absence of a centralized database of court cases which diminishes the ability to improve protection systems. It is noticeable that the first ever consolidated national register of paedophiles in Spain (exclusively for use by judges and police) was only created in 2009.

The First Spanish Association for Adult Victims of Childhood Sexual Abuse

Fada Association, literally translated as 'angel', started in 1997 in Barcelona with professionals from the fields of psychology, psychiatry and law in order to fill the lack of specialized resources on the prevention and counselling of adults who have suffered sexual abuse during childhood (Pereda et al. 2007). Fada offered two integral services, psychological and legal advice on CSA; it also worked on policy formation and campaigns for greater awareness of CSA in Spanish society.

In 2005 Fada collaborators monitored the public who had contacted them during January to December and found that Fada dealt with 593 cases. Twenty-eight per cent were under age and 72 per cent over 18, confirming that sexually abused children do not feel secure in reporting their abuse. It is worth noting that only 6 underage children asked for legal advice. The majority of adults contacting Fada were unable to bring cases against their abusers as they related to events which were more than 20 years old. Therefore, the vast majority of victims requested psychological support. According to the reports in this study, dealing only with sexual abuse during childhood, the two most common sexual acts the victims revealed were fondling under and on top of clothes (64.4 per cent) and vaginal penetration (9.27 per cent). Other acts, like masturbation, anal and oral penetration, and abuses without physical contact were between 2 and 4 per cent (Pereda et al. 2007). This study confirms the estimation of the Council of Europe that in 70 per cent to 85 per cent of cases the abuser is someone the victim knows and is likely to trust. For Pereda et al. (2007), approximately 85 per cent of the perpetrators were in this group: (34 per cent) father figures, (29 per cent) members of extended family and 18 per cent (people known by the victim). According to Pereda et al. (2007) the work of Fada highlighted the urgent and specialized attention needed to support victims of CSA in Spain. In 2006, Fada became Vicky Bernadet Foundation. It is still the only organization in Spain which uniquely deals with CSA experiences either when they are already adults or still children.

Victim disclosure and concealment in sport: responses and policy development

Hartill (2013: 250) argues that the concealment of CSA in sport by adults does not correspond to being seen 'simply as a "cover-up"' by individuals. It is a deeper and extended practice, which is related to 'the culturally sanctioned exploitation and abuse of children within sports' (Hartill 2013: 250). This is illustrated by the fact that investigations of CSA in sport frequently reveal that many other adults (in some cases, families, in other cases coaches or sport managers) had been aware of the abuse but had failed to report it. For example, Ayala and Ayala (2013) confirm that at least five families knew about Torres Baena's abuses since the late 1980s. One of the mothers even went to the police in 1988 when her daughter was 12. According to this mother the answer of the police was 'nothing can be done regarding this because [they] did not have proof or witnesses [...] it is the child's word against that of the coach' (Ayala and Ayala 2013: 148–9).

Moreover, in the Jesus Carballo case, ex-coach Toni Llorens recently revealed that during a 1979 training camp in Gijón, 'I saw Carballo touch her breast and kiss her on the neck. I couldn't believe it.' Llorens also said that he alerted two directors of the Spanish Gymnastics Federation of what he saw in Gijón, but 'they hit the roof and didn't do anything about it' (Iríbar 2013c). In the Rayo Vallecano case, de las Heras had been already expelled from another football club in Madrid, La Chopera, his director did not like his attitude with the boys: 'I have never seen anything but he had a very strange attitude with the boys. I sensed it could be something else' (Miguélez 1993). Rather than report the issue, the club fired him.

Therefore, according to one specialist in sexual abuse in sects in Spain

> there are some others who with their silence, concealment or inhibition have been the necessary aiders and abettors for the sect of karate to act in the way it did under the light of day during more than three decades.
>
> (Rodriguez in Ayala and Ayala 2013: 22)

This supports the argument that CSA in sport is not only an issue between the perpetrator and the victim, the whole institution of sport needs to examine the discourses and messages it is sending to society, but mainly to child athletes, families, coaches and sport directors (Brackenridge 2001; Hartill 2013).

As noted above, the duration of the judicial process for CSA is troubling. The Torres Baena case – referred to as 'the karate case' – took two years and three months of investigation before coming to trial; the trial itself lasted six months, and it took a further three months to hand down the sentence: a total of three years. Torres Baena was detained on the 3 February 2010 and sentenced to 302 years in prison on 15 March 2013 (Ayala and Ayala 2013). In another recent case, Martin Pajuelo, a football coach, was accused of having sexually abused four 14–16 years old boys in mid-2008 but he was not sentenced until July 2013 (Diario de Cádiz 2013).

Furthermore, when Gloria Viseras reported, at the end of 2012, that Jesús Carballo had sexually abused her between the ages of 12 and 15 in the late 1970s, the CSD advised her to go to the police. The CSD then initiated action against Carballo and subsequently dismissed him. Carballo is a famous coach in Spain so the case received a great deal of media coverage. In response to these allegations, supported by the Spanish Gymnastic Federation, the president of which is Carballo's son, over 40 former national gymnasts from the last 30 years who trained at some point in their careers with Carballo signed a letter of support stating that he 'has never exercised any humiliating treatment towards us and moreover against our sexual freedom' (La Gaceta 2013). Supporters of Carballo have also used social media tools (Facebook and Twitter) to insult Viseras and accuse her of destroying the image of Spanish gymnastics (personal correspondence).

Despite the cases of CSA that have come to light within Spanish sport, authorities within Spain have, so far, failed to introduce policy responses to this serious problem. Research and victim accounts in relation to the difficulty of disclosing abuse clearly indicate that appropriate educational provision for adults who work with children, or have responsibility for children's environments, is crucial in efforts to reduce CSA (Echeburúa and Guerricaechevarría 2011). Whilst it is clear that adults in sport (such as coaches) have abused and continue to abuse children (physically and emotionally as well as sexually), sports coaches are also central to efforts to safeguard children from abuse in (and through) sport. Coaches have an insider's view of the organizational culture within a sport or individual club which is invaluable to the task of constructing a child-centred sports system and combatting abuse (David 2005). Moreover, s/he may also be the first adult to whom an abused child turns.

According to Pereda et al. (2007) the wider socio-cultural context influences the availability of support for victims of sexual violence. While it is crucial, to tackle the taboo and silence that surrounds CSA in Spanish sport, through awareness-raising campaigns, it is also necessary to promote gender equality in sport (Puig and Soler 2004; Vázquez 2002). Competitive sport in Spain is still considered a safe haven for hyper-masculinist behaviour and only 3 per cent of female sports participants play competitively, compared to 25 per cent of men (García-Ferrando and Llopis-Goig 2011).

Actions taken regarding child sexual abuse in sport

Whilst the International Olympic Committee (2007) was adamant about instigating national Committees to deal with sexual harassment and abuse in sport, Spain has no policies protecting athletes from any kind of abuse, including child athletes. Frequently in high-level sport, athletes are regarded as machines, as objects to produce achievements for the pride of the country. The wellbeing and the needs of the human being driving these achievements is often a long way down the list of priorities. These abuses generally go unpunished by the judicial system and the sports field/community has so far failed to coordinate unitary action to address them. One response of note is a new CSD programme called PROAD:

'Attention to under age high-level athletes' which was launched in February 2013 (CSD 2013a). The goal of PROAD is to ensure the safe educational, formative and emotional development of children and youngsters who are in intense high-level sport programmes. It does not, however, deal specifically with sexual abuse.

Whilst there is no sociological research on athletes' sexual abuse in sport in Spain yet, there have been some initiatives to bring sport agents' attention to the negative impact of the issue on young athletes. For instance, Professor Celia Brackenridge visited Barcelona in November 2007 (Catalan School of Sport 2007). In October 2012, Dr Mike Hartill delivered a seminar on child sexual abuse at the University of Vic (see Hartill 2012 for details), and in June 2013 a seminar on the prevention of CSA in sport was held in CSD with the participation of English and German sport sociologists (CSD 2013b). As a result of this seminar a multi-disciplinary group (academics, coaches, sport managers, athletes, victims, journalists, psychologists and medical doctors) called GAPAS (D) – 'Support Group to Prevent Sexual Abuse in Sport', was created at the beginning of September 2013 with the intention of becoming a pressure group which gathers key CSA in sport information. For instance, the journalist Cristina Gallo is meticulously gathering and following up all the CSA in sport cases covered in the media. The ultimate goal is to pressure the governing institutions to develop initiatives, including but not limited to: (1) policies of child safeguarding in sport; (2) creating awareness campaigns of the existence of CSA in sport; (3) revising legal aspects regarding the protection of children; and (4) investing in research on the issue.

Final thoughts

Spain still has a long way to go to be able to establish a decent and efficient system of preventing, identifying and punishing offenders of CSA in sport. As noted above, following some high-profile cases of sexual abuse, the Spanish High Sports Council, the CSD, seems to be reacting to the issue. Undoubtedly more cases will follow, but the speed and extent to which this occurs will depend on the responses by sport agencies and wider Spanish society. As stated above, some of the reactions to Gloria Viseras' allegations against Jesús Carballo are not promising and will certainly cause many victims (current and historic) to maintain their silence.

Thus, one cannot be too naïve about the likelihood of this issue becoming a priority for sport politics. Whilst media coverage helps to make the issue more visible, the risk of secondary victimization is still high. As stated by several studies, deficiencies in the legal and child protection systems in Spain can have very damaging outcomes – in some cases as damaging as the actual sexual abuse experiences themselves. The victim who reveals such a painful experience needs to feel supported by her/his sports organization. Equally, the sports community (volunteers, coaches, etc.) also need to be supported to understand and have confidence in handling disclosures and allegations. Spanish sport needs to create mechanisms to raise awareness on all forms of maltreatment in sport, and should consider carefully how they can best support their various communities to address this issue in light of the growing realization that children and young people in sport can be sexually exploited and abused by those in whose care they are entrusted.

References

Aguilar-Cárceles, M. M. (2009) 'Sexual abuse in childhood', *Anales de Derecho*, 27: 210–40.

Ayala, M. F. and Ayala, M. (2013) *The Karate Sect*, Madrid: Mercurio Editorial.

Brackenridge, C. H. (2001) *Spoilsports: understanding and preventing sexual exploitation in sport*, London: Routledge.

Cantón, J. and Cortés, M. R. (2000) *Guide to Assess Child Sexual Abuse*, Madrid: Pirámide.

Catalan School of Sport (2007) *Sexual Harassment in Sport Seminar*. Online. Available HTTP: <www.donesenxarxa.cat/IMG/pdf/JORNADES_ESPORT.pdf> (accessed 21 September 2013).

Consejo Superior de Deportes (2013a) *PROAD Programme: attention to the minor*. Online. Available HTTP: <proad.csd.gob.es/noticias/item/911–presentacion-del-nuevo-programa-proad-atencion-al-menor> (accessed 27 May 2013).

— (2013b) *Child Sexual Abuse Prevention in Sport Seminar*. Online. Available HTTP: <www.csd.gob.es/csd/salud/seminario-sobre-prevencion-del-abuso-sexual-infantil-en-el-deporte/> (accessed 5 September 2013).

David, P. (2005) *Human Rights in Youth Sport: a critical review of children's rights in competitive sports*, London: Routledge.

De Paúl, J., Milner, J. S. and Múgica, P. (1995) 'The potential of childhood maltreatment, childhood social support, and child abuse in the Basque country', *Child Abuse and Neglect*, 19: 907–20.

Diario de Cádiz (2013) *Sentencing the Ex-Football Player Pajuelo for the Sexual Abuse of Four Minors*. Online. Available HTTP: <www.diariodecadiz.es/article/provincia/1569491/condenan/ex/futbolista/pajuelo/por/abusos/sexuales/menores.html> (accessed 23 September 2013).

Echeburúa, E. and Guerricaechevarría, C. (2011) 'Psychological treatment of intrafamalilial victims of sexual abuse', *Behavioural Psychology*, 19: 469–86.

El País (1995) *An Ex-Rayo Coach Accused of Abusing Minors*. Online. Available HTPP: <elpais.com/diario/1995/12/20/madrid/819462264_850215.html> (accessed 16 September 2013).

García-Ferrando, M. and Llopis-Goig, R. (2011) *Democratic Ideal and Personal Welfare*, Madrid: CSD.

Guillén-Sádaba, E., Aleman, M. C., Arias, A., Murillo, F. and Pérez, D. (2002) 'The detection of child sexual abuse cases in social services: difficulties and suggestions', *Cuadernos de Trabajo Social* (Journal of Social Work), 10: 241–51.

Government of Spain (2013) *Plan of Childhood and Adolescence 2013–2016*. Online. Available HTTP: <www.lamoncloa.gob.es/ConsejodeMinistros/Enlaces/050413enlaceinfancia.htm> (accessed 31 May 2013).

Hartill, M. (2012) '*Sexual harassment and abuse in sport*', seminar presented at the University of Vic, Catalonia, 17 October. Online. Available HTTP: <www.uvic.es/sites/default/files/acAssetjamentIAbusSexual.pdf> (accessed 29 September 2013).

— (2013) 'Concealment of child sexual abuse in sports', *Quest*, 65: 241–54.

Hervada, M. (2003) *The Provincial Court of Soria Will not Ask for the Extradition of the Sexual Abuse Offender*. Online. Available HTTP: <www.abc.es/hemeroteca/historico-31-05-2003/abc/CastillaLeon/la-audiencia-provincial-de-soria-no-solicitara-la-extradicion-del-condenado-por-abusos-sexuales_184670.html> (accessed 16 September 2013).

International Olympic Committee (2007) *IOC Adopts Consensus Statement on Sexual Harassment and Abuse in Sport*. Online. Available HTTP: <www.olympic.org/content/news/media-resources/manual-news/1999-2009/2007/02/08/ioc-adopts-consensus-statement-on-sexual-harassment-and-abuse-in-sport/> (accessed 10 July 2012).

Iríbar, A. (2013a) 'The police totally believe that Carballo has abused child gymnasts', *El País*, 19 May. Online. Available HTTP: <deportes.elpais.com/deportes/2013/05/19/actualidad/1368994806_207923.html> (accessed 5 July 2013).

Iríbar, A. (2013b) 'The CSD supports the continuation of the investigation of Carballo', *El País*, 20 May. Online. Available HTTP: <deportes.elpais.com/deportes/2013/05/20/actualidad/1369081563_252933.html> (accesed 5 July 2013).

Iríbar, A. (2013c) 'He wouldn't let us talk to the girls', *El País*, 9 July. Online. Available HTTP: <elpais.com/elpais/2013/07/09/inenglish/1373372172_899333.html> (accessed 9 September 2013).

La Gaceta (2013) *Jesús Carballo: reaction against the accusations*, 21 May. Online. Available HTPP: <www.intereconomia.com/noticias-gaceta/deporte/jesus-carballo-reaccion-su-linchamiento-20130521> (accessed 5 July 2013).

La Nueva España (1991) 'A Soria football coach has been sentenced to 15 years for sexual abuse', *La Nueva España*, 19 April.

Law 1/1996 of Child Protection (1996). Online. Available HTTP: <www.boe.es/diario_boe/xml.php?id=BOE-A-1996-1069> (accessed 15 February 2013).

López, F. (1994) *What the Adults Remember*, Madrid: Ministry of Social Affairs.

López, F., Hernández, A. and Carpintero, E. (1995) 'Child sexual abuse: concept, prevalence and effects', *Infancia y Aprendizaje* (Children and Learning), 18: 77–98.

Miguélez, J. (1993) '15 children accuse their coach of abuse', *El País*, 18 September. Online. Available HTTP: <elpais.com/diario/1993/09/18/madrid/748351456_850215.html> (assessed 29 September 2013).

Pereda, N. and Forns, M. (2007) 'Prevalence and characteristics of child sexual abuse in Spanish university students', *Child Abuse and Neglect*, 31: 417–26.

Pereda, N., Guilera, G., Forns, M and Gómez-Benito, J. (2009a) 'The prevalence of child sexual abuse in community and student samples: a meta-analysis', *Clinical Psychology Review,* 29: 328–38.

— (2009b) 'The international epidemiology of child sexual abuse: a continuation of Finkelhor (1994)', *Child Abuse and Neglect,* 33: 331–42.

Pereda, N., Polo, P., Grau, N., Navales, N. and Martínez, M. (2007) 'Child sexual abuse victims', *Revista d'Estudis de la Violència* (Journal for the Study of Violence), 1: 1–18.

Puig, N. and Soler, S. (2004) 'Women and sport in Spain: state of the matter and interpretative proposal', *Revista Apunts Educacion Fisica y Deportes* (Physical Education and Sport), 76: 71–8.

Rodríguez, P. (2013) 'Preface: the web of the nascissist and the silence of his victims', in M. F. Ayala and M. Ayala (eds.) *The Karate Sect,* Madrid: Mercurio Editorial.

Save the Children (2012) *Spanish Justice in Cases of Child Sexual Abuse in the Family Environment*, Ministry of Health, Social Politics and Equality. Online. Available HTTP: <www.savethechildren.es/docs/Ficheros/553/Informe_JUSTICIA_ESP_ABUSO_SEXUAL_INFANTIL_vOK-2.pdf> (accessed 17 March 2013).

Televisión Canaria Dos (2010) *Karate Case (Interview with José Pérez, the President of the Karate Canary Island Federation)*, 24 March. Online. Available HTTP: <www.youtube.com/watch?v=qaUnSCROHWQ> (accessed 25 September 2013).

United Nations General Assembly (1989) Convention on the Rights of the Child. Online. Available HTTP: <www.unhcr.org/refworld/docid/3ae6b38f0.html> (accessed 15 March 2013).

Vázquez, B. (2002) 'Women in competitive domains: the domain of sport' *Faisca: Revista de Altas Capacidades* (Journal of High Abilities), 9: 56–69.

Widdup, E. (2009) 'Paedophile who fled Spain was cleared to run children's football team in Britain', *The Mail Online*, 27 January. Online. Available HTTP: <http://www.dailymail.co.uk/news/article-1128734/Paedophile-fled-Spain-cleared-run-childrens-football-team-Britain.html#ixzz2nwLyhdKw> (accessed 17 December 2013).

8 Safeguarding children from violence and abuse in Slovenian sport

Joca Zurc, Daniel J. A. Rhind and Melanie Lang

Slovenia is a central European nation at the crossroads of the main European cultural and trade routes. The country has been a member of the European Union since 2004 and is a regular participant at the summer and winter Olympic Games, where it is one of the most successful countries in terms of the number of medallists per resident (Olympic Committee of Slovenia 2011). Indeed, sport is a central part of the Slovene national identity (Olympic Committee of Slovenia 2011). Yet despite this focus on sport, developments to safeguard and protect athletes, both adults and children, are limited. Nevertheless, as this chapter highlights, attitudes to this issue from both sports organizations and the police and judiciary may be on the cusp of change, driven by high-profile media coverage of sexual violence in sport.

Children's and athletes' rights in Slovenia

The term 'safeguarding' as it is understood in England (see Chapter 1) is not yet embedded in child welfare legislation, policy and practice in Slovenia. However, the country ratified the United Nations Convention on the Rights of the Child (United Nations General Assembly 1989) in 1991 and has been bound by all the rights guaranteed by the Convention since 2004. It has a good record of incorporating provisions on children's rights into domestic law (Longchampt 2013), although some non-governmental organizations (NGOs) argue such laws are often flouted, putting the legal protections in place for children at risk (Slovene NGO Coalition ZIPOM 2013).

In sport, the 1998 Sports Act was enacted in part to safeguard athletes, especially children, young people and elite athletes (Jagodic 2010). It contains measures to prevent athletes from being forced to compete or train during injury or illness, mandates preventative medical exams for athletes participating in all levels of sport, and states that participation in sport should not be detrimental to an individual's health (The Sports Act 1998). The law also provides a national system for regulating the status of elite athletes, among other things setting the minimum age at which athletes can turn professional as 15 years old (INEUN Consulting/Taj 2008). Any abuses of an athlete's human rights are prosecuted by the Inspectorate for Education and Sport of the Republic of Slovenia, a body affiliated to the Ministry for Education and Sport (The Sports Act 1998).

Meanwhile, the National Programme of Sport, which was established in 2000 under the Sports Act, provides additional safeguards for all athletes, including children. For example, it mandates that the state should pay for athletes to have medical, social and injury and disability insurances, and sets the minimum age for athletes to commence high-level training at 6 years old (INEUN Consulting/ Taj 2008).

Legislating against violence and child abuse

While the legislation noted in the previous section offers certain protections and rights to athletes of all ages, Slovenia has also enacted laws specifically to protect against what is termed 'violence' and 'abuse'. The Family Violence Prevention Act (Ministry of Labour, Family, Social Affairs and Equal Opportunities 2008) defines the following forms of violence: physical, sexual, psychological or economic violence (European Network for Ombudspersons for Children 2013).

In terms of sexual violence towards children, which is deemed taboo and rarely reported or prosecuted in Slovenian society (Bašič 1993), Article 171 of the Penal Code establishes sexual violence against any person as a criminal offence punishable by up to 15 years in prison (Ministry of Justice 2005). It defines sexual violence as when one person forces another person, whether of the same or opposite sex, to perform any sexual act (Ministry of Justice 2005). Meanwhile, Article 172 criminalizes the 'sexual abuse of defenceless persons', meaning people with 'mental disease, temporary or graver mental disorder or sickness or any other state' (Ministry of Justice 2005: 71).

In relation to children, the Slovenia Constitution and its related legislation guarantee children special protection from violence and abuse, with a child defined under the Slovenian Penal Code as a person under 15 years old (Ministry of Justice 2005). Article 173 of the Penal Code states that any sexual activity with a child under 15 years old is punishable by imprisonment of between three and eight years, with special provisions to increase the sentence to a maximum ten years if the offence is perpetrated by someone in a position of authority over the child, such as a teacher, parent or guardian, priest or doctor (Ministry of Justice 2005). Cases of sexual violence against children in sport can be prosecuted under Article 171 and/or under Article 173, in the latter case particularly using the clause on abuse of a position of authority.

The Family Violence Prevention Act (Ministry of Labour, Family, Social Affairs and Equal Opportunities 2008) also defines sexual violence. However, its provisions extend only to violence perpetrated within the family, such as a family member forcing a child to experience sexual content or behaviour. Limiting the definition of sexual violence in this way has resulted in criticism from some NGOs for failing to offer protection from violence to children in all contexts (European Network for Ombudspersons for Children 2013; Slovene NGO Coalition ZIPOM 2013). Nevertheless, the Act offers children in sport some protection. It mandates that all citizens, and in particular social workers, health workers and those in the education sector, must report suspicions of child abuse, regardless of where the abuse is suspected of occurring, to either the police, the state prosecutor's office or one of the national network of Centres for Social Work, state-run centres that oversee social welfare issues, including child protection (Ministry of Labour, Family, Social Affairs and Equal Opportunities 2008).

Media coverage and growing awareness of abuse in sport

In recent years, awareness of violence and abuse in sport has been raised following high-profile media coverage. The first such case to be covered by the Slovenian media appeared in 2007, when national volleyball player Jana Vernig alleged she had been sexually abused by her high jump coach when she was 12 years old. Vernig, who was 30 years old at the time of the allegations, trained as a high jumper from the sixth grade of primary school under coach Slavko Malnar. In a series of articles in the Slovene newspaper *Daily News*, Vernig accused Malnar of sexually abusing her for one and a half years, explaining that the alleged abuse prompted her to give up high jumping and take up volleyball (*Daily News* 2007). The story sparked significant public reaction, and Vernig was commended for going public with the allegations (*Daily News* 2007). The allegations also prompted a flood of newspaper articles on child abuse, particularly child sexual abuse, in sport in Slovenia, although the initial media interest failed to provoke any reaction from sports organizations in the country.

The following year the public prosecutor rejected all charges against Malnar because the statute of limitations for the alleged offence had expired. Malnar later took the publishers of the *Daily News* to court for defamation, arguing he had been unfairly labelled a paedophile, but he lost the case. As this chapter went to press, Malnar was still working as a senior coach at an athletic club in Novo Mesto in south-east Slovenia. Vernig has expressed disappointment at the club allowing Malnar to continue to coach and called on sports organizations in the country to face up to the existence of child abuse in their ranks (*Dolenjska Newspaper* 2008).

Then in 2010 the police in Piran on the Slovenian coast received an anonymous letter alleging children were being sexually assaulted by a 35–year-old coach from a well-known acrobatic-dance club in the town called Flip. Later that year, Mitja Mehora was convicted on 39 counts of sexually assaulting 14 girls under the age of 15 during training, leisure time and at competitions or trips abroad (*Primorske Info* 2010). Mehora was sentenced to seven and a half years in prison (*Daily News* 2010) but on appeal, eight of the 39 counts against him were rejected on the grounds that there was a lack of credible evidence. Mehora was re-tried on the remaining 31 counts but the court was unable to find further evidence to substantiate the claims and Mehora was released from prison in April 2011 (*Primorske News* 2011).

The next high-profile case came in 2012 when a 14–year-old boy alleged he had been sexually assaulted by Sašo Kisela, a 43–year-old coach at a summer camp run by the Slovenia Basketball Federation (POP TV 2012). The police investigated the allegations against Kisela and passed the case to the prosecutor's office and the Disciplinary Board of the Slovenia Basketball Federation initiated a review into the allegations. In 2013 Kisela was excluded from the Basketball Coach Society of Slovenia and the prosecutor requested further investigation of the allegations, including the questioning of additional witnesses (*Slovenian News* 2012). The case was unusual because the Slovenia Basketball Federation was quick to react to the allegations, publicly condemning sexual assault, suspending Kisela pending the outcome of the criminal investigation against him, and offering professional support to the boy who made the allegations. Indeed this case, and in particular the way the Slovenia Basketball Federation managed it, suggests sports organizations may be beginning to take seriously allegations of (sexual) violence in sport.

Most recently, the *Daily News* newspaper published an article claiming six girls were being sexually assaulted by their 61–year-old karate coach, Josip Kovšca (*Daily News* 2012). Kovšca, who was the head coach at a karate club in Postojna in south-west Slovenia and one of the club's presidents, was charged in March 2013 with sexually assaulting children under the age of 15 and abusing his position of authority (*Daily News* 2012).

The high media profile given to these cases signals a growing awareness of sexual violence and abuse in sport in Slovenia. Indeed, while the Vernig case did little at the time to drive child protection developments in sport in the country, it was instrumental in increasing public and media awareness of sexual violence in sport, and may yet mark the turning point for how violence and abuse is managed in Slovenian sport. In addition although anecdotal, the variety of sports involved in these cases suggests that violence and abuse can occur in any sport and that those targeted can be boys or girls of any age from very young children through to teens. Indeed, this mirrors research evidence from studies of the prevalence and incidence of (sexual) violence and abuse in other countries (Fasting and Knorre 2005; Fasting et al. 2000; Kirby and Greaves 1996; Leahy et al. 2002; Yorganci 1993). However, while in Slovenia the alleged perpetrators reported in media cases have, so far, been male coaches, it is important to recognize that violence, harassment and abuse are not the preserve of men; women and children themselves have been identified as perpetrators of such violence in and beyond sport (Gannon and Cortoni 2010; Kirby and Greaves 1996; Sahlstrom and Jeglic 2008).

Campaigns to raise awareness of sexual violence

Prompted in part by the media coverage discussed above, in recent years the Slovenian Government embarked on a series of public campaigns aimed at raising awareness of violence and abuse, although the focus so far has been on sexual abuse at the expense of other forms of abuse and broader safeguarding issues, and none of the campaigns have yet specifically tackled sport as a context for such violence. As an example, the Ministry of the Interior, in conjunction with the police, publicized an educational campaign called 'Some secrets should not remain hidden!'. The campaign involves advertising on social media, television and radio as well as distributing posters, leaflets and a children's book on the topic. The book, which describes experiences of abuse through the story of a sexually abused child (Vojnović 2011), was distributed to pupils in Slovenian primary schools along with a presentation advising pupils on how to manage sexual abuse (Ministry of the Interior 2013).

Another such campaign is fronted by Slovenian boxer Dejan Zavec, who also works for the Ministry of Interior. The campaign, which is based around a video titled 'Sexual abuse should not stay hidden', addresses sexual violence in a variety of settings and is aimed at children aged between 10 and 14 years old, but again does not specifically address the context of sport (Gotal 2011).

Country-specific empirical evidence

To date, there are only limited empirical studies of violence, child abuse and broader safeguarding and children's rights issues in sport in Slovenia, so there remain significant gaps in our knowledge about these issues in the cultural context of Slovenian sport, not least about the prevalence and incidence of violence and child abuse in sport in the country. To the best of our knowledge, only one study has explored violence in sport, and that had a focus on sexual violence such as sexual harassment and child sexual abuse. Kozina (2009) investigated physical education (PE) teachers' knowledge of sexual harassment and child abuse in sport and physical activity, and found that 62 per cent of PE teachers had no knowledge about sexual harassment and child abuse in sport. In total, 57 per cent said they were not aware of any regulations relating to the prevention of harassment and child abuse in sport, and 66 per cent said they believed such problems did not exist in Slovenia. These findings are obviously worrying but perhaps unsurprising given that sport departments in the country do not include these issues in their curriculum.

More recently, Zurc (2013) conducted an exploratory study into a broad range of child welfare issues in sport in Slovenia. In the study, the first author of this chapter conducted retrospective interviews with 11 female former Slovenian child athletes on their experiences of elite youth gymnastics. The study identified several themes relating to safeguarding children in sport. Among these, two in particular – managing injuries and mitigating pain through the use of legal drugs – will be discussed in detail here.

Managing injury

As Abernethy and Bleakley (2007: 627) note, 'young people are at particular risk of sports injury because of high levels of exposure at a time of major physiological change'. Injury is a particular risk in gymnastics because of the nature of the sport. In this exploratory study, as has been found elsewhere (Zurc 2010), it often ended the gymnasts' careers. However, participants described how their risk of picking up an injury was magnified by their desire to comply with coaches' demands. As one participant explained:

> If I had the opportunity to live my life in gymnastics again, I would definitely change it if I knew it was going to be like this. For sure, I would say no sometimes, I don't want to, I can't, whatever, because maybe these injuries wouldn't happen then. Because I'm quite persistent and if the coaches say something, I go for it and I want to reach the goal. But you mustn't go beyond your limits and unfortunately I did. And unfortunately, I am where I am now … When there was pain, I should have said, I'm sorry, no I can't.
>
> (Jana)

Hughes and Coakley (1991: 308) refer to athletes' 'uncritical acceptance of and commitment to what they have been told by important people in their lives', such as coaches, as 'positive deviance'. Equally, Lang (2010) and Johns and Johns (2000) argue that common coaching practices, underpinned by understandings of coaches as 'experts' and athletes as 'novice recipients of this authoritative expertise' (Johns and Johns 2000: 231), encourage athletes to conform to normative behaviours in sport, leading them to submit to intensive and sometimes dangerous training protocols. Given these points, it is unsurprising that these gymnasts wished to comply with their coaches' demands (Burke 2001). Crucially, however, it is only with hindsight, as adults, that they are able to reflect critically on their behaviour and its potential impact on their health.

Mitigating pain through legal drug use

Athletes in a range of sports have been found to continue to train and complete while injured (Murphy and Waddington 2007; Papaefstathiou et al. 2013), in some cases taking prescription and non-prescription drugs to numb their pain and enable them to keep playing (Ryan 1995; Tscoll et al. 2009). Similarly, the athletes said they often continued to train through injury and health problems and self-medicated with painkillers to facilitate this. While in most cases the athletes took the decision to use such drugs themselves, one said she had been made to do so by her coach, against her wishes:

> I was injured. I had a torn muscle in the lumbar area, but I had to do it [compete] with different injections because it was a national championship. At that point, it all became a little negative for me … Anyway, before the competition they drugged me, numbed me a little less … At the end, I didn't win anything but I still had to go because it was a group event – we actually won … and then I quit gymnastics forever.
>
> (Nina)

Although the participants in this study were reflecting back on experiences when they were children, more recent studies of youth athletes have found that similar practices still occur (Tscoll et al. 2009). Athletes have reported receiving 'official recognition' from coaches and other athletes for their willingness to continue playing while injured, while coaches have been found to ignore or deny athletes' pain and injury in an attempt to encourage them to continue playing (Roderick et al. 2000). Given this context, and the culture of sport that demands conformity and compliance to the coaches' demands (Lang 2010), it is easy to see why some athletes are willing to put their health at risk in this way.

Despite the experiences detailed above, all the former gymnasts said participating in the sport had been fulfilling and provided them with a sound foundation for their future. In particular, they highlighted their positive memories of being part of the sport and the benefits they perceived they had gained from it, such as developing life experience and life skills. It has long been acknowledged that sport can be beneficial to children; as well as being fun, it has the potential to positively affect health and fitness (Bertelloni et al. 2006), increase bodily awareness and self esteem (Engh 2002), and teach rules, respect, sportsmanship and social interaction (Donnelly 1993). Yet as noted above, 'uncritical acceptance of and commitment to' the norms of sports cultures (Hughes and Coakley 1991: 308) can result in athletes normalizing negative and potentially dangerous behaviours. It may be that, even after retiring from the sport, these norms continue to influence these former athletes' perceptions of gymnastics, encouraging them to normalize their negative experiences.

Future developments and concluding comments

Recent media coverage of allegations of violence and child abuse in sport in Slovenia has ensured that violence, and particularly sexual violence, is beginning to be recognized as an issue in sport in the country. However, much more empirical research is needed to explore child welfare in Slovenian sport. Indeed, although some researchers have begun to take steps in this direction, there remain many gaps in our knowledge, including understandings of the extent of violence and abuse endured by athletes in sport, whether as children or adults. There is also an urgent need to look beyond cases of sexual violence and consider other forms of violence and abuse (physical, psychological, economic) as well as broader safeguarding issues.

The data reported in the second part of this chapter is a first, exploratory step towards this goal. Enhanced understanding of these and other child welfare issues should be used, in tandem with the opinions and wishes of children and young people, to inform strategies to safeguard and protect children in sport. We recognize that the need to develop standardized approaches to these issues at the global level, combined with the need for tailored approaches at the micro level that take into consideration the specificities of a country's culture, history and sport organization structures, is a key tension still to be managed. However, we recommend that Slovenian sports authorities develop and implement a strategy that should, as a minimum, incorporate clear policies and guidelines for safeguarding and protecting children in sport, and education programmes that include the views of children, their parents, coaches and other sport support staff (Bochaver and Kasatkin 2010; McArdle and Duda 2008).

References

Abernethy, L. and Bleakley, C. (2007) 'Strategies to prevent injury in adolescent sport: a systematic review', *British Journal of Sports Medicine,* 41: 627–38.

Bašič, K. (1993) 'Sexual assaults on children', *Journal of Police,* 13: 36–51.

Bertelloni, S., Ruggeri, S. and Baroncelli, G. I. (2006) 'Effects of sports training in adolescence on growth, puberty and bone health', *Gynecological Endocrinology,* 22: 605–12.

Bochaver, A. and Kasatkin, V. (2010) '*The characteristics of attitudes towards performance-enhancing drugs in sport in Russia*', paper presented at the 24th European Health Psychology Society conference, Cluj-Napoca, Romania.

Burke, M. (2001) 'Obeying until it hurts: the coach-athlete relationship', *Journal of the Philosophy of Sport,* 28: 227–40.

Daily News (2007) 'Confession: I was told, "you will make people disgusted" – me, the victim', *Daily News,* 15 September. Online. Available HTTP: <www.dnevnik.si/objektiv/vec-vsebin/268767> (accessed 8 July 2013).

Daily News (2010) 'Judgement on Mitja Mehora from Piran acrobatic-dance sport club Flip for abusing 16 girls', *Daily News* 27 October. Online. Available HTTP: <www.dnevnik.si/kronika/1042398614> (accessed 8 July 2013).

Daily News (2012) 'Head coach of Postojna karate club suspected of sexually harassing six young female athletes', *Daily News,* 18 August. Online. Available HTTP: <www.dnevnik.si/kronika/1042547260> (accessed 8 July 2013).

Dolenjska Newspaper (2008) 'Jana Vernig: "probably I will go for a civil lawsuit"', *Dolenjska Newspaper,* 27 May. Online. Available HTTP: <www.dolenjskilist.si/2008/05/27/4398/novice/clanek/Jana_Vernig_Verjetno_se_bom_odlocila_za_civilno_tozbo/> (accessed 8 July 2013).

Donnelly, P. (1993) 'Problems associated with youth involvement in high-performance sport', in B. R. Cahill and A. J. Pearl (eds) *Intensive Participation in Children's Sports,* IL.: Human Kinetics.

Engh, F. (2002) *Why Johnny Hates Sports: why organized youth sports are failing our children and what we can do about it,* New York: Square One.

European Network for Ombudspersons for Children (2013) *Slovenia: national laws on children's rights.* Online. Available HTTP: <www.crin.org/enoc/resources/infodetail.asp?id=31249> (accessed 11 December 2013).

Fasting, K. and Knorre, N. (2005) *Women in Sport in the Czech Republic: the experiences of female athletes,* Oslo: Norwegian School of Sport Sciences/Czech Olympic Committee.

Fasting, K., Brackenridge, B. and Sundgot-Borgen, J. (2000) *Sexual Harassment in and Outside Sport,* Oslo: Norwegian Olympic Committee.

Gannon, T. A. and Cortoni, F. (2010) *Female Sexual Offenders: theory, assessment and treatment,* Chichester, UK: Wiley-Blackwell.

Gotal, M. (2011) 'Attention! Some secrets should not remain hidden!', *Journal of Security,* 59: 22–3.

Hughes, R. and Coakley, J. (1991) 'Positive deviance among athletes: the implications of over-conformity to the sport ethic', *Sociology of Sport Journal,* 8: 307–25.

INEUN Consulting/Taj (2008) *Study on Training of Young Sportsmen/Women in Europe: final report.* Online. Available HTTP: <http://ec.europa.eu/sport/library/documents/c3/doc512_en.pdf> (accessed 11 December 2013).

Jagodic, T. (2010) 'National models of good governance in sport: Slovenia', *The International Sports Law Journal*, 3–4: 118–22.

Johns, D. P. and Johns, J. S. (2000) 'Surveillance, subjectivism and technologies of power: an analysis of the discursive practice of high-performance sport', *International Review for the Sociology of Sport*, 35: 219–34.

Kirby, S. and Greaves, L. (1996) '*Foul play: sexual abuse and harassment in sport*', paper presented at the Pre-Olympic Scientific Congress, Dallas, USA, July 1996.

Kozina, A. (2009) '*The role of the Physical Education teacher in recognizing child abuse*', unpublished BSc thesis, University of Ljubljana.

Lang, M. (2010) Surveillance and conformity in competitive youth swimming', *Sport, Education and Society*, 15: 19–37.

Leahy, T., Pretty, G. and Tenenbaum, G. (2002) 'Prevalence of sexual abuse in organized competitive sport in Australia', in C. Brackenridge and K. Fasting (eds) *Sexual Harassment and Abuse in Sport: international research and policy perspectives*, London: Whiting and Birch.

Longchampt, P. (2013) *Children of Slovenia: realizing children's rights in Slovenia*. Online. Available HTTP: <www.humanium.org/en/slovenia/> (accessed 10 December 2013).

McArdle, S. and Duda, J. L. (2008) 'Exploring the etiology of perfectionism and perceptions of self-worth in young athletes', *Social Development*, 17: 980–97.

Ministry of Justice (2005) *Criminal Code of the Republic of Slovenia*. Online. Available HTTP: <http://tinyurl.com/ptyum9w> (accessed 11 December 2013).

Ministry of Labour, Family, Social Affairs and Equal Opportunities (2008) *The Family Violence Prevention Act*. Online. Available HTTP: <sgdatabase.unwomen.org/uploads/Family%20Violence%20Prevention%20Act%202008.pdf> (accessed 16/12/13).

Ministry of the Interior (2013) *Campaign on Raising Awareness of the Sexual Abuse of Children*. Online. Available HTTP: <www.mnz.gov.si/si/medijsko_sredisce/teme_in_programi/kampanja_o_osvescanju_o_spolnih_zlorabah_otrok/> (accessed 15 July 2013).

Murphy, P. and Waddington, I. (2007) 'Are elite athletes exploited?', *Sports in Society*, 10: 239–55.

Olympic Committee of Slovenia (2011) *Olympic Committee of Slovenia – Association of Sports Federations 1991–2001: sport story, woven from thousands actions*, Ljubljana: Olympic Committee of Slovenia.

Papaefstathiou, M., Rhind, D. and Brackenridge, C. (2013) 'Child protection in ballet: experiences and views of teachers, administrators and ballet students', *Child Abuse Review*, 22: 127–41.

POP TV (2012) 'Are basketball coaches sexual harassing young people in Postojna?', *24ur.com*. Online. Available HTTP: <www.24ur.com/novice/crna-kronika/kosarkarski-trener-naj-bi-na-taboru-v-postojni-spolno-nadlegoval-mladoletnega-udelezenca.html> (accessed 8 July 2013).

Primorske Info (2010) 'The serial sexual abuse of children in sport club Flip in Piran', *Primorska Info*, 4 February. Online. Available HTTP: <www.primorska.info/novice/7001/serijsko_spolno_zlorabljal_otroke_piranskega_drustva_flip> (accessed 8 July 2013).

Primorske News (2011) 'Former Flip coach at liberty', *Primorska News*, 22 April. Online. Available HTTP: <www.primorske.si/Kronika/Nekdanji-trener-Flipa-na-prostosti.aspx> (accessed 8 July 2013).

Roderick, M., Waddington, I. and Parker, G. (2000) 'Playing hurt: managing injuries in English professional sport', *International Review for the Sociology of Sport*, 35: 165–80.

Ryan, J. (1995) *Little Girls in Pretty Boxes*, New York: Doubleday.

Sahlstrom, K. J. and Jeglic, E. L. (2008) 'Factors affecting attitudes toward juvenile sex offenders', *Journal of Child Sexual Abuse*, 17, 180–96.

Slovene NGO Coalition ZIPOM (2013) *NGO Report to the Implementation of the Convention on the Rights of the Child and its Optional Protocols in Slovenia*. Online. Available HTTP: <www2.ohchr.org/english/bodies/crc/docs/ngos/Slovene_ZIPOM_Slovenia_CRC63.docx> (accessed 11 December 2013).

Slovenian News (2012) 'The investigation against the coach is completed', 25 July.

The Sports Act (1998) *Official Gazette of the Republic of Slovenia*, No. 22/1998. Online. Available HTTP: <http://www.uradni-list.si/1/objava.jsp?urlid=199822&stevilka=929> (accessed 15 November 2013).

Tscoll, P., Feddermann, N., Junge, A. and Dvorak, J. (2009) 'The use and abuse of painkillers in international soccer: data from 6 FIFA tournaments for female and youth players', *The American Journal of Sports Medicine*, 37: 260–5.

United Nations General Assembly (1989) *Convention on the Rights of the Child*. Online. Available HTTP: <www.unhcr.org/refworld/docid/3ae6b38f0.html> (accessed 15 March 2013).

Vojnović, G. (2011) *Some Secrets Should not Remain Hidden*, Ljubljana: Ministry of the Interior.

Yorganci, I. (1993) 'Preliminary findings from a survey of gender relationships and sexual harassment in sport', in C. Brackenridge (ed.) *Body Matters: leisure, images and lifestyles*, Brighton: Leisure Studies Association.

Zurc, J. (2010) 'The price behind the beauty of the Olympic performance in women's artistic gymnastics during the period 1972–88', in C. Brackenridge and D. Rhind (eds) *Elite Child Athlete Welfare: international perspectives*, Uxbridge: Brunel University Press.

Zurc, J. (2013) 'The challenges of safeguarding children in elite sport: a case study of Slovenian women's gymnastics', in I. Zagorac and I. Martinović (eds) *22nd Days of Frane Petrić: Perspectives of philosophy*, Cres, Croatia: Croatian Philosophical Society.

9   Protecting children from abuse and exploitation in South African sports

Rudolph Leon Van Niekerk

A democratic South Africa emerged from its Apartheid past in 1994, carrying with it a history of violence and disregard for the person in all areas of life, including sport. South Africa considers itself a sporting nation and aims to have at least 50 per cent of citizens participating in sport or active recreation by 2020 (National Sport and Recreation Indaba 2011). Sport in South Africa is organized by the various national sport federations and, in schools, by the Education Department. Although Physical Education was removed from the curriculum in 1994, various national sports such as rugby, football, field hockey, and track and field have, over decades, developed as school sports.

However, despite this sporting history, during Apartheid most Black people did not have access to recreational or competitive sport opportunities, and facilities and sport development were neglected (National Sport and Recreation Indaba 2011). Consequently, Merrit et al. (2011) argue that some sports became 'racialized'; rugby and cricket were played primarily by Whites while other sports, namely football, by Blacks. Failure to achieve equality of representation and opportunity for all ethnic groups in sport resulted in interventions such as affirmative action, but the socio-economic imbalance between former White (advantaged) and Black (disadvantaged) schools still causes inequalities in school sport participation and competition today (Du Toit 2012).

Recently, sport has become an important instrument in social transformation (National Sport and Recreation Indaba 2011), with the government's goal to maximize sport participation among young people (Morodi 2011). Sport in South Africa is organized by federations affiliated to the South African Sports Confederation and Olympic Committee under the Ministry of Sport, Arts and Culture. With sport centrally positioned to help develop a more equal South Africa, advocates have noted that sports organizations need to wake up to their responsibility to protect children and young people (Bryson 2012).

Indeed, as South Africa has shifted from Apartheid, the country has also seen the beginnings of a shift in cultural understandings of children and their rights. Increased media coverage of child abuse, growing interest in abuse and children's rights from academics, and ongoing pressure from children's charities has put children's rights on the agenda. This chapter explores the context of children's welfare in South African society, both in sport and beyond.

The legal framework for safeguarding children

In South African law, the terms 'child abuse' and 'child protection' are predominantly used. The Children's Act (2005) provides the framework for the protection of children and is underpinned by the Constitution of South Africa (1996: 1255), which states that 'every child has the right to be protected from maltreatment, neglect, abuse or degradation'. Specifically, the term 'child abuse' is defined as 'any form of harm or ill-treatment deliberately inflicted on a child' (Children's Act 2005: 9–10), where a child is defined as anyone under 18 years old. This definition encompasses sexual, physical, emotional and moral ill-treatment as well as discrimination and exploitation. The Children's Act sits alongside the Criminal Law Amendment Act (2007) which specifically codifies sexual offences against children, including the sexual assault or molestation of a child, encouraging or forcing a child to be used for sexual gratification, using a child for or exposing a child to sexual activity, and procuring a child for commercial sexual exploitation.

Child protection in South Africa is primarily the function of the Department of Social Development within the Ministry for Welfare and Population Development, but both state and private welfare agencies are involved in protecting children against abuse. Private welfare agencies, including non-governmental organizations such as the South African Society for the Prevention of Child Abuse and Neglect (SASPCAN), Child Line South Africa, Women and Men against Child Abuse, and The Teddy Bear Clinic for Abused Children, have long provided child protection services along with state departments.

Statistics suggest the prevalence of sexual offences against children in South Africa is higher than other crimes against children that involve some form of contact. Murder (1.56 per cent), attempted murder (1.49 per cent), assault with the intent of inflicting grievous bodily harm (20.97 per cent) and common assault (24.91 per cent) constituted half of the 50,688 reported so-called 'contact crimes' against children in 2011–12. Meanwhile, 51.02 per cent of such crimes were sexual offences (South African Police Services 2012). Meanwhile, there were 25,862 reported sexual offences against children in 2012 (South African Police Services 2012). As in other countries, though, the true extent of child sexual abuse in South Africa is difficult to establish due to underreporting (Mathews et al. 2012). Sport-specific data on child sexual abuse does not yet exist.

Within sport, there have been no large-scale prevalence studies on child abuse. However, research has identified child physical abuse (Rossouw 2006), child sexual abuse (Van Niekerk and Rzygula 2010) and sexual harassment (Burnett 2004) in sport. Burnett (2004) found female athletes in all provinces of South Africa reported experiencing sexual harassment or abuse by male coaches and authority figures in sport. Meanwhile in the first study of its kind in sport, Van Niekerk and Rzygula (2010) found that 21.9 per cent of male student athletes surveyed had experienced unwanted sexual behaviour from their coach during their sports career, with 41.7 per cent reporting physical and verbal behaviour of a sexual nature and 78.1 per cent reporting sexist and discriminatory behaviour

(Van Niekerk and Rzygula 2010). According to these figures, by the time an athlete leaves school, one in five will have experienced serious unwanted sexual behaviour from their coach. A similar study of male students within school, where most children participate in sport, found that 9 per cent of the 10–19–year-olds surveyed reported experiencing forced sex in the year before the study, with the figure highest (44 per cent) among males aged 18 (Anderson and Ho-Foster 2008). The perpetrators of such abuse were predominantly adults, including family members (18 per cent), teachers (20 per cent) and strangers (28 per cent), although other school students were also implicated (28 per cent). Most students who had experienced forced sex reported the perpetrator was female – 41 per cent compared to 32 per cent who reported the perpetrator was male – while 26 per cent reported multiple instances with both males and females as perpetrators (Anderson and Ho-Foster 2008). Given that most young people participate in sport through school, these figures highlight the urgent need for abuse prevention programmes to be implemented in school sport.

Measures to safeguard children in South African sport

Legislation aimed at protecting children and young people from abuse within a sports context has only existed in South Africa since the late 1990s, when the National Sport and Recreation Act (1998) and the South African Council for Educators Act (2000) came into law. Both make provision for the protection of children against abuse: individuals working in schools and sports federations must behave in a way that is conducive to keeping children safe at all times, and adults responsible for children's welfare, such as parents, teachers and coaches, are required to report complaints of child sexual abuse to the police. In addition, the National Sport and Recreation Act (1998) gives the national sport confederation the right to investigate when, among others, a child alleges their rights and freedoms have been violated or malpractice has occurred. Since its inception, however, no allegations of sexual offences have been investigated under this law even though criminal cases have been brought against coaches. Consequently, critics argue the sports world has yet to face up to the challenge of protecting children (Bryson 2012). Following an assessment of the measures in place to protect children and young people from abuse and other forms of maltreatment and exploitation in sport, Brook (2009) noted that sport is failing children and young people and called on sport federations to place child protection protocols on their agenda. Similarly an audit of South African coaches (Duffy 2010) highlighted the need for child protection policies and codes of ethics. In addition, Singh (2006) identified the measures needed to prevent child sexual abuse in South African sport. These include: acknowledgement from key stakeholders such as the South African Sport Confederation and Olympic Committee (SASCOC) that child sexual abuse is an issue for sport; identifying key stakeholders in sport with responsibility for child protection; introducing criminal record checks for coaches and volunteers; developing child protection policies and disciplinary procedures; appointing named individuals in clubs with the responsibility for promoting child protection and managing suspected abuse; educating athletes on child protection; developing codes of conduct and implementing a national register of offenders in sport.

In response, there have been developments in recent years, prompted primarily by a concern about child sexual abuse in sport because this is regarded in South Africa as the most severe crime against children. In 2013, the CEO of SASCOC announced that:

> SASCOC is totally against abuse in whatever shape or form and takes a very firm stance on this. Sport has a great role to play in the correct and moral upbringing of our youth and must be used as a form of nation building and unifying of our children.
>
> (Association Internationale de la Press Sportive 2013)

In addition, preventing the sexual abuse of children and young people in sport is now included in a code of conduct for sport officials (National Sport and Recreation Indaba 2011) and in the national coaching framework (Vardhan and Duffy 2011). Nevertheless, despite clear suggestions for progressing this issue and the responsibility of national sport and recreation federations for safety in sport, only a handful have taken action. In part, this is due to a lack of understanding about the relevance of child protection to sport organizations and denial that child abuse occurs within sport, as well as a lack of coordination on child protection within the sports sector and a fear that implementing protection measures in sport would highlight the problem and attract negative publicity.

Child protection in school sport

Many of the most popular sports in South Africa are played in schools, where teachers often double up as coaches and competition takes place through intra-school leagues. In this context, the position of authority and trust coach-educators find themselves in, and the close physical and emotional relationship between educator-coaches and student-athletes renders young people particularly vulnerable to abuse (Brackenridge 2001). Consequently, under the Employment of Educators Act (1998) sexual relations between teachers and students, including coach-educators and student-athletes, are banned. Similarly, the Council for Educators Act (2000) mandates that teachers 'avoid any form of humiliation and refrain from any form of child abuse, physical or psychological' (South African Council for Educators Act 2000). However, there have been suggestions that the rights of children are sometimes ignored in schools (Rossouw 2006). In particular, in a review of court cases, Rossouw (2006) found abuse occurs in school sport and contended such cases were increasing. Without baseline prevalence figures, however, this claim cannot be substantiated.

It has been suggested that the social context in South Africa, where social norms require the respect of one's elders and dominant constructions of masculinity position men as superior to women and children and thus 'entitled' to control them, perpetuate child sexual abuse (Mathews et al. 2012). In a society with such low status, children are rarely given decision-making rights and frequently complain they are not listened to or taken seriously (Jamieson et al. 2011). In addition, Van der Bijl and Rumney (2010) argue that decision makers in the South African police, prosecution service and judicial service are too often influenced by prevailing social attitudes that portray sexual violence as at least in part the fault of the victim, undermining victims' credibility and making prosecution difficult. If we are to prevent all forms of abuse and exploitation, it is crucial we take such social constructs into consideration and work to change attitudes through education and advocacy.

Abuse cases in sport media

Cases of abuse in and beyond sport are widely covered by the media in South Africa, which has the benefit of raising awareness of child abuse and children's rights and breaking some of the silence around the issue. The case of Joe Lourenco is one of the earliest to have been featured in the South African press. In 2002, the 45–year-old male gymnastics coach received a five-year suspended sentence for the historic sexual abuse of two male gymnasts he worked with 22 years earlier (Singh 2006). He was also ordered to pay damages of R135,500 (approximately £8,942) to his victims. One of the victims, Glenn Joselowitz, who was 11 years old when he started training with Lourenco, went public with his story to raise awareness of sexual abuse in sport. Joselowitz, who was training to win a place on the national team at the time of the abuse, told South Africa television programme Carte Blanche that he saw Lourenco as a trusted father figure, someone who would help him achieve his aim of making the national team but that he also feared him:

> Joe was everything to us. He was a father figure in a sense. He was the person who was going to get me to the top. … My not saying 'no' was not consent. It was me not knowing better. It was me fearful of what was going on.
>
> (Joselowitz speaking to Carte Blanche 2000)

More recently, 68–year-old male karate coach Peter Foyn pleaded guilty to inappropriately touching 11 female current and former athletes as well as rape, and was convicted in 2012 on 10 counts of sexually assaulting athletes aged between 8 and 34 (South African Press Association 2012a and 2012b). Foyn, who had 43 years' experience as a coach, was sentenced to three years of correctional supervision and community service and his name was recorded on the national sexual offenders register. The sentence provoked anger from athletes' parents and child abuse advocates such as the charity Women and Men Against Child Abuse. They argued it was overly lenient, but the presiding magistrate said she had taken into account Foyn's age and the fact that he was a first-time offender when passing sentence.

The most high-profile case of a South African accused of abusing athletes came to light in 2011 when an American former youth tennis player alleged to the *Boston Globe* newspaper that tennis icon Bob Hewitt began a sexual relationship with her in the 1970s when she was 15 years old and he was a world-renowned doubles player (Hohler 2013b). Hewitt, now 74, migrated from his native Australia to South Africa in the 1960s. He represented South Africa as a doubles player and was inducted into the International Tennis Hall of Fame in 1992 – an honour that was suspended indefinitely in 2012 following the abuse allegations (Hohler 2012). Following the *Boston Globe*'s coverage of the allegations against Hewitt, US cable TV channel HBO aired a documentary in which several women from South Africa and the United States alleged Hewitt had abused them in the 1980s and 1990s when Hewitt was their tennis coach. The South African authorities subsequently investigated the allegations involving South African citizens, and Hewitt was charged in August 2013 with two counts of rape and one count of sexually assaulting a minor (Hohler 2013b). The abuse allegedly began when the women were 12, 13 and 16 years old, respectively, and Hewitt was in his thirtiess and forties (Cronin 2012; Hohler 2013b). Hewitt denies the charges. Meanwhile, several other women in the United States also allege they were abused by Hewitt when he coached them as children between the 1970s and 1990s. No charges are likely to be made, however, as the statute of limitations for criminal charges there has expired (Leonard 2012).

Worryingly, an investigation by the *Boston Globe* newspaper, where the allegations against Hewitt first surfaced, found that complaints had been made against Hewitt to South African tennis officials in the 1970s but were largely ignored, apparently due to Hewitt's status as a successful tennis player (Leonard 2012); South African tennis authorities argued nothing could be done until someone pressed charges (Bryson 2012). Indeed, when the family of one victim, Twiggy Tolken, pressed charges against Hewitt, they were later dropped because they did not want her to face Hewitt and his lawyers in court (Bryson 2012).

As these three high-profile cases illustrate, coaches are in a position of authority over athletes and, through this privileged status, are well placed to induce fear in athletes to silence them if they are intent on abuse. The absence of policies in sport that could empower children and young people to take action against abusive coaches, and the lack of clear guidelines in sport for reporting suspicions of abuse further contribute to the silence of young athletes. It is no surprise, then, that in some cases such as those reported above, athletes have not reported their abuse until many years later.

Future directions

Despite legislation and guidelines from the South African government, few sport federations have developed policies for protecting youth athletes from abuse and exploitation. Some federations still do not understand the legal and ethical consequences of ignoring abuse and exploitation in sport and continue to deny the abuse of children in their ranks because they do not know how to deal with it or they believe that addressing such concerns will generate negative publicity (Singh 2006). One exception is Swimming South Africa, which published a child protection policy on its website in 2010 in response to calls for clearer regulations for coaches working with children, and out of awareness that close but professional interaction between children and adults is crucial to the sport's development. The policy, which represents the first of its kind in a South African sport federation, includes sections on the rights of children and young people and the process for reporting child abuse. However, while it marks a step in the right direction, there is concern this may be more a tick-box exercise than a genuine attempt to enact change as the policy does not appear to be accompanied by a campaign to raise awareness of the policy or a strategy to educate swimming stakeholders about the policy.

Finally, the recently proposed National Development Plan for South Africa (Manuel and Chabane 2013) introduces the long-term strategic goal of ensuring all South Africans attain a good standard of living through the elimination of poverty and the reduction of inequality by 2030. In particular the plan identifies, among others, social protection and recreation and leisure as core indicators of a good standard of living. The aim is to integrate the plan's proposals into all government structures and departments, which could help ensure that more child protection policies are developed and embedded within sport federations.

References

Anderson, N. and Ho-Foster, A. (2008) '13,915 Reasons for Equity in Sexual Offences Legislation: a national school-based survey in South Africa', *International Journal for Equity in Health*, 20. Online. Available HTTP: <www.ncbi.nlm.nih.gov/pmc/articles/PMC2515838> (accessed 3 October 2013).

Association Internationale de la Presse Sportive (2013) *South Africa Olympic Back 'Stop Rape' Campaign*. Online. Available HTTP: <www.aipsmedia.com/index.php?page=news&cod=10065&tp=n&allcomm=1> (accessed 13 July 2013).

Brackenridge, C. H. (2001) *Spoilsports: understanding and preventing sexual exploitation in sport*, London: Routledge.

Brook, N. (2009) 'Child protection in sport in South Africa', *Brook Sport and Leisure News* 4 June.

Bryson, D. (2012) *South Africa Tennis Star Bob Hewitt Probed on Child Rape Allegations*. Online. Available HTTP: <www.independent.co.uk/news/world/africa/south-african-tennis-star-bob-hewitt-probed-on-child-rape-allegations-7920521.html> (accessed 21 September 2013).

Burnett, C. (2004) *The Status of South African Women in Sport and Recreation: 1994–2004*, Cape Town: Department of Sport and Recreation South Africa.

Carte Blanche (2000) *Boys Betrayed*. Online. Available HTTP: <www.beta.mnet.co.za/carteblanche/Article.aspx?Id=1454> (accessed 5 May 2013).

Children's Act, No. 38 of 2005 (2005). Cape Town: Government Gazette.

Constitution of the Republic of South Africa, No. 108 of 1996 (1996). Cape Town: Government Gazette.

Criminal Law Amendment Act, No. 30 of 2007 (2007). Cape Town: Government Gazette

Cronin, M. (2012) *Bob Hewitt Responds to Sexual Abuse Allegations*. Online. Available HTTP: <www.bob-hewitt-responds-sexual-abuse-allegations> (accessed 21 September 2013).

Du Toit, T. (2012) '2012: the year of school sport', *Sport Trader*, March: 58.

Duffy, P. (2010) *South African Coaching Framework: scoping report*, London: UK Sport.

Employment of Educators Act, No. 76 of 1998 (1998). Cape Town: Government Gazette.

Fourie, J., Slabbert, E. and Saayman, M. (2011) 'The leisure and sport participation patterns of high school learners in Potchefstroom', *South African Journal for Research in Sport, Physical Education and Recreation*, 1: 65–80.

Hohler, B. (2012) *Tennis Hall of Fame Removes Bob Hewitt*. Online. Available HTTP: <www.bostonglobe.com/sports/2012/11/15/bob-hewitt-suspended-from-tennis-hall-fame-after-allegations-sexual-abuse/QxC7zbtLwwsHCjDY5wdkJK/story.html> (accessed 21 September 2013).

— (2013a) *Bob Hewitt Faces Rape Charges in South Africa*. Online. Available HTTP: <www.bostonglobe.com/sports/2013/06/19/former-tennis-star-bob-hewitt-faces-sexual-abuse-charges/TPFi5DoDq489trcC4pI1IJ/story.html> (accessed 21 September 2013).

— (2013b) *Rape Charges Lodged Against Former Tennis Great Bob Hewitt*. Online. Available HTTP: <www.bostonglobe.com/sports/2013/08/16/rape-charges-lodged-against-former-tennis-great-bob-hewitt/tGB8vGfMjXeO9BLcgbAD2I/story.html> (accessed 21 September 2013).

Jamieson, L., Bray, R., Viviers, A., Lake, L., Pendlebury, S. and Smith, C. (eds) (2011) *South African Child Gauge 2008/2009*, Cape Town: University of Cape Town.

Leonard, T. (2012) 'Tennis champion Bob Hewitt under investigation over claims he sexually abused young girls that he coached', *The Daily Mail*. Online. Available HTTP: <www.dailymail.co.uk/news/article-2168662/South-African-tennis-champion-Bob-Hewitt-investigation-claims-sexually-abused-young-girls-coached.html#ixzz2fWdmtRIN> (accessed 21 September 2013).

Manuel, T. and Chabane, C. (2013) *Implementation of the National Development Plan*, press release 19 February 2013.

Mathews, S., Loots, L., Sikweyiya, Y. and Jewkes, R. (2012) 'Sexual abuse', in A. Van Niekerk, S. Suffla and M. Seedat (eds) *Crime, Violence and Injury in South Africa: 21st century solutions for child safety*, Pretoria: Psychology Society of South Africa.

Merrit, C., Tatz, C. and Adair, D. (2011) 'History and its racial legacies: quotas in South African rugby and cricket', *Sport in Society*, 6: 754–78.

Morodi, L. (2011) 'The reconstruction, development and transformation of South African diversified society through sport: Cherished ideals of Nelson Mandela and their challenges', *International Journal of Sport and Society*, 3: 11–20.

National Sport and Recreation Act no 110 of 1998 (1998). Cape Town: Government Gazette.

National Sport and Recreation Indaba (2011) *The National Sport and Recreation Plan (Draft 20)*, Cape Town: Department of Sport and Recreation South Africa.

Rossouw, J. P. (2006) '*Emotional and physical abuse of a non-sexual nature by educator-coaches in school sport*', paper presented at SAELPA International Conference, East London, September 2006.

Singh, P. (2006) *The Protection of Children in Sport*, Cape Town: Department of Sport and Recreation South Africa.

South African Press Association (2012a) 'Child abuse karate coach in court', *South African Press Association*. Online. Available HTTP: <www.sowetanlive.co.za/news/2012/12/05/child-abuse-karate-coach-in-court> (accessed 21 September 2013).

South African Press Association (2012b) 'Shock at non-custodial sentence in sex assault case', *South African Press Association*. Online. Available HTTP: <http://www.iol.co.za/pretoria-news/shock-at-non-custodial-sentence-in-sex-assault-case-1.1436870> (accessed 21 September 2013).

South African Council for Educators Act No 31of 2000 (2000). Cape Town: Government Gazette.

South African Police Services (2012) *Crime Statistics Overview RSA 2011/2012*, Pretoria: South African Police Services.

Statistics South Africa (2012) *Victims of Crime Survey*, Pretoria: Statistics South Africa.

Swimming South Africa (2011) *The Constitution of Swimming South Africa, Appendix V: child protection policy*. Online. Available HTTP: <www.swimsa.org/Modules_BE/AdminConsole/Contentmanager/data/SSA_Constitution%20–%20November%20 2011.pdf> (accessed 10 February 2013).

Van der Bijl, C. and Rumney, P. (2010) 'Attitudes, rape and law reform in South Africa', *Journal of Criminal Law*, 5: 414–49.

Van Niekerk, R. L. and Rzygula, R. (2010) 'The perceptions and occurrence of sexual harassment among male student athletes with male coaches', *African Journal for Physical, Health Education, Recreation and Dance*, December (Supplement): 49–62.

Vardhan, D. and Duffy, P. (2011) *The South African Coaching Framework*, Johannesburg: SASCOC.

10 Athlete welfare and protection policy development in the USA

Donna A. Lopiano and Connee Zotos

Until recently, there has been little movement on athlete welfare in the United States (US). Lawsuits involving coach abuse of youth sport programme participants in high-profile college football programmes and in open amateur swimming and gymnastics were accompanied by sustained media coverage, which put pressure on the United States Olympic Committee (USOC) to address athlete welfare. This resulted in state and federal governments strengthening child welfare laws and better enforcing laws prohibiting sexual harassment in education.

The legislative framework

The child welfare system in the United States is reactive rather than preventive, highly fragmented and does not specifically address children and young people in sports programmes. The US Constitution recognizes that parents have a fundamental right to decide how to raise their children so the government interferes only when necessary to protect the child's safety and wellbeing. Thus, the child welfare system focuses its work on protection from harm rather than on promoting healthy development more broadly.

US federal and state laws prohibit the causing of harm to others, however, the responsibility for establishing and enforcing child welfare laws rests with each of the 50 states, the District of Columbia and the five territories comprising the United States of America (hereafter referred to as the 'states'). Therefore, arrangements for child welfare, including definitions of child abuse, differ by state.

At a federal level, the government has indirectly established minimum child welfare standards and guidelines for states via the Child Abuse Prevention and Treatment Act (CAPTA). CAPTA defines child maltreatment as:

> Any recent act or failure to act on the part of a parent or caretaker which results in death, serious physical or emotional harm, sexual abuse or exploitation, or an act or failure to act, which presents an imminent risk of serious harm.
>
> (CAPTA 2010: 6)

Most states interpret this as including 'four major types of maltreatment: neglect, physical abuse, psychological maltreatment, and sexual abuse' (US Department of Health and Human Services 2012: 22) and report annually on these.

Meanwhile, the US Department of Health and Human Services (USDHHS) established mandatory reporters of child maltreatment which, in most states, includes school teachers and administrators. However, in most schools, coaches of sport programmes are not required to be teachers and are often part-time employees or volunteers. Only three states specifically name school coaches as mandatory reporters alongside teachers, while five states include employees of summer or day camps, which includes non-school sport camps. In addition, ten states either name all citizens as mandatory reporters or specify individuals working in non-school organized programmes for children. Consequently, only 18 per cent of states have child welfare laws that cover children participating in sport programmes in both school and non-school settings (USDHHS-State Statutes 2012).

There are, then, specific laws to protect children and young people from maltreatment. However, devolving responsibility for the implementation of these laws to states has resulted in a fragmented system whereby understandings of, and arrangements for, child welfare differ by state. This has resulted in criticism because such differences undermine the seriousness of child maltreatment (National Coalition to End Child Abuse Deaths 2010) – after all, a child's life or death is at stake. Meanwhile the system has also suffered criticism because there has been no evaluation of its primary strategies for managing offenders or of school-based education programmes, meaning their effectiveness remains unproven (Finkelhor 2009).

Protections in schools and colleges

In addition to CAPTA and state child welfare laws, Title IX of the Education Amendments Act 1972 prohibits sex discrimination, including sexual harassment and abuse, in educational programmes that are recipients of federal funds. Title IX, which applies to all states, protects children and adults participating in primary, secondary and post-secondary education, including curricular programmes such as physical education and extra-curricular activities such as sport.

Title IX mandates immediate action to remove all sexual harassment and abuse, forcing institutions to deal with perpetrators even if the abuse or harassment falls short of the legal definition. So rather than 'beyond a reasonable doubt', under Title IX action can be taken where there is a 'preponderance of evidence' (US Department of Education Office for Civil Rights 2011: 11). This obligation for immediate action to protect student victims and the inclusion of measures that allow educational institutions to quickly suspend or terminate the employment of alleged abusers affords a higher standard of protection than the criminal or civil court system.

In 2001 and 2011, the Government Office for Civil Rights issued letters to all schools and colleges about their obligations under Title IX (US Department of Education OCR 2001, 2011). These letters drew specific attention to schools' and colleges' responsibilities regarding sexual harassment and abuse. The 2011 letter was in part precipitated by a report for the National Institute of Justice that revealed one in five women and one in sixteen men had experienced real or attempted sexual assault in college (Krebs et al. 2007). Sexual assault also appears to be an issue for younger students: 'During the 2007–08 school year, there were 800 reported incidents of rape and attempted rape and 3,800 reported incidents of other sexual batteries at public high schools in the USA' (Robers et al. 2010: 104). Nationally, sexual abuse is the third most prevalent form of child abuse – neglect is first and physical abuse second – with the largest study indicating that one in four girls and one in six boys will suffer sexual abuse before adulthood (CDC 2006).

Media coverage precipitating sport policies

Media coverage often drives political action in the US. Generally, the media cover child welfare issues only sporadically and often focus on horrific and relatively unusual cases, while the child welfare system itself receives little attention. Recently, coverage of high-profile cases of abuse and harassment in sport has increased public awareness of the problem, resulting in increased pressure on non-school amateur sport organizations to address the issue and minor changes to state laws, such as including sports officials as mandatory reporters.

In 2010, the case of assistant football coach Jerry Sandusky caused a media storm and emerged as a 'tipping point' for child welfare in sport. Sandusky, who worked for the most revered college football coach in the US, Joe Paterno, was convicted of sexually abusing ten young boys. Paterno was implicated in a cover-up as he failed to report Sandusky as required under state laws (Freeh 2012). The media focused on the downfall of Paterno and on the rampant homophobia in men's sport (Messner and Sabo 1994). In response to the Sandusky case, many states initiated legal amendments to include coaches and sport administrators in public and private sports programmes as mandatory reporters (USDHHS-State Statutes 2012), although notably state legislatures led these actions, not sport governance associations. In addition, the Sandusky case has resulted in more regular media attention being paid to athlete abuse by coaches.

Research on abuse in sport

Research on the prevalence and incidence of abuse in sport in the US is non-existent. However, anecdotal data from media reports abound (for example Kozen 2012; Frere 2012) and appear to represent the proverbial 'tip of the iceberg'. Over the past decade until the time of writing, 159 coaches in Washington State public schools alone had been fired or reprimanded for sexual misconduct ranging from harassment to rape (Willmsen and O'Hagan 2003). Nearly all were male perpetrators while victims were girls. Meanwhile, as of 2 May 2013, the national governing body (NGB) USA Swimming had declared 84 coaches or others permanently ineligible for membership, with 70 males listed as committing code of conduct violations or felonies relating to sexual abuse or sexual misconduct (USA Swimming 2013). The NGB of gymnastics, USA Gymnastics, only began reporting misconduct violations in 2012, but as of 27 April 2013 had declared 89 coaches or others permanently ineligible for membership (USA Gymnastics 2013). A review of court and media records revealed that 69 of the 89 coaches – 68 males and one female – had been accused or convicted of sexual misconduct, while in the remaining 20 cases the type of misconduct was not recorded.

Current state of sport policy

While criminal background checks are already mandatory for teachers, increased attention by the media and increased emphasis on enforcing Title IX in schools and colleges has created the impetus for background checks of full-time, part-time and volunteer coaches who are not teachers. In addition, many athletic departments are creating policies that address sexual harassment, sexual abuse and emotional and physical abuse in the sport setting. The fact that schools and colleges must comply with Title IX's sexual abuse and harassment provisions is significant. The US is one of the few countries where competitive sport exists as a school sponsored co-curricular or extra-curricular activity, with one out of every two boys and two out of every five girls at a secondary school participating in such programmes (NFSHA 2012).

Yet while school and college sport programmes have government-mandated Title IX protections in place, the same is not true for amateur sports clubs that operate outside the school setting. No sport ministry or similar national governmental agency has central control over all sports in the US. Rather, governance of amateur sport is fragmented among hundreds of state and national associations and thousands of independent commercial and not-for-profit local sports clubs and programmes. The largest group of such organizations, including the school/college group covered by Title IX, is assembled under the auspices of USOC. USOC consists of NGBs for those sports on the programmes of the Olympic, Pan- American and Paralympic Games, Community-Based Multisport Organizations (CBMO), Education-based Multi-sport Organizations (EBMO), Armed Forces Organizations (AFO) and other recognized sport organizations that do not represent sports in the Olympic, Pan American or Paralympic Games.

The Ted Stevens Olympic and Amateur Sports Act (1978) is a federal law that gives USOC responsibility, among others, for recognizing one NGB in each sport in the Olympic, the Pan American and the Paralympic Games and for coordinating their activities related to amateur international competition. Although the USOC is also charged with promoting and encouraging amateur sports activities and advancing sport safety, its focus has been on elite sport competition and development. Thus, although the issue of athlete protection is now an important focus of USOC in relation to elite athlete programmes, little attention is being paid to the needs of the much larger youth sport population served by community-based multisport organizations.

In 2005, the USOC adopted its first comprehensive code of ethics for coaches, the Coaching Ethics Code (USOC 2005). Among others, it prohibits coaches from engaging in sexual and other forms of harassment and bans coaches from entering into sexual or romantic relationships with anyone over whom they have supervisory control. It also prohibits coaches from sexual intimacy with one of their current athletes, with any athlete they have coached in the previous two years, and from coaching athletes with whom they have previously been sexually intimate. However, the code only applies to coaches employed by USOC, working with athletes in USOC programmes or at USOC training centres. Adoption of the code outside these domains remains voluntary and it does not address athlete-on-athlete sexual harassment or abuse.

In 2010, USOC appointed a Working Group for Safe Training Environments. The Group, which consisted of individuals from within the Olympic movement and external experts on sexual and physical misconduct (USOC 2010), released its first report later that year. Six recommendations from the report were made to the USOC's Board of Directors, urging the organization to: (1) play a leadership role in promoting safe training environments, (2) lead by example, (3) develop a centralized set of training and educational resources that could be adopted by NGBs, clubs and grassroots sports organizations and (4) have materials be accessible online, (5) work with NGBs to standardize the delivery of services to promote safe training environments and (6) encourage NGBs to adopt policies, practices and tools to address sexual and physical misconduct and that could be used by NGBs to encourage grassroots organizations to adopt similar measures. Emotional and verbal abuse were identified as longer-term areas for attention. Overall, then, the recommendations focused on encouraging NGBs and their members to act, rather than on requiring policies and programmes.

In 2011, USOC established the post of Director of Ethics and Sport to oversee implementation of these recommendations and direct continued educational programming. It also created its own child protection policy, SafeSport (USOC 2012–13), which specifically addresses child physical and sexual abuse, emotional and physical misconduct, bullying, hazing and harassment. Yet although comprehensive in scope, the policy only applies to:

> USOC employees, coaches, contracted staff, volunteers, board members, committee and task force members, and other individuals working with athletes or other sport participants while at an OTC, whether or not they are employees of the USOC and athletes training and/or residing at a USOC Olympic Training Centre.
>
> (USOC 2012: 3)

In late 2012, USOC extended the protection afforded to athletes under the SafeSport policy to participants in its affiliated NGBs by adopting the USOC Minimum Standards Policy for Athlete Safety Programmes (USOC 2013). This programme requires USOC-affiliated NGBs, which include those for Olympic and non-Olympic sports, to adopt an athlete welfare strategy with the following minimum components by 31 December 2013:

1   A policy that prohibits bullying; hazing; harassment; emotional, physical and sexual misconduct, including child sexual abuse; and romantic or sexual relationships between NGB programme participants and coaches or other supervisory personnel with direct supervisory control, or who are in a position of power or trust, over the participant.

2   A requirement for 'criminal background checks for those individuals it formally authorizes, approves or appoints (a) to a position of authority over, or (b) to have frequent contact with athletes' (USOC 2013: 2).

3   Beginning 1 January 2014, implementation of 'education and training concerning the key elements of their safety programme for those individuals it formally authorizes, approves or appoints (a) to a position of authority over, or (b) to have frequent contact with athletes' (USOC 2013: 2).

4   A procedure for reporting misconduct.

5   A grievance process to address misconduct allegations that have not been adjudicated under a criminal background check, and that includes the opportunity for independent review.

Failure to comply with this policy could result in disciplinary action against the NGB, including the withdrawal of high-performance funding – a significant penalty. However, the reach of the policy is again limited to those working in elite programmes sponsored by the NGB, specifically, '(1) NGB employees; (2) the athletes the NGB designates for in and out-of-competition testing by the US Anti-Doping Agency; and (3) individuals the NGB formally authorizes, approves or appoints to a position of authority over, or to have frequent contact with, athletes' (USOC 2013: 1). In other words, NGBs are not required to extend the policy to local clubs or individual coaches outside NGB-sponsored programmes, weakening the protection available. Of course, clubs should ideally have their own child welfare strategy so they can be immediately responsive to conduct violations. For example, Safe4Athletes recommends that if an allegation is made or an athlete is deemed to be at risk, the perpetrator should be removed by the local club until an investigation is completed, and where allegations are proven, the club should ban the perpetrator and ask the NGB for a more permanent penalty such as banning the perpetrator from further participation in any NGB member programme.

It is too early to say how many NGBs will voluntarily extend the policy to individual and club members. As of May 2013 some NGBs, such as USA Swimming and USA Gymnastics, had adopted the Minimum Standards policy and required their individual and local club members to follow the Minimum Standards policy and report misconduct to the NGB for investigation. However, local clubs do not always have their own investigation and disciplinary processes and if a club does not, it may be left waiting for the NGB to act while the individual accused remains working with athletes. The practical application of the policy, then, remains unclear.

In early 2013, the USOC launched an online version of the SafeSport Programme, which includes sample policies and education materials for NGBs to help them meet the Minimum Standards policy and for clubs and other sport organizations that voluntarily seek to adopt such policies (USOC SafeSport Programme 2012–13). This online version also provides the details of law firms who have offered to work *pro bono* for NGBs investigating misconduct investigations. The first editions of these sample policies and materials are commendable, although there remains some work to be done in several areas. Notably, the school/college community is realizing the need for an athlete-employee welfare advocate who can assist victims in navigating the complaint process as there remains a perception that those designated by the sport organization to manage complaints may be more concerned with protecting the organization's reputation than with the victim's welfare. In addition, education materials need to be developed to enable local clubs with no professional managers to administer an effective training programme and manage reports and investigations of misconduct.

Many children remain without policy protection

The number of NGBs that have signed up to the USOC's SafeSport mandate is as yet unknown as the deadline for implementation is not until 31 December 2013, after this book went to print. USOC admits it is difficult to identify how many people are served by all NGBs, but estimates the most recent USOC quadrennial census report suggests there are 3,220,988 NGB-affiliated athletes (USOC 2008: 29). Consequently, even if NGBs enforce USOC's policy at a local level, a relatively small number of youth sports participants will be affected as USOC can only enforce the policy on NGBs in its four member categories – in NGBs of sports on the programmes of the Olympic, Pan American and Paralympic Games and other recognized sports competitions. Many more non NGB-affiliated youth sport participants fall outside USOC's SafeSport mandate because it is not applicable to non-NGB organizations. For example, the estimated number of youth participants served by CBMOs – a non-NGB USOC membership category – is 60 million (USOC Multi-Sport Organization Council 2012). No information is yet available to indicate if or how these organizations will be required to implement policies to protect athletes. One suggestion is that USOC require all members to adopt and enforce an athlete welfare strategy as a condition of membership and/ or funding. Meanwhile, some non-profit organizations, like Safe4Athletes (2012), are working to get local sport programmes to adopt policies and prevention programmes. However, these efforts are stymied by a lack of finances and the lack of practical incentives, such as requirements for such programmes at a community level.

Meanwhile at a grassroots level, NGBs do not have a system for notifying other clubs of pending criminal or civil lawsuits against coaches, and small youth sport clubs often do not require criminal background checks as a condition of employment. Therefore, if a coach abuses but leaves a club before the abuse is detected, or if an allegation is not reported to the police, they can be hired by another club or programme or open their own independent youth sport business without anyone knowing their background. In addition, some clubs may be afraid of firing an abusive coach for fear they will be sued for wrongful termination of contract, and some clubs may not report misconduct to protect their reputation, believing instead that as long as they remove the coach their job is done. Smaller community clubs may not even be aware of state mandatory reporting laws. Furthermore, most parents associated with local clubs are volunteers, not professional sport administrators, and are therefore not trained to deal with abuse allegations.

Summary

The story of athlete protection in the US is a rapidly evolving one. State laws governing child welfare are highly fragmented and do not address children participating in youth sport programmes in a clear or comprehensive way. However, more and more states are including coaches and sport programme administrators in their list of mandatory reporters of child abuse, although even if these state laws are used the response remains reactive rather than proactive in nature.

Title IX offers strong prevention, protection and enforcement measures for school and college athletes at institutions receiving federal funding. The USOC has established strong minimum athlete protection standards for a relatively small number of athletes participating in USOC and NGB elite athlete programmes and is providing educational tools for clubs who voluntarily wish to adopt similar standards. However, athlete protection policies and procedures for many of the 60 million youth athletes participating in community-based multi-sport sport programmes are non-existent. Much work remains to be done.

References

Centre for Disease Control and Prevention (2006) *Adverse Childhood Experiences Study: data and statistics.* Online. Available HTTP: <www.cdc.gov/nccdphp/ACE/prevalence. htm> (accessed 16 May 2013).

Child Abuse Prevention and Treatment Act (2010). 42 U.S.C. 5101 et seq; 42 U.S.C. 5116 et seq.

Finkelhor, D. (2009) 'The prevention of childhood sexual abuse', *The Future of Children: preventing child maltreatment,* 2: 169–94. Online. Available HTTP: <www.futureofchildren. org/futureofchildren/publications/docs/19_02_08.pdf> (accessed 16 May 2013).

Freeh Sporkin and Sullivan, LLP (2012) *Report of the Special Investigative Counsel Regarding the Actions of The Pennsylvania State University Related to the Child Sexual Abuse Committed by Gerald A. Sandusky.* Online. Available HTTP: <www.health-equity.pitt.edu/3956/1/REPORT_FINAL_071212.pdf> (accessed 16 May 2013).

Frere, E. (2012) *Santa Ana Boxing Club Coach Accused of Sexual Abuse.* Online. Available HTTP: <www.abclocal.go.com/kabc/story?section=news/local/orange_county&id=8738059> (accessed 16 May 2013).

Kozen, K. (2012) 'More coaches accused of sexual abuse', *Aquatics International*, 1 September. Online. Available HTTP: <www.aquaticsintl.com/2012/sep/1209n_abuse. html#.UAqTNaNRC1g> (accessed 16 May 2013).

Krebs, C. P., Lindquist, C. H., Warner, T. D., Fisher, B. S. and Martin, S. L. (2007) *The Campus Sexual Assault Study: final report xiii*. Online. Available HTTP: <www.ncjrs. gov/pdffiles1/nij/grants/221153.pdf> (accessed 16 May 2013).

Messner, M. and Sabo, D. (1994) *Sex, Violence and Power in Sports: rethinking masculinity*. California: Crossing Press.

National Coalition to End Child Abuse Deaths (2010) *Coalition Recommendations*. Online. Available HTTP: <www.everychildmatters.org/storage/documents/pdf/coalition/coalitionrecommendations.pdf> (accessed 16 May 2013).

National Federation of State High School Associations (2012) *2011–12 High School Participation Data*. Online. Available HTTP: <www.nfhs.org/content.aspx?id=3282> (accessed 16 May 2013).

Robers, S., Zhang, J. and Truman, J. (2010) *Indicators of School Crime and Safety 2010*. Online. Available HTTP: <www.nces.ed.gov/pubs2011/2011002.pdf> (accessed 16 May 2013).

Safe4Athletes (2012) *Local Sport Club Policies and Procedures*. Online. Available HTTP: <www.safe4athletes.org/4–clubs/model-policy> (accessed 16 May 2013).

Ted Stevens Olympic and Amateur Sports Act (1978). 36 U.S.C. Sec. 220521 et seq.

Title IX of the Education Amendments (1972), 20 U.S.C. § 1681 et seq.

United States Olympic Committee (2005) *Coaching Ethics Code*. Online. Available HTTP: <www.usacoaching.org/resources/Coaching%20Ethics%20Code_new.pdf> (accessed 16 May 2013).

United States Olympic Committee (2008) *United States Olympic Committee Report to the President and Congress for the Period of 2005–2008*. Online. Available HTTP: <www.teamusa.org/About-the-USOC/Legal/Quadrennial-Congressional-Reports. aspx> (accessed 16 May 2013).

United States Olympic Committee (2010) *Working Group for Safe Training Environments' Recommendations to the USOC Board of Directors*. Online. Available HTTP: <www. assets.teamusa.org/assets/documents/attached_file/filename/31322/USOC_Working_ Group_Safe_Training_Environments_Final_Recommendations_to_the_USOC_ Board_of_Directors_9282010__2_.pdf> (accessed 16 May 2013).

United States Olympic Committee (2012) *Multi-Sport Organizations*. Online. Available HTTP: <www.teamusa.org/About-the-USOC/In-the-Community/Partner-Programs/ Multi-Sport-Organizations.aspx> (accessed 16 May 2013).

United States Olympic Committee (2012–13) *Governance Documents. USOC bylaws (8 March 2013)*. Online. Available HTTP: <www.teamusa.org/Footer/Legal/Governance-Documents.aspx> (accessed 16 May 2013).

United States Olympic Committee (2013) *SafeSport*. Online. Available HTTP: <www. safesport.org/what-is-safesport/the-usoc-program/> (accessed 29 September 2013).

United States Olympic Committee (2013) *USOC Minimum Standards Policy for Athlete Safety Programmes*. Online. Available HTTP: <www.usfsa.org/content/Minimum%20 Standards%20Policy%20from%20USOC.pdf> (accessed 16 May 2013).

US Department of Education Office for Civil Rights (2001) *Revised Sexual Harassment Guidance: harassment of students by school employees, other students or third parties – Title IX*. Online. Available HTTP: <www2.ed.gov/offices/OCR/archives/pdf/shguide. pdf> (accessed 16 May 2013).

US Department of Education Office for Civil Rights (2011) *'Dear Colleague' Letter on the Sexual Harassment of Students as Prohibited by Title IX of the Education Amendments of 1972*. Online. Available HTTP: <www2.ed.gov/about/offices/list/ocr/letters/colleague-201104.html> (accessed 16 May 2013).

US Department of Health and Human Services, Administration for Children and Families, Administration on Children, Youth and Families, Children's Bureau (2012) *Child Maltreatment 2011*. Online. Available HTTP: <www.acf.hhs.gov/programs/cb/research-data-technology/statistics-research/child-maltreatment> (accessed 16 May 2013).

US Department of Health and Human Services, Administration for Children and Families, Administration on Children, Youth and Families, Children's Bureau (2012) *State Statutes Search*. Online. Available HTTP: <www.childwelfare.gov/systemwide/laws_policies/state/index.cfm> (accessed 16 May 2013).

USA Gymnastics (2013) *Individuals Permanently Suspended or Ineligible (as of 2 May 2013)*. Online. Available HTTP: <www.usagym.org/pages/aboutus/pages/permanently_ineligible_members.html> (accessed 16 May 2013).

USA Swimming (2013) *Permanently Ineligible Members (as of 27 April 2013)*. Available HTTP: <www.usagym.org/pages/aboutus/pages/permanently_ineligible_members.html> (accessed 16 May 2013).

Willmsen, D. and O'Hagan, M. (2003) 'Coaches Who Prey: the abuse of girls and the system that allows it', *Seattle Times*, 15 December. Online. Available HTTP: <www.seattletimes.com/news/local/coaches/news/daytwo.html > (accessed 16 May 2013).

11 Athlete welfare and safeguarding in sport in Canada

Sylvie Parent

In Canada, two million children aged 5 to 14 participated in organized sport activities (Warren 2005). Overall, boys made up 56 per cent of this group and girls 44 per cent. Sport Canada is the organization mandated by the Canadian Government to enhance opportunities for all Canadians to participate and excel in sports. The Canadian sport system is composed of 61 national governing bodies and 22 national multisport service organizations (Sport Canada 2013).

As in some other countries, the media interest in child sexual abuse in sport has been considerable. Indeed, a seminal case in the development of child protection in sport is that of ex-professional hockey player, Sheldon Kennedy (Kennedy and Grainger 2006). Kennedy reported his sexual victimization at the hands of his coach Graham James in 1996. Some years later another high-profile ex-player, Theoren Fleury, disclosed that James had abused him also (Fleury and McLellan Day 2009). Combined with cyclist Geneviève Jeanson's claims of being physically abused and forced to dope by her coach (Gravel 2008), these cases have generated a great deal of attention in Canada and have pushed child abuse onto the Canadian sports agenda. Thus, the issue of protection of young people in sport and the emphasis on well-being is increasingly evident in Canada, illustrated by initiatives focused on improving behaviour in sport (see the Canadian Center for Ethics in Sport (CCES) and True Sport) and a focus on the long-term development of athletes. This chapter provides an overview of the protection of youth in Canadian sport.

Terms and definitions

Common terminology within this area is 'child' or 'youth protection' (Clément and Dufour 2009). This incorporates the prevention of maltreatment as well as official responses when abuse or neglect is identified. In Quebec, the Youth Protection Act (YPA) (Government of Quebec 2013a) 'applies to a child whose security or development is or may be considered compromised' (Moreau et al. 2009: 180) and covers: abandonment, neglect, emotional abuse, sexual abuse, physical abuse and serious behavioural problems. The concept of maltreatment is also widely used in Canada and 'refers to situations which seriously threaten the security or development of a child' (Dufour 2009: 5). It may take the form of physical, psychological or sexual abuse or neglect (Krug et al. 2002).

Whilst the term 'safeguarding' is not in common use in Canada, the principles of safeguarding as defined in England (see Chapter 1) have also permeated Canadian sport. For instance, Kerr and Stirling (2008) advocate the importance of adopting an 'athlete-centered' philosophy in sport where 'the health and well-being of the athlete takes precedence over performance outcomes and is the primary focus in the development of policies, programmes, and procedures' (Kerr and Stirling 2008: 316). According to these authors, this philosophy is the best means to protect youth in sport.

Research on youth protection in Canadian sport

Child abuse in Canada and Canadian sport

A major study reported on the (corroborated) incidence of maltreatment against children in Canadian society. Trocmé et al. (2005) found that for every 1,000 children: 4.4 experience physical violence; 0.6 experience sexual abuse; 6.3 experience neglect; and 2.6 experience emotional abuse. As a percentage of all confirmed reports, 34 per cent related to neglect, 23 per cent to physical abuse, 14 per cent to psychological abuse and 3 per cent to sexual abuse. Whilst the scientific evidence in relation to violence against young people in sport is sparse, the Canadian research community has produced studies in the areas of sexual abuse and harassment (Kirby et al. 2000; Parent 2011, 2012), emotional abuse (Stirling and Kerr 2013), bullying (Gendron et al. 2011) and hazing (Kirby and Wintrup 2002).

The only study to provide an overview of the prevalence of sexual abuse of young athletes is that of Kirby et al. (2000). In a sample of 266 adult male and female elite Canadian athletes, they found that 1.9 per cent (n = 3 males and 2 females) reported sexual abuse in a sporting context before the age of 16. In addition, 6.8 per cent of athletes reported having had forced sex after the age of 16 in this same context (n = 4 males and 14 females) and 2.3 per cent of sexually active athletes had their first sexual intercourse with their coach. It is also noted that certain widespread myths and beliefs about abuse prevent disclosure. For example, assumptions that children make things up; boys cannot be victims of sexual abuse; athletes can defend themselves physically; and having a married, gay or female coach will preclude abuse from occurring – all operate to sustain a culture of silence and inaction (Parent 2011, 2012).

Emotional abuse has also received attention in the Canadian scientific community, particularly through the work of Stirling and Kerr (see Chapter 15). Gendron et al. (2011) also conducted a major study into young soccer players experiences of bullying. The results indicated that youth who played soccer in Quebec experienced various forms of bullying during the game and 75 per cent (of 609 players questioned) witnessed physical or verbal bullying during the game at least once during the previous year. Moreover, 53 per cent of this sample reported having been the victim of one of these two forms of bullying and 45 per cent admitted to acts of bullying in this context. Although some researchers are interested in the issue of violence against youth in sport, very few data are currently available to help understand the different forms of violence that can take place in this context.

Prevention measures in Canadian sport

The author has conducted research into the preventative measures implemented by sports organizations and the impact they have on the protection of young people. In a study of 81 local and regional sports and leisure organizations that work with vulnerable clients in Quebec, 69 per cent of the organizations surveyed did not have a designated individual responsible for dealing with incidents of violence; 35 per cent did not have a code of ethics; 70 per cent did not conduct a criminal background check before recruiting; and 80 per cent had no policy regarding this problem (Parent 2005).

At the provincial level, the data are not better. A recent survey of 49 Quebec sports federations showed that only 10 per cent had a policy on the prevention of abuse and harassment as recommended by the Ministry of Education, Leisure and Sport (MELS) (Directorate for the Promotion of Safety 2012). Moreover, only 18 per cent of sport organizations ran a criminal record check at the regional and provincial levels and 57 per cent had no codes of conduct relating to transportation, locker room or to overnight trips.

Although striking, these data do not provide information about the nature of the measures that are in place or how effective they are. A Quebec study aimed to better understand these issues through the examination of case studies (Parent and Demers 2011). This study, conducted on six provincial and local sports organizations, revealed several factors affecting the implementation of prevention measures. These include: (1) a negative view of prevention, for example, a perception that raising awareness of sexual abuse would lead to malicious allegations against coaches; and (2) a lack of leadership, competence and resources. In addition, few measures exist to prevent and manage cases of sexual abuse in these organizations. More specifically, the organizations studied had little pre-employment screening; stakeholders were not well trained, informed or aware; and there was a lack of explicit codes or guidelines for ethical behaviour (Parent and Demers 2011).

Parent (2011) also found few complaint procedures in relation to these issues in sports organizations, and where they exist, athletes and parents are often unaware of them. In addition, the administrators responsible for delivering these policies and procedures feel unprepared to deal with this type of problem (Parent 2011).

Parent and El Hlimi (2012) analysed the legal, political, and socio-cultural context of sport in Quebec in an attempt to better understand the existing problems and challenges regarding the protection of athletes. Based on their analysis, three main conclusions were drawn regarding youth protection in Quebec sport. First, it appears that greater attention should be paid to youth protection in sport, which remains an important area to be developed by the authorities responsible for sport and youth protection. Second, useful mechanisms and means of leverage to better protect youth in sport already exist but are underused. Finally, action plans and government policies exist to protect youth against various forms of violence, however, some of these do not refer specifically to the sport context and in those that do, many of the sport-related objectives or actions are difficult to implement. Studies conducted in Quebec reflect Kerr and Stirling's (2008: 311) conclusion that 'the child protection policies established so far in Canadian sport are lacking in accountability and universality.' The next section presents a brief background on the system of the protection of young Canadians and the current Canadian efforts in youth protection in sport.

Policies for the protection of youth in Canadian sport

Youth protection in Canada

Canada has established mechanisms for the protection of children and young people from abuse and neglect. Article 153 of the Criminal Code of Canada states 'the age of consent is 18 years where the sexual activity […] occurs in the context of a relationship of authority, trust or dependence' (Department of Justice Canada 2013a). This provision clearly applies to the coach-athlete relationship. The Sex Offender Information Registration Act (SOIRA) (Department of Justice Canada 2013b) requires convicted sex offenders to register annually with the Canadian Police. Moreover, each province has its own laws, measures and services to protect children from abuse, exploitation and neglect. To illustrate, I will briefly discuss the situation in Quebec.

In Quebec, the 'Governmental orientations concerning sexual assault' emphasized the need for an intersectoral approach (Ministry of Health and Social Services 2001a), stating that sport and leisure associations have a role to play in this regard. Thus, a multi-sector Agreement in regard to child victims of abuse, maltreatment and neglect (Ministry of Health and Social Services 2001b) states the responsibilities and commitments of the different ministries and all agencies involved as well as the intervention process where cases arise. MELS is a co-signatory of this agreement, thus, it applies to schools, colleges, recreational organizations and sports clubs. Unfortunately, the actions planned in these documents relating to sport are not, for the most part, applied or implemented (Parent and El Hlimi 2012).

A similar problem is present for criminal background checks. The Education Act (Ministry of Education, Recreation and Sports 1988) in Quebec states that any person who wishes to teach in Quebec must hold a teaching licence, which is now accompanied by a criminal background check (Ministry of Education, Leisure and Sport 2006). This also applies to pre-school facilities (Government of Quebec 2013b). However, the government has not established any similar requirements within sport (Parent and El Hlimi 2012).

The protection of young athletes in Canada

The National Summit of Sport in April 2001 was the impetus for the Canadian Sport Policy (Sport Canada 2002a). One of the challenges identified in this policy was 'to enhance ethical conduct at all levels and in all forms of sport in Canada' (Sport Canada 2002a). These priorities were introduced in the Canadian Strategy on Ethical Conduct in Sport (Sport Canada 2002b) and include a commitment from government to creating a sport environment free of violence (Canadian Minister of Sport 2001: 2). Yet child protection is not specifically addressed. However, the government's stance on ethical conduct nevertheless led to the development of child protection mechanisms within Canadian sports federations. Thus, national sport organizations are now required by Sport Canada to have 'a formal policy on harassment and abuse, including procedures for the reporting and for the investigation of complaints' in order to receive funding (Sport Canada 2011: 2).

Other initiatives include two training programmes on ethics and protection of youth, aimed mainly at coaches. The first is a specific module of the National Coaching Certification Programme (NCCP, established 1974) 'Make Ethical Decisions' (provided and managed by Coaching Association of Canada). NCCP train more than 60,000 coaches (CAC 2013) and all coaches wishing to receive NCCP accreditation must complete this module. NCCP accreditation is not mandatory in all sports organizations, however, it is well recognized in Canada and coaches increasingly require this certification in order to practice.

Stirling et al. (2012) conducted an evaluation of this module and found that the vast majority of the 30 interviewed coaches who completed the training 'were satisfied with the module and reported that the module impacted their decision-making' (Stirling et al. 2012: 45). However, coaches also stated that the module would benefit from the 'addition of more content information on ethical dilemmas in sport' (Stirling et al. 2012: 45). A second phase of the study (an online questionnaire completed by 3,742 coaches) found that a large majority of the sample wanted more information on the maltreatment of athletes, doping and on issues relating to health and safety (Stirling et al. 2012).

The second training programme is 'Respect in Sport', an interactive online programme intended for 'raising awareness, acquiring knowledge and giving tools to prevent bullying, abuse, harassment and neglect – mainly in sport but also in any other community activity' (Martin 2012: 38). The programme targets coaches, managers, trainers, administrators, volunteers and even parents. Created in 2004 by Sheldon Kennedy and Wayne McNeil, this training is mandatory for coaches in some provinces and some sports organizations. Nirmal conducted a study in 2010 among 1,091 coaches that showed that participants perceive the Respect in Sport programme had an impact on their practices that related to the main themes of the training. For example, approximately 75 per cent of participants indicated that they felt competent or very competent to report abuse, harassment or neglect after the training (Nirmal 2010). Maybe alliances could be created between these two programmes to standardize and reinforce the service offer in regard to the protection of young people in sports organizations.

Conclusion: developments and future prospects

Currently in Canada, several interesting initiatives are present to promote a healthy and safe environment for young athletes. However, as this chapter has explained, improvements in terms of interventions and research seems necessary to overcome the current shortcomings. First, there is a lack of empirical data on this subject and a pressing need for research to better document the phenomenon of violence against youth in sports in a comprehensive and systematic manner (types of violence, extent, characteristics, recurrence, etc.). In addition, sports policy-makers are often poorly informed about this topic and, therefore, not proactive in seeking change. According to Krug et al. (2002: 272) 'the support of political leaders is necessary not only to ensure adequate funding and effective laws, but also to give further legitimacy to prevention and to attract more public interest toward them.' Thus, more systematic inclusion of the sport context in the government action plans related to the issue of violence against young people, and a better exploitation of existing legislative mechanisms or policies, would generate more effective interventions.

The sport community in Canada often work alone in the area of youth protection. Establishing partnerships with child protection and public health bodies is recommended as it would: '(a) increase efficiency, (b) avoid intervention repetition, (c) increase the availability of resources by pooling funds and personnel in joint actions, and (d) ensure that research and prevention measures are conducted in a more collective and coordinated manner' (Krug et al. 2002: 270). Given the lack of resources and relatively low levels of knowledge around this problem within Canadian sport, such partnerships could provide important support for sports organizations in their prevention efforts. Finally, most interventions in Canadian sport have not been evaluated. This is a significant shortcoming which must be addressed, as further initiatives are developed, if we are to understand more clearly the impact and effectiveness of the programmes we implement.

References

Canadian Minister of Sport (2001) *The London Declaration: expectations for fairness in sport*. Online. Available HTTP: <www.truesportsecretariat.ca/files/Documents/FPT-CCES-LondonDeclaration-F.pdf> (accessed 4 April 2013).

Clark, W. (2008) 'Kid's sports', *Statistics Canada Catalogue*, 11: 53–61.

Clément, M-E. and Dufour, S. (2009) *Violence against Children in the Family Environment*. Québec: Les Éditions CEC inc.

Coaching Association of Canada (2013) *Who We Are*. Online. Available HTTP: <http://www.coach.ca/who-we-are-s13411> (accessed 4 April 2013).

Department of Justice Canada (2013a) *Age of Consent to Sexual Activity*. Online. Available HTTP: <www.justice.gc.ca/eng/rp-pr/other-autre/clp/faq.html> (accessed 4 April 2013).

— (2013b) *Sex Offender Information Registration Act*. Online. Available HTTP: <http://laws-lois.justice.gc.ca/PDF/S-8.7.pdf> (accessed 4 April 2013).

Directorate for the Promotion of Safety (2012) *Survey Conducted of National Agencies for Recreation and Sport on the Prevention Measures Put in Place in Order to Ensure the Security and Integrity of Participants*, Ministry of Education, Leisure and Sport.

Dufour, S. (2009) 'Issues related to the study of family violence', in M-E. Clément and S. Dufour (eds) *Violence against Children in the Family Environment*, Québec: Les Éditions CEC.

Fleury, T. and McLellan Day, K. (2009) *Playing with Fire: the highest highs and lowest lows of Theo Fleury*, USA: Harper Collins Publishers.

Gendron, M., Frenette, É., Debardieux, É. and Bodin, D. (2011) 'Behaviours of intimidation and violence in amateur soccer in Quebec: the situation of the players and players from 12 to 17 years enrolled in a sport-studies programme', *International Journal of Violence and School*, 12: 90–111.

Government of Quebec (2013a) *Youth Protection Act*. Online. Available HTTP: <http://www2.publicationsduquebec.gouv.qc.ca/dynamicSearch/telecharge.php?type=2&file=/P_34_1/P34_1.html> (accessed 4 April 2013).

— (2013b) *Educational Childcare Act*. Online. Available HTTP: <www2.publicationsduquebec.gouv.qc.ca/dynamicSearch/telecharge.php?type=2&file=//S_4_1_1/S4_1_1.htm> (accessed 4 April 2013).

—(2013c)*Law on Security in Sport*. Online. Available HTTP: <www2.publicationsduquebec.gouv.qc.ca/dynamicSearch/telecharge.php?type=2&file=/S_3_1/S3_1.htm> (accessed 4 April 2013).

Gravel, A. (2008) *The Jeanson Affair: the gears*, Québec: Les Éditions voix parallèles.

Kennedy, S. and Grainger, J. (2006) *Why I Didn't Say Anything: the Sheldon Kennedy story*, Toronto: Insomniac Press.

Kerr, G. and Stirling, A. E. (2008) 'Child protection in sport: implications of an athlete-centered philosophy', *Quest*, 60: 307–23.

Kerr, G. A. and Stirling, A. E. (2012) 'Parents' reflections on their child's experiences of emotionally abusive coaching practices', *Journal of Applied Sport Psychology*, 24: 191–206.

Kirby, S. and Wintrup, G. (2002) 'Running the Gauntlet: an examination of initiation/hazing and sexual abuse in sport', in C. Brackenridge and K. Fasting (eds) *Sexual Harassment and Abuse in Sport: international research and policy perspectives*, London: Whiting and Birch.

Kirby, S., Greaves, L. and Hankivsky, O. (2000) *The Dome of Silence: sexual harassment and abuse in sport,* Halifax: Fernwood Publishing Ltd.

Krug, E. G., Dalhberg, L. L., Mercy, J. A., Zwi, A. and Lozano-Ascensio, R. (2002) *World Report on Violence and Health*, Genova: World Health Organization.

Martin, M. (2012) 'Respect in Sport: Canada's online programme', in S. Chroni, K. Fasting, M. Hartill, N. Knorre, M. Martin, M. Papaefstathiou, D. Rhind, B. Rulofs, J. Toeftgaard Støckel, T. Vertommen and J. Zurc (eds) *Prevention of Sexual and Gender Harassment and Abuse in Sports: initiatives in Europe and beyond*, Frankfurt: Deutsche Sportjugend.

Ministry of Education, Leisure and Sport (2006) *The Verification of Legal History: information document for applicants and holders of an authorization to teach*. Online. Available HTTP: <http://www.mels.gouv.qc.ca/dftps/interieur/PDF/Antecedents_judiciaires_f.pdf> (accessed 4 April 2013).

— (2007) *Criteria for the Recognition of Québec Organizations to Govern Sports*. Online. Available HTTP: <http://www.mels.gouv.qc.ca/en/athletes-coaches-and-referees/athletes-dexcellence/partenaires/quebec-sports-federations/> (accessed 5 January 2013).

Ministry of Education, Recreation and Sports (1988) The Education Act. Online. Available HTTP:<http://www2.publicationsduquebec.gouv.qc.ca/dynamicSearch/telecharge.php?type=2&file=/I_13_3/I13_3_A.html> (accessed 4 April 2013).

Ministry of Health and Social Services (2001a) *Government Guidelines on Sexual Assault*, Québec: Government of Quebec.

— (2001b) *Multi-Sectoral Agreement Concerning Children Who are Victims of Sexual Abuse or Physical Ill-Treatment or Whose Physical Health is Threatened by a Lack of Physical Care*, Québec: Government of Quebec.

Moreau, J., Cabaret, M. and Carignan, L. (2009) 'The system of protection of youth in Québec', in M. E. Clément and S. Dufour (eds) *Violence Against Children in the Family Environment*, Québec: Les Éditions CEC.

Nirmal, R. (2010) *'Coaches' perceived impact of the Respect in Sport (RiS) program on bullying, abuse, neglect, and harassment in sports'*, unpublished master's thesis, University of British Columbia.

Parent, S. (2005) *The Prevention of Harassment and Sexual Abuse in Leisure and Sport: we are working*, Québec: Regional Unit of Leisure and Sport of Quebec.

— (2011) 'Disclosure of sexual abuse in sport organizations: a case study', *Journal of Child Sexual Abuse*, 20: 322–37.

— (2012) 'The issue of sexual abuse in sport: perceptions and realities', *Revue Canadienne de Service Social*, 29: 205–27.

Parent, S. and Demers, G. (2011) 'Sexual abuse in sport: a model to prevent and protect athletes', *Child Abuse Review*, 20: 120–33.

Parent, S. and El Hlimi, K. (2012) 'Athlete protection in Quebec's sport system: assessments, problems and challenges', *Journal of Sport and Social Issues*, DOI: 10.1177/0193723512467358.

Sport Canada (2002a) *The Canadian Sport Policy 2002*. Online. Available HTTP: <http://pch.gc.ca/eng/1374688900142/1374689425694> (accessed 4 April 2013).

— (2002b) *The Canadian Strategy for Ethical Conduct in Sport*. Online. Available HTTP: <www.pch.gc.ca/eng/1376330638168/1376398861384> (accessed 4 April 2013).

— (2011) *Sport Funding and Accountability Framework 2013–2017*. Online. Available HTTP: <http://pch.gc.ca/pgm/sc/pgm/cfrs/sfafelig13–eng.cfm> (accessed 4 April 2013).

— (2012) *Canadian Sport Policy 2012*. Online. Available HTTP: <http://sirc.ca/CSPRenewal/documents/CSP2012_EN.pdf> (accessed 4 April 2013).

— (2013) *Introduction*. Online. Available HTTP: <http://www.pch.gc.ca/eng/1268160670172/1268160761399> (accessed 4 April 2013).

Stirling, A. (2010) 'Elite child athletes' narratives of emotional abuse', in C. H. Brackenridge and D. Rhind (eds) *Elite Child Athlete Welfare: international perspectives*, London: Brunel University Press.

Stirling, A. E. and Kerr, G. (2013) 'The perceived effects of elite athletes' experiences of emotional abuse in the coach-athlete relationship', *International Journal of Sport and Exercise Psychology*, 11: 87–100.

Stirling, A. E., Kerr, G. A. and Cruz, L. C. (2012) 'An evaluation of Canada's national coaching certification program's "Make Ethical Decisions" coach education module', *International Journal of Coaching Science*, 6: 45–60.

Trocmé, N., Fallon, B., MacLaurin, B., Daciuk, J., Felstiner, C., Black, T., Tommyr, L., Blackstock, C., Barter, K., Turcotte, D. and Cloutier, R. (2005) *Canadian Incidence Study of Reported Child Abuse and Neglect – major findings – 2003*, Ottawa: Minister of Public Works and Government Services Canada.

Warren, C. (2005) *Physical Activity Among Children*, Canada: Statistics Canada.

12 Child safety and wellbeing in Australian sport

Kate Russell

Sport is central to the lives of Australians, woven into the fabric of the nation's collective identity (Georgakis and Russell 2011). But even in this 'paradise of sport' (Cashman 1995) in recent years questions have been raised about the widely held belief of the innate 'goodness' of sport. Concerns about child abuse within and beyond sport and about sexism, doping and wider ethical issues have, in recent years, led to legislative and policy changes aimed at improving children's safety and promoting wellbeing in and beyond sport.

From child protection to promoting children's wellbeing

Australia comprises six states and two territories – the Australian Capital Territory, New South Wales, Tasmania, South Australia, Western Australia, Victoria, Queensland and the Northern Territory – and each has its own legal jurisdiction. Consequently, there are differences in legislation and practice relating to children's services across the country. However, all services for children are underpinned by the principle that a child is anyone under the age of 18 and the notion that 'the best way to protect children is to prevent child abuse and neglect from occurring in the first place' (Commonwealth of Australia 2009: 1), where child abuse is understood as comprising four categories of maltreatment – sexual, physical and emotional abuse plus neglect.

Since the end of the 1980s, definitions of child abuse in each state and territory have been broadly consistent. As an example, the Australian Institute of Health and Wellbeing (AIHW) (AIHW 2013a) defines child sexual abuse as any act by a person having the care of the child that 'exposes a child to, or involves a child in, sexual processes beyond his or her understanding or contrary to accepted community standards' (AIHW 2013b: 75). Meanwhile, child neglect is defined as:

> ...any serious omissions or commissions by a person having the care of a child that, within the bounds of cultural tradition, constitute a failure to provide conditions that are essential for the healthy, physical and emotional development of a child.
>
> (AIHW 2013b: 75)

However, while children's services have historically focused on the protection of children from abuse and the development of prevention strategies to meet this aim, there has recently been a shift towards a more holistic, proactive approach. In 2009, all Australian governments endorsed the National Framework for Protecting Australia's Children 2009–2020 (Commonwealth of Australia 2009). The central premise of the framework is that 'protecting children is everyone's responsibility … not simply a matter for the statutory child protection systems' (Commonwealth of Australia 2009: 6). In particular, the framework notes that, 'Australia needs to move from seeing "protecting children" merely as a response to abuse and neglect to one of promoting the safety and wellbeing of children' (Commonwealth of Australia 2009: 7). So under the pre-framework system, statutory services could only be provided to children and families in need of additional help or intervention to protect against abuse. However, under the new focus of promoting children's safety and wellbeing, universal support can be provided for *all* children and their families through programmes on, say, education and health. A consequence of this, including for sporting organizations, is that securing children's welfare requires a proactive approach and is the responsibility of the whole of society rather than a handful of child protection specialists.

Legislation

The National Framework (Commonwealth of Australia 2009) states that every child has a right to be safe from harm and that protecting children is a public responsibility (Community and Disability Services Ministers 2005). Consequently, everyone in organizational settings, including sport, has a legal duty to ensure they provide a safe environment for children. The extent to which individuals in sport are aware of these responsibilities is unknown. As volunteers run much of sport in Australia, it may be that training and resources are needed to inform them of their legal duties. Sporting organizations, such as Play by the Rules (see below), provide a range of online and face-to-face training resources to inform individuals of their roles and responsibilities.

But while promoting children's safety and wellbeing is now part of all services for children, concerns about child abuse remain high following a series of high-profile scandals (see below). To encourage the identification of abuse, legislation mandates that certain individuals report suspicions of abuse. States and territories have slightly different laws about who is named a mandatory reporter and different rules about the stage at which suspicions should be reported. In some cases, individuals in sport are included as mandatory reporters, while in others they are not. For brevity I highlight the differences between three states/territories and refer readers to the Australian Institute of Family Studies (2013) for further detail.

In the Northern Territory, all adults are named as mandatory reporters and should report suspicions of abuse and neglect when there are 'reasonable grounds' that a child has suffered or is likely to suffer harm. This means employees and volunteers who work with children in sport are classified as mandatory reporters in this territory. In South Australia, individuals in sport also have this responsibility as the law relates to:

> ...any person who is an employee of, or volunteer in, a non-government organization that provides sporting or recreational, services wholly or partly for children, being a person who: (1) is engaged in the actual delivery of those services to children; or (2) holds a management position in the relevant organization the duties of which include direct responsibility for, or direct supervision of, the provision of those services to children.
>
> (Play by the Rules 2013a)

Meanwhile, in New South Wales, adults in sport are excluded from mandatory reporting responsibilities as the law only applies to individuals who in the course of their work deliver health care, welfare, education, children's services, residential services or law enforcement wholly or in part to children, or to anyone who holds a management position in an organization that includes direct responsibility for or direct supervision of those services to children.

Finally, regardless of the state or territory, anyone working with or supervising children must undergo a Working with Children Check (WWC). WWC checks aim to ensure children's safety 'by helping to prevent people who have a criminal history that indicates they may harm children from working with children' (Western Australia Department of Child Protection 2008). While there are some state/territory differences, the checks cover all convictions, including those that are spent as well as charges that are still pending and that did not result in a conviction (Western Australia Department of Child Protection 2008). Checks cost around $80 (approximately £47) for employees but are free for volunteers (Play by the Rules 2013b), and applicants are either cleared to work with children for three years or banned from ever working with children (Western Australia Department of Child Protection 2008).

WWC checks have faced criticism. It has been suggested that organizations rely too heavily on the checks and that they have obfuscated wider discussions about how to create safe and positive sporting environments for all members (McAllion 2013a). In addition, the checks only identify individuals already convicted of offences against children; first-time offenders and those yet to be caught offending would not be identified (Brackenridge 2001). Meanwhile, the CEO of the Royal Commission into the Institutional Responses to Child Sexual Abuse, Janette Dines, identified potential loopholes in WWC checks (Fife-Yeomans 2013), noting the potential for sports not to be told immediately if a current WWC holder has been charged, convicted or sentenced for a relevant offence against a child, especially if the individual did not specify in their WWC application that they work in a sports environment (McAllion 2013a).

High-profile inquries into child abuse

In 2012, state- and national-level inquiries into child abuse in institutions including sport were launched. In the state of Victoria, the Parliamentary Inquiry into the Handling of Child Abuse by Religious and Other Organizations is charged with investigating how non-government organizations, including religious and sports organizations, respond to allegations of child abuse (Family and Community Development Committee 2012). The inquiry was established following revelations about child sexual abuse in the Roman Catholic Church and a string of other religious and non-religious institutions. To date, only one sports organizations has submitted to this inquiry – vicsport, the leading sports organization in Victoria. While the final report is not due until 2014, initial reports suggest systemic failures including the covering up of abuse and failures to refer suspicions of abuse to the police or other relevant authorities: 'practices and processes within these organizations discouraged reporting to state authorities and possibly contributed to both the incidence of offending and the effective denial of justice to victims' (Family and Community Development Committee 2012: 2).

Meanwhile, the Royal Commission into Institutional Responses to Child Sexual Abuse (Royal Commission 2013a) was initiated following the inquiry in Victoria to 'inquire into the experience of people directly or indirectly affected by child sexual abuse and related matters in institutional contexts' (Family and Community Development Committee 2012: 2–3). Under its remit is 'any institution which provides the means through which adults have contact with children' (Royal Commission 2013c: 32), meaning sports organizations are included as well as other recreational groups such as the Girl Guides, Boys Scouts, religious organizations and schools (Royal Commission 2013a). Despite its title, the Royal Commission will report on all forms of unlawful or improper treatment of children, including physical and emotional abuse and neglect as well as sexual abuse. It aims to recommend changes to policy and practice to 'better protect against and respond to child sexual abuse in an institutional context' (Royal Commission 2013b:10). At the time of writing, hearings in both these inquiries were just beginning so there was no information available on the extent of child abuse identified by the commissions within sports organizations.

Abuse in sport

There is very little empirical evidence of the extent of child abuse in Australian sport, although anecdotal cases have appeared in the media. In 1999, for example, the world-renowned Australian triathlete coach Brett Sutton admitted five sexual offences against a teenage girl under his care in the 1980s (Downes 2002). Sutton received only a suspended sentence partly because, in the words of the judge, 'a large number of leading athletes will suffer disadvantage from your absence from the scene' (Downes 2002). Sutton also received a life ban from coaching in Australia but he moved to Europe and took up coaching in Spain and Switzerland (Downes 2002).

Another infamous case involved former head coach and ex-team manager of the Australian national swim team, Terry Buck. In 2009, four years after Buck's death, Olympic swimmer Greg Rogers accused Buck of sexually abusing him in the 1960s (Jeffery 2009). Rogers alleged he was 11 years old at the time of the abuse while Buck was 16 years old. No criminal charges were ever brought against Buck (Jeffery 2009). Meanwhile, in 2013 Brazilian-born Australian Football League star Harry O'Brien told reporters he had been abused as a child (Brodie 2013). While O'Brien did not clarify whether or not the abuse took place in a sporting context, the case further raised the profile of child sexual abuse in sport in Australia.

The only large-scale empirical study in Australian sport on the prevalence of abuse found that of the 370 regional- and elite-level adult athletes questioned, 31 per cent of females and 21 per cent of males reported experiencing sexual abuse at some point in their lives (Leahy et al. 2002). Of those who had experienced sexual abuse, 41 per cent of females and 29 per cent of males reported the abuse occurred in a sports setting. Meanwhile, of the elite athletes in the study, 48.8 per cent of females and 40 per cent of males reported the perpetrator was a member of sports personnel, while among the regional-level athletes the figure was 29.1 per cent among females and 21 per cent among males.

Meanwhile, sport is beginning to acknowledge its responsibility for proactively promoting the safety and wellbeing of children. Consequently, it has begun to explore issues that relate to all athletes, not just children, under the banner of 'sports ethics'. In 2010 the Australian Sports Commission (ASC) (ASC 2010: 3), the country's key sports agency with a remit to increase sports participation and excellence, published a report into 'the most prevalent and serious ethical and integrity issues' across all levels of sport. The Ethics in Sport report drew on evidence gathered from 3,700 players, coaches, administrators and officials. Among the six most commonly witnessed ethical and integrity issues were: sledging (also called hazing); juniors participating against more physically developed opponents; juniors participating against more skilled opponents; and athletes being pushed too hard by coaches and parents. Meanwhile the national crime agency, the Australian Crime Commission (ACC), also looked into sports ethics. The Organized Crime and Drugs in Sport report (ACC 2013) highlighted the use of performance-enhancing drugs; excessive alcohol consumption, primarily among male athletes; and match fixing as key areas for concern. As a result of the ACC report, the Australian Sports Anti-Doping Agency has already handed down infraction notices for doping to a member of the Canberra Raiders National Rugby League (NRL) club (Fox Sports 2013) and is reportedly ready to hand out more to players and officials in the Australian Football League or Aussie Rules (AFL) club Essendon, which could result in lifetime bans (ABC News 2013).

Policy developments in sport

There have also been policy developments within sport that reflect the Australian government's proactive approach to children's welfare. For example, all National

Sporting Organizations (NSOs) funded by the ASC are required to have a Member Protection Policy in place to show how they will meet their obligations to ensure their sports are safe, fair and inclusive for everyone, not just children (ASC 2013a). Each NSO's Member Protection Policy covers how they will prevent and address discrimination, harassment and child protection concerns and refers to the relevant state/territory child welfare laws, depending on where the NSO is based, including laws around who is classed as a mandatory reporter of abuse and which adults must undergo WWC checks.

However, while having a Member Protection Policy creates some consistency across sports, organizations not funded by the ASC are exempt from this requirement so there is no guarantee all sports will have similar protections in place, and there are also likely to be differences in understandings and implementation of safeguards for children across sports (McAllion 2013b). Speaking at the Parliamentary Inquiry into the Handling of Child Abuse by Religious and Other Organizations the CEO of vicsport, Mark McAllion, also noted that some sports organizations believe they have met their responsibilities simply by having a Member Protection Policy. He argued that a further step of educating sports stakeholders about their responsibilities and raising awareness of child welfare issues in sport is also required to develop understandings of:

> how to create an environment where, if an issue takes place, a child or parent feels comfortable enough to raise it with the hierarchy of the club or knows the steps to take it further, if appropriate, and when that does happen, the club knows how to appropriately deal with the situation.
>
> (McAllion 2013b: 3)

In other words, there is a need for sports organizations to understand the importance of prevention work to children's welfare in sport and a need for sport to go beyond policy creation and compliance. Admittedly this creates additional pressure on the largely volunteer workforce operating within sport to act in increasingly professionalized ways to implement and maintain safe environments. The difficulty for organizations is the level of monitoring this requires, particularly given that the sports workforce often changes and is already stretched for resources.

Meanwhile, initiatives such as Play by the Rules offer nationwide training and advice on child protection and other welfare issues in sport. Play by the Rules is a collaboration between the ASC, the Australian Human Rights Commission, the New South Wales Commission for Children and Young People, the Australian and New Zealand Sports Law Association, state and territory departments of sport and recreation, and state and territory anti-discrimination and human rights agencies (ASC 2013b). It aims to 'build the capacity and capability of sport and recreational clubs/associations to prevent and deal with discrimination, harassment and child safety issues in sport' (Play by the Rules 2013c). While the initiative uses the term 'child protection,' it also refers to 'child safety' because it aims to promote good coaching practice in general rather than only protect children from sexual abuse. To this end, Play by the Rules serves as a hub for training, resources and advice relating to discrimination, harassment, child protection and child safety (ASC 2013b). It also trains people who wish to act as Member Protection Information Officers (MPIO) either at NSO or at club level. MPIOs are responsible for 'providing information about a person's rights, responsibilities and options to an individual making a complaint or raising a concern' about discrimination, harassment and child safety (Play by the Rules no date).

Meanwhile, some sports have also developed their own initiatives and policies to foster positive environments for their members. For example, in 2005 the Australian Football League (AFL) developed a 'Respect and Responsibility' policy aimed at creating a safe and inclusive environment for women at all levels of the game (AFL 2005). Likewise, a similar policy was developed by the National Rugby League (NRL), following high-profile allegations of sexual assault by players from the Sydney Bulldogs team in 2004 (Krien 2013). The allegations negatively impacted on the reputation of NRL and its players, who were 'widely depicted as rapists and thugs' (Albury et al. 2011: 339). In response, the NRL ran a series of Play By The Rules workshops for players on ethics and sexual behaviours (Lumby et al. 2004). The workshops sought to problematize a range of sexual behaviours, such as the 'sharing' of a sexual partner among teammates. However, the notion that men should have to undergo training to know how to treat women appropriately is inherently problematic as this does not occur outside of a sport context. This may suggest a more disturbing rhetoric around the argument that such behaviours are 'part of the game'. Krien (2013) notes that many former and current players believe that behaviour such as this supports team dynamics and that the workshops are simply to appease the wider public. While the policy and workshops are primarily related to improving the way AFL and NRL players view women, there are also concerns about the impact of the apparent culture of sexism in some football codes on children and young people.

Recommendations

Although advances have been made regarding children's welfare in sport in recent years, more remains to be done. For example, an evaluation of the implementation of the National Framework for Protecting Australia's Children 2009–2020 (Commonwealth of Australia 2009) is needed to understand the extent of collaboration between government and non-government agencies, the impact of the framework on protecting children from harm, and the usefulness of a national approach to children's welfare in the context of varying geographical, economic and health drivers.

To further build safer environments for youth athletes there is also an urgent need for empirical data on the incidence and prevalence of child abuse within sport in Australia to provide baseline data for future strategies. Data on the knowledge and implementation of child welfare strategies among sports stakeholders is also needed, as are studies exploring the effectiveness of coach education and WWC checks and to determine what constitutes good practice for coaches, parents, officials, administrators and peer athletes. An evaluation of perceptions around current coaching practice, parental engagement and official responses to incidences of poor practice would, therefore, provide a far broader understanding of the importance and impact of changes on welfare policy.

References

ABC News (2013) 'ASADA preparing action against Essendon AFL players and officials: reports', *ABC News*, 19 September. Online. Available HTTP: <www.abc. net.au/news/2013–09–19/asada-preparing-action-against-essendon-players-and-officials3/4968740> (accessed 20 September 2013).

Albury, K., Carmody, M., Evers, C. and Lumby, C. (2011) 'Playing by the rules: researching, teaching and learning sexual ethics with young men in the Australian National Rugby League', *Sex Education*, 3: 339–51.

ACC (Australian Crime Commission) (2013) *Organized Crime and Drugs in Sport: new generation performance and image enhancing drugs and organized criminal involvement in their use in professional sport*, Canberra: Australian Crime Commission.

Australian Football League (2005) *Respect and Responsibility: creating a safe and inclusive environment for women at all levels of Australian football*. Online. Available HTTP: <www.afl.com.au/staticfile/AFLpercent20Tenant/AFL/Files/Respect_&_Responsibility_Policy.pdf> (accessed 15 August 2013).

Australian Institute of Family Studies (2013) *Mandatory Reporting of Child Abuse and Neglect*. Online. Available HTTP: <www.aifs.gov.au/cfca/pubs/factsheets/a141787/> (accessed 10 July 2013).

Australian Institute of Health and Welfare (2013a) *Child Protection Australia 2011–12*, Canberra: Australian Institute of Health and Welfare. Online. Available HTTP: <www.aihw.gov.au/WorkArea/DownloadAsset.aspx?id=60129542752> (accessed 1 June 2013).

Australian Institute of Health and Wellbeing (2013b) *Appendix 1*. Online. Available HTTP: <www.aihw.gov.au/WorkArea/DownloadAsset.aspx?id=6442455165> (accessed 4 October 2013).

Australian Sports Commission (2010) *Australian Sport Commission: ethics in sport*. Canberra: Colmar Brunton Social Research. Online. Available HTTP: <secure.ausport. gov.au/__data/assets/pdf_file/0003/417117/ASC_Ethics_report.pdf> (accessed 28 August 2010).

— (2013a) *National Member Protection Policy Template*. Online. Available HTTP: <www. ausport.gov.au/supporting/integrity_in_sport/resources/national_member_protection_policy_template> (accessed 6 October 2013).

— (2013b) *Play by the Rules*. Online. Available HTTP: <www.ausport.gov.au/supporting/integrity_in_sport/get_involved/play_by_the_rules> (accessed 6 October 2013).

Brackenridge, C. H. (2001) *Spoilsports: understanding and preventing sexual exploitation in sport*, London: Routledge.

Brodie, W. (2013) 'O'Brien battling personal demons, begs for space from media', *The Age*, 9 July. Online. Available HTTP: <www.theage.com.au/afl/afl-news/obrien-battling-personal-demons-begs-for-space-from-media-20130709–2pn11.html> (accessed 6 October 2013).

Cashman, R. (1995) *Paradise of Sport*, Melbourne: Oxford University Press.

Commonwealth of Australia (2009) *Protecting Children is Everyone's Business – National Framework for Protecting Australia's Children 2009–2020: understanding the approach*, Canberra: Commonwealth of Australia. Online. Available HTTP: <www.fahcsia.gov.au/our-responsibilities/families-and-children/publications-articles/protecting-children-is-everyones-business> (accessed 1 July 2013).

Community and Disability Services Ministers (2005) *Creating Safe Environments for Children: organizations, employees and volunteers*. Online. Available HTTP: <www.checkwwc.wa.gov.au/NR/rdonlyres/E1B2D479-B4EE-4119-9944-28C3E478EBA5/0/childsafe_framework.pdf> (accessed 6 October 2013).

Downes, S. (2002) 'Every parent's nightmare', *Observer Sport Monthly*, 7 April. Online. Available HTTP: <http://observer.theguardian.com/osm/story/0,,678189,00.html> (accessed 1 October 2009).

Family and Community Development Committee (2012) *Opening Statement*. Online. Available HTTP: <www.parliament.vic.gov.au/fcdc/article/1786> (accessed 15 November 2013).

Fife-Yeomans, J. (2013) 'Royal commission into child sex abuse targets employment loopholes', *The Daily Telegraph*, 17 June. Online. Available HTTP: <www.dailytelegraph.com.au/news/nsw/royal-commission-into-child-sex-abuse-targets-employment-loopholes/story-fni0cx12-1226664710581> (accessed 23 July 2013).

Fox Sports (2013) *NRL Hands Down First Infraction Notice of ASADA Drugs Inquiry to Canberra Raiders Star Sando Earl*. Online. Available HTTP: <www.foxsports.com.au/league/live-nrl-snap-press-conference-with-ceo-dave-smith/story-e6frf3ou-1226706766537#.Ujug6GT-L2E> (accessed 20 September 2013).

Georgakis, S. and Russell, K. (2011) 'Introduction', in S. Georgakis and K. Russell (eds) *Youth Sport in Australia*, Sydney: University of Sydney Press.

Jeffery, M. (2009) 'Swim coach Terry Buck denied date of meeting', *The Australian*, 10 December. Online. Available HTTP: < www.theaustralian.com.au/sport/swim-coach-terry-buck-denied-date-of-meeting/story-e6frg7mf-1225808818398> (accessed 4 October 2013).

Krien, A. (2013) *Night Games: sex, power and sport*, Collingwood, Vic.: Black Inc. Books.

Leahy, T., Pretty, G. and Tenenbaum, G. (2002) 'Prevalence of sexual abuse in sport in Australia', *Journal of Sexual Aggression*, 2: 16–36.

Lumby, C. K., Albury, C. and McCarthy, Q. (2004) *Playing by the Rules: on and off the field research report for the National Rugby League*. Sydney: University of Sydney.

McAllion, M. (2013a) *Submission to the Parliamentary Inquiry into the Handling of Child Abuse by Religious and Other Non-government Organizations*, Melbourne: vicsport. Online. Available HTTP: <www.parliament.vic.gov.au/images/stories/committees/fcdc/inquiries/57th/Child_Abuse_Inquiry/Submissions/vicsport.pdf> (accessed 2 June 2013).

McAllion, M. (2013b) 'Transcript', *Family and Community Development Committee: inquiry into the handling of child abuse by religious and other organizations*. Online. Available HTTP: <www.parliament.vic.gov.au/images/stories/committees/fcdc/inquiries/57th/Child_Abuse_Inquiry/Transcripts/vicsports_12–April-13.pdf> (accessed 20 June 2013).

Play by the Rules (2013a) *Reporting Child Abuse Info Sheets*. Online. Available HTTP: <www.playbytherules.net.au/resources/reporting-child-abuse-info-sheets> (accessed 15 July 2013).

— (2013b) *Working with Children Checks Fact Sheets*. Online. Available HTTP: <www.playbytherules.net.au/legal-stuff/child-protection/child-protection-laws-explained/screening> (accessed 15 July 2013).

—— (2013c) *Our Strategic Plan*. Online. Available HTTP: <www.playbytherules.net.au/home/our-strategic-plan> (accessed 6 October 2013).

—— (no date) *Member Protection Information Officer Training*. Online. Available HTTP: <www.playbytherules.net.au/assets/WEB_MPIO_Training_DL.pdf> (accessed 6 October 2013).

Royal Commission (2013a) *Royal Commission into the Institutional Responses to Child Sexual Abuse: formal opening of the inquiry*. Online. Available HTTP: <www.childabuseroyalcommission.gov.au/Hearings/Pages/Hearings-transcripts.aspx> (accessed 30 May 2013).

—— (2013b) *Royal Commission into the Institutional Responses to Child Sexual Abuse: terms of reference*. Online. Available HTTP: <www.childabuseroyalcommission.gov.au/our-work/terms-of-reference/> (accessed 30 May 2013).

—— (2013c) *Royal Commission into the Institutional Responses to Child Sexual Abuse: transcript day two*. Online. Available HTTP: <www.childabuseroyalcommission.gov.au/public-hearings/transcripts/> (accessed 17 September 2013).

Western Australia Department of Child Protection (2008) *Working with Children*. Online. Available HTTP: <www.dsr.wa.gov.au/working-with-children> (accessed 6 October 2013).

13 The protection of young athletes in China

Policy and practice

Fan Hong and Zhang Ling

China's sporting success has largely been accredited to its state-driven elite sports system, which was instigated in the 1980s to realize the Chinese government's aim of making the country a sporting superpower. Under the system, which came to prominence in the 1980s, thousands of children are identified as having elite sport potential and moved to train in programmes aimed at producing future Olympic champions. The system has undoubtedly made China one of the world's most successful medal-winning nations. But it has also come under intense criticism in recent years from academics, journalists and sports insiders concerned about the human cost of a system that has been accused of putting the interest of the state ahead of the welfare of its athletes (see for example British Broadcasting Corporation 2005; Wu 2002).

Unbeknownst to many, however, the Chinese Government has enacted legislation in recent years to safeguard the welfare of child athletes in its specialist sports system. The 2011 law Regulations on Managing Young People and Children's Sports Schools (Chinese Sport Ministry/Ministry of Education 2011a) is perhaps the most significant of these and has come to be seen as landmark legislation for the welfare of athletes under the age of 18, the age of majority in China. The act ensures that children in the sports school system should continue to receive a formal academic curriculum alongside their sports training, mandates that athletes are provided with medical insurance in case of injury, and prohibits sports schools from using corporal punishment (Chinese Sport Ministry/Ministry of Education 2011a). Related legislation from the same year, the Regulation on Managing Young People and Children's Sports Schools at the Middle Level (Chinese Sport Ministry/Ministry of Education 2011b), requires that sports schools ensure their young students' diets contain sufficient nutrition to allow them to undergo the training required and that sports schools provide regular medical checks for athletes to prevent injuries (Chinese Sport Ministry/Ministry of Education 2011b).

This chapter considers these and other measures aimed at protecting the welfare of children and young people in the specialist sports school system in China. It focuses specifically on issues relating to athletes' selection, training, education, medical injury and insurance, and also discusses anti-doping legislation and enforcement.

Talent identification, training and education in China

Identifying a steady stream of talented athletes is crucial to the success of the elite sports system in China. Talent identification begins early; indeed, research suggests that more than 90 per cent of those in the system are children (Yang 2010). This is especially true in sports such as gymnastics, diving and table tennis, where athletes start their training from age 4 to 6. At this first stage, school Physical Education teachers and coaches from local sports clubs nationwide select talented athletes aged between 5 and 16 years old, depending on the sport, from primary schools, local clubs and competitions. Those selected register in specialist sports schools in their local area that are run by local sports commissions. Here selected athletes study an academic programme in the morning, either at the sports school or at a local non-specialist sports school, and sports training, led by full-time professional coaches employed by the sports commissions, takes place before school and in the afternoons.

The 1986 Compulsory Education Law (National People's Congress 2006) enshrined in law equal rights for all citizens to education and mandated nine years of compulsory schooling for children and young people. As a result, all children up to the age of 15, including those in the elite sports training system, are required to study at secondary level. Equally, under the Regulations on Managing Young People and Children's Sports Schools law (Chinese Sport Ministry/Ministry of Education 2011a), the government mandates that children receive sports training alongside a formal academic curriculum, stating that, 'sports training for young athletes should be systematic and scientific and, in principle, the training time should be under 2.5 hours per day (including morning training). The sports schools should arrange both training and academic study time sensibly' (Chinese Sport Ministry/Ministry of Education 2011a). To support this, the law requires local education departments to regularly inspect sports schools' academic classes and standards, and punishments can be handed down to schools that fail to meet the minimum standards (Chinese Sport Ministry/ Ministry of Education 2011a).

There are indications the law is flouted in some specialist sports schools, however. In non-specialist sports schools, pupils usually play sports two days per week; by comparison, children in specialist sports schools train between three and four hours per day, five days per week. At the same time, pupils in non-specialist sports schools follow an academic programme for between five and six hours per day, while children in specialist sports schools have been found to spend only three hours a day on academic study (Hong 2004). In addition, to fit in their training regime children at sports schools are often limited in the number and range of subjects they can study, meaning they have fewer qualifications than their non-sporting peers when their sports career is at an end. Further concerns have been raised about the standard of academic study in elite sports training schools, where it has been suggested that sports training is prioritized over academic study, as an athlete in Zhang's (2013) study suggests:

I had trained in Guangzhou Weilun Sports School for six years. Although there were academic classes, the main priority was sports training. Study was never comprehensive and basically of little value. The [sports] training was semi-professional, and during competition we did not have to attend the classes. However, at the end of our schooling, we passed our final exam like normal students. If we were taking part in competitions at national, city or provincial level, training could take from half a year to one year, during which we did not attend any [academic] classes.

(Zhang 2013: 121)

For the young people in specialist sports schools, the next step towards becoming an elite athlete comes if, after several years of specialist training, they are selected for provincial training centres or academies. In most cases, the children selected are between age 9 and 18 (Zhang 2013). Only around 12 per cent of sports school pupils make it to this next stage (Liu 2010); the rest leave sports school behind and return to their local school to continue their academic studies. The provincial training centres and academies follow their own academic programme; students are assigned a group based on their age and academic level, and attend academic classes on Tuesday and Thursday mornings. Alongside this, students train for between six and eight hours per day, six days per week (Zhang 2013). As with elite training schools, however, concerns have been raised that provincial training centres and academies prioritize students' athletic training and put students' academic education at risk (Zhang 2013). For example, academic classes are frequently cancelled to allow students to prepare for and to attend national and international competitions and students, exhausted from long hours of training, have been found to struggle to maintain their studies (Zhang 2013).

National team members are selected from provincial-level training centres and academies. Only a handful receive this 'honour' – about 2 per cent – and many are children under the age of 18, especially those selected in sports such as gymnastics, diving and table tennis (Zhang 2013). For those selected to move up to this level, academic study is not required and instead youngsters train full time – at least eight hours a day, six days per week, increasing to up to ten hours per day ahead of major competitions, even if they are still of school age (Zhang 2013).

Safeguarding athletes against injury and illness

A crucial point about the current state-supported system of sports training in China is that those identified as potential future elite athletes are often children, whose young bodies and minds are still under development. Involvement in such intense training regimes means injuries are common – Lu (2010) found that every player in the national badminton team was carrying an injury at the time of the study. In addition, the high-intensity training normalized in China's sports schools has the potential to hinder children's physical development. For example, Olympic gymnast Fan Ye has described how she did not begin menstruating until age 20 following years of intense training and dieting (Reuters 2012). Her mother is reported as saying that she regrets allowing Fan to join the sports school system after seeing the impact of her intense training in the Hebei provincial team (Reuters 2012). Other athletes have described how these young athletes' bodies are shaped through intense training into the 'ideal' for their sport, even if this causes serious injury:

> During normal training, it is advantageous for wrestlers to have a short rather than a long neck. To do this we use a position from gymnastics called the 'bridge', but instead of using our feet and hands we use the feet and neck to support the body. This compresses the neck to make it shorter. To increase the effect, we sometimes have one of our colleagues sit on our stomach. Over time, our neck becomes very short and many [athletes] have varying degrees of cervical vertebra disease.
>
> (Female wrestler, quoted in Zhang 2013: 132)

In recognition of this issue, in 1998 the Chinese Sports Foundation set up a system to insure athletes in case of injury, providing one million Chinese renminbi (approximately £100,000) to insure the 1,400 Chinese athletes on national teams in an Olympic discipline. Further financial support was provided in 2008 through the establishment of a special fund for retired elite athletes. The fund, which is managed by the Sports Ministry, provides elite athletes with compensation if they have to leave sport due to injury and also offers financial assistance and education grants to athletes retiring from elite sport. Similarly, the 2011 law Regulations on Managing Young People and Children's Sports Schools (Chinese Sport Ministry/ Ministry of Education 2011a) obliges sports schools to take out insurance for their young athletes to cover them for injuries suffered during training and competition, and the Improvement of the Education and Welfare System for Elite Athletes law (Chinese Sport Ministry 2010c) obliges athletes and sports schools to pay social insurance to provide athletes with medical cover and financial benefits if they are injured during training or competition.

Safeguarding against doping in youth sport

Since China re-joined the Olympics in 1980, allegations about the systematic doping of athletes, including children, have blighted the country's sports teams (Hong 2004). To protect the health of all athletes and promote fair play, in 1992 the Chinese Olympic Committee formed the Anti-Doping Commission. Three years later, the Sport Ministry passed the Interim Provisions to Prohibit the Use of Drugs in Sports law (Chinese Sport Ministry 1995), which bans all forms of doping, including forcing, instigating, inducing, guiding and tacitly supporting illegal drug use in sport. Under the law, athletes found guilty of a doping violation are referred to their respective international sports organization to be sanctioned. Sanctions can include withdrawal of medals, annulling of results, temporary suspensions and life bans from sport. Importantly, the law also covers coaches, team doctors and team leaders involved in doping athletes, mandating that punishment for aiding and abetting doping should be equal to that handed down to an athlete (Chinese Sport Ministry 1995).

In addition, revisions to the Regulation on Managing Young People and Children's Sports Schools law (Chinese Sport Ministry/Ministry of Education 2011a) also banned doping in sports schools, where children are selected to train in the hope of reaching the national team. Furthermore, a 2004 policy update from the State Council of China, the Anti-Doping Regulations (State Council of China 2004), mandated that sports schools educate athletes on doping and reinforced the earlier ban on the use of performance-enhancing drugs and enforced doping. In response to allegations of state-sponsored doping, this policy also prohibits sports organizations or sports administrative departments from providing advice or support to athletes using banned substances or to those seeking to evade drug testing or trying to mask evidence of the use of illegal substances (State Council of China 2004). The sanction for violations of this policy include a ban from working in sports management or with athletes for four years, while individuals found guilty of enforced doping may be prosecuted and can be sued for compensation if an athlete's health has been affected (State Council of China 2004).

Yet despite this legislative and policy framework to protect athletes, there is evidence that the win-at-all-costs culture within the sports system means some coaches and doctors are flouting the rules. In one case from 2002, a routine inspection of Shenyang Sports School by officials from the Chinese Olympic Committee's anti-doping commission found that the school doctor injected child athletes with drugs such as human growth hormone before they participated in the Ninth Liaoning Provincial Games. By way of sanction, the Sport Ministry and the Liaoning Provincial Sports Committee demoted the principal, vice-principal and other sport staff in the school (Shi 2003). Similarly, in 2006, the anti-doping commission found some staff at the Anshan Sports School in Liaoning province used the hormone erythropoietin, also known as EPO, on ten athletes aged between 15 and 18 years old ahead of the Tenth Liaoning Provincial Games (Ma and Li 2006). In a search of the school, other drugs were also found, including in the principal's office – in total, 450 types of banned substance were seized. The Liaoning Sports Commission investigated the case and those involved were fired (Ma and Li 2006).

Zhao Jian, a member of the Chinese Olympic Committee's anti-doping commission, notes that the fight against doping is facing new challenges. For one, dope testing predominantly takes place during competitions because of the logistical and resource difficulties of testing the tens of thousands of young people involved in sports schools (Li 2006). But preventing doping requires more than an effective testing system; a change of attitude about the purpose of sport and about the win-at-all-costs mentality of some coaches and sports authorities is also needed. In addition, there needs to be a greater understanding of the dangers of doping for all athletes and heightened awareness of, and support for, the rights of children, both in sport and in wider society.

Conclusion

Since the 1980s, young athletes have been co-opted into a system that puts athletic achievement ahead of academic scholarship to help China achieve its dream of becoming a sporting superpower. These children, often undergoing intensive training for long hours day in day out, risk physical and mental burnout, injury and, in some cases, pressure to take illegal substances. Although legislation and policies have gone some way to protecting and promoting young people's welfare in sport, not enough has been done and the call to recognize that healthy, rounded athletes are central to the future success of Chinese sport has, so far, fallen on deaf ears.

References

British Broadcasting Corporation (2005) *Pinsent Shocked by China Training*. Online. Available HTTP: <http://news.bbc.co.uk/sport1/hi/other_sports/gymnastics/4445506.stm> (accessed 10 December 2013).

Chinese Sports Ministry (1995) *Interim Provisions to Prohibit the Use of Drugs in Sports*. Online. Available HTTP: <http://2004.sina.com.cn/other/2004–08–09/55687.html> (accessed 10 December 2012).

Chinese Sport Ministry (2010) *Suggestions on the Improvement of the Education and Welfare System for Elite Athletes*, Beijing: Chinese Sport Ministry.

Chinese Sport Ministry/Ministry of Education (1999) *Regulations on Managing Young People and Children's Sports Schools*. Online. Available HTTP: <http://www.china lawedu.com/news/1200/22598/22620/22880/2006/3/wc1274465656141360021120–0.htm> (accessed 21 February 2013).

—— (2011a) *Regulations on Managing Young People and Children's Sports Schools*. Online. Available HTTP: <www.sport.gov.cn/n16/n1092/n16864/2653206.html> (accessed 21 February 2013).

—— (2011b) *Regulation on Managing Young People and Children's Sports Schools at the Middle Level*. Online. Available HTTP: <www.sport.gov.cn/n16/n1092/n16864/2653226.html> (accessed 15 February 2013).

Hong, F. (2004) 'Innocence lost: child athletes in China', in J. Mangan (ed.) *Sport in Society*, Abingdon: Taylor & Francis.

Li, Y. (2006) *The Problem of Drug Abuse in China*. Online. Available HTTP: <http://news.sports.cn/others/track/2006–08–24/914144.html> (accessed 20 February 2013).

Liu, P. (2010) *Speech on the Policy on Athlete's Education and Welfare*. Online. Available HTTP: <www.sport.gov.cn/n16/n1077/n1467/n1701156/n1701221/1750122.html> (accessed 12 May 2012).

Lu, Y. (2010) 'The institutional price paid by the competitive sports management system currently effective in China', *Journal of Physical Education*, 17: 7–12.

Ma, X. and Li, Z. (2006) *Report into the Anshan Sports School's Drug Case*. Online. Available HTTP: <http://sports.sohu.com/20060831/n245099642.shtml> (accessed 12 February 2013).

National People's Congress (2006) *The Compulsory Education Law of the People's Republic of China*. Online. Available HTTP: <www.gov.cn/ziliao/flfg/2006–06/30/content_323302.html> (accessed 25 November 2012).

Reuters (2012) 'Memoirs of a top Chinese gymnast', *The Age*, 27 July. Online. Available HTTP: <www.theage.com.au/olympics/off-the-field/memoirs-of-a-top-chinese-gymnast-20120727–22xnt.html> (accessed 15 November 2012).

Shi, Z. (2003) *Report into the Shenyang Sport School's Drug Case*. Online. Available HTTP: <http://mil.eastday.com/epublish/gb/paper347/20030519/class034700010/hwz1124832.html> (accessed 12 February 2013).

State Council of China (2004) *Anti-Doping Regulations*. Online. Available HTTP: <www.sport.gov.cn/n16/n1092/n16834/312929.html> (accessed 2 December 2012).

Wu, S. (2002) *History of Sport in the People's Republic of China*, Beijing: China Book Press.

Yang, Z. (2010) 'Alienation of competitive sports viewed from the perspective of body theory', *Journal of Chengdu Sport University*, 36: 55–8.

Zhang, L. (2013) '*A study of retired elite athletes' re-employment in China: system, policy and practice*', unpublished PhD thesis, Cork: University College Cork, Ireland.

14 Who safeguards the child in Japanese sports?

Aaron L. Miller and Atsushi Nakazawa

In January 2013, another Japanese teen took his life. This time the boy, a second-year high school student at Sakuranomiya High School in Osaka, committed suicide after his basketball coach, Komura Hajime, repeatedly beat him. After the incident, Komura admitted to having beaten and wounded the 17–year-old team captain when the boy failed to meet his expectations (Aquino 2013). Komura told authorities that he had used corporal punishment, known as 'taibatsu' in Japanese, to 'guide his pupil strictly', in large part because he was the team captain and thought he could handle it (Osaka Board of Education 2013). Just a few weeks later, news surfaced that Japan's National Women's Judo coach, Ryuji Sonoda, had allegedly physically abused his players before the 2012 London Olympics. Sonoda defended his actions by saying that he felt pressure to bring home a gold medal. Sonoda has since resigned.

Around the same time that these incidents took place, the Japanese government learned that the suicide of another teenager, this time in Otsu City in 2011, had been the direct cause of bullying, or 'ijime' in Japanese, and that the incident had been covered up by the local Board of Education. The board feared the incident might incite a media firestorm, so it chose to hide the issue.

These recent incidents, which were all over the Japanese news, galvanized the Japanese government into swift action. In February 2013, Prime Minister Abe Shinzō and his cabinet entrusted the specially appointed Education Rebuilding Realization Council (ERRC) to draft and release policy recommendations regarding appropriate responses to bullying and corporal punishment. The ERRC recommended that Japanese schools strengthen their moral education curriculum, and that lawmakers pass an anti-bullying measure (The Office of the Prime Minister of Japan and his Cabinet 2013). The latter recommendation resulted in the passing of the Bullying Prevention Act in 2013.

The Prime Minister's Office also advised the Ministry of Education, Culture, Sports, Science and Technology (MEXT) to undertake a survey of sports coaching and set stricter guidelines for coaches (MEXT 2013a). In its report, MEXT (2013a: 2) noted that:

> Sports ... based upon the enjoyment of spontaneous exercise ... develop character, foster respect for discipline and justice, produce a collaborative

spirit and friendliness toward others ... The act of corporal punishment within sports instruction negates these sporting values ... We must eradicate corporal punishment in all sports settings.

The MEXT survey identified 6,721 cases of corporal punishment in the academic year 2012 (MEXT 2013b, MEXT 2013c), despite the fact that corporal punishment is officially illegal in Japanese schools and has been for many decades. This figure was considerably higher than the number of cases reported up to 2004, the last year for which MEXT collected such statistics before it stopped between 2005–11 (MEXT 2013b, MEXT 2013c). This increase in the number of cases in 2012 could be attributed to heightened media attention being paid to, and therefore public awareness of, the issue.

In general, the recommendations MEXT makes to schools are not binding, although in certain circumstances it can choose to mandate that schools follow its orders by issuing a 'memo'. Following the incident at Sakuranomiya, MEXT published two memos and undertook a survey of sports coaching (MEXT 2013b, 2013e), placing the issues of corporal punishment and bullying back in the national spotlight.

Tragedies like the Sakuranomiya suicide happen all over the world, of course, but in Japan they are part of a sports culture that often encourages, if not outright reveres, strict training regimens and strict vertical hierarchal relations. Sadly, Japanese authorities – teachers, coaches, parents, and government officials – do not do enough to safeguard and protect their children from these dangers in sport. Even when they do take steps to reduce the risks, what they do does not always translate easily from the level of policy rhetoric to ground-level practice (Miller 2013). While authorities at MEXT, the Japan Sports Association and other national sports organizations insist that corporal punishment and authoritarian coaching regimes are unnecessary and indeed dangerous to young athletes, at a grassroots level Japanese sports coaches in a wide range of sports continue to believe they must be 'strict' in order to guide effectively.

Definitions

The safeguarding of youth in Japanese sports is covered by various legislation, so there are several important definitions to be considered. Regarding the protection of children in the home, the relevant Japanese terminology is as follows: child welfare or 'jido fukushi', care/nursing or 'yōgo', protection or 'hogo' and care/fostering or 'yōiku'. No equivalent to the term 'safeguarding' is commonly used in the Japanese sports, education or welfare sectors. Regarding the failure to protect children, several terms are relevant. Abuse or 'gyakutai' is defined in Japanese law as physical injury, indecency, neglect, or any act that causes post-traumatic stress disorder (cf. Child Abuse Protection Act 2000), although the term is usually used only in the context of the family. In sport, abuse is not considered a significant problem – more concerns are raised about bullying and corporal punishment – but at present little is known about the extent of abuse in Japanese sport as research is limited. Meanwhile, bullying or 'ijime' is defined as 'an act in which any student ... feels physical or mental pain because he is influenced by physical or psychological acts (including over the Internet) in his peer relationships' (MEXT 2013d: 4). This definition is subjective and empowers the person being bullied to define any act as bullying if they see fit, potentially disempowering the person doing the bullying. In this sense, it is perhaps more progressive than comparative definitions of bullying from other countries, although in Japan bullying is commonly understood as occurring only between students.

This chapter focuses on corporal punishment or 'taibatsu' in order to shed light on safeguarding children in Japanese sport. In the West, corporal punishment is commonly defined as beating, hitting, or kicking, to discipline or punish, by a person in a position of authority relative to a person in a subordinate position (Donnelly and Straus 2005). However, this definition is highly contested in Japan. The term 'taibatsu' was only coined in the late-nineteenth century during the Meiji Period, and has never been clearly defined by the government (Miller 2013). To this day understandings and definitions of corporal punishment in Japan overlap considerably with definitions of abuse and bullying mentioned above, and with understandings of the terms 'choukai' and 'shitsuke', which both broadly refer to the act of an adult disciplining a child. Consequently, corporal punishment is ill defined and remains ambiguous in Japan.

What is clear, however, is that it raises serious educational questions because of its perceived educational purpose. After the teen suicide in Sakuranomiya in 2013, MEXT attempted to clarify understandings by defining specific acts that should be considered corporal punishment in sport. These included the failure to provide athletes with water during training or making them sit in difficult positions for long periods of time, but excluded behaviours implicit in sport, such as receiving a strong volleyball serve or being thrown on the mat during judo (MEXT 2013e). It remains to be seen whether these definitions will settle the longstanding debates among the Japanese regarding the meaning of 'corporal punishment'.

Policy

Safeguarding the welfare of children in Japanese sport involves several government agencies, including MEXT, the Ministry of Health, Labour and Welfare (MHLW), the Office of the Prime Minister of Japan and his Cabinet, and the Ministry of Justice. Each have jurisdiction for specific areas of Japanese life; the MHLW deals with safeguarding issues in the home, whereas MEXT handles such issues in schools, for example. In terms of safeguarding and protecting children in sport, the two most relevant governmental agencies are MEXT and the Office of the Prime Minister of Japan and his Cabinet. Both these conduct surveys of and issue reports on the state of Japanese education, including issues such as the state of extra-curricular club activities, youth and bullying.

Similarly, various laws are relevant to safeguarding and protecting Japanese youth, depending on the context. These include the School Education Act (1947), the Child Welfare Act (1947), the Child Abuse Protection Act (2000), the Basic

Act on Sport (2011) and the Bullying Prevention Countermeasure Promotion Act (2013). The liability of adults for safeguarding and protecting children depends upon the circumstances under which the individual oversees children, for example, whether they are a teacher, a coach, a youth leader, etc.

In the following discussion, we examine how previous legislation and policy developments have failed to stop the use of corporal punishment in Japanese schools and sport, and consider the issue of whether recent policies will succeed in strengthening the safeguarding of Japanese youth in and beyond sport.

Case study: corporal punishment in Japanese sports

Corporal punishment remains a widely used disciplinary practice throughout the world, most commonly used by parents at home but also by teachers at school, and it represents an important crossroads at which the policies of schools and sports meet (Donnelly and Straus 2005; Miller 2013). It also raises important issues regarding power, the body and human rights.

The physical discipline of children has been used in Japan for centuries, although it was only labelled 'taibatsu' in the late-nineteenth century (Miller 2009, 2013). Incidents of corporal punishment in Japan today follow a strikingly similar pattern, especially in the case of fatal or severe incidents: after the media begins to publicize a case of corporal punishment, the perpetrator, whether coach or teacher, commonly argues that the 'victim' is actually not a victim at all but rather a specially 'chosen pupil' who must be strictly trained to maximize their potential. Coaches, therefore, often do not regard corporal punishment as problematic, and they use it to set an example to the team of steadfast perseverance in the face of hardship, absolute obedience to authority and constant loyalty to the team. Many Japanese coaches believe this teaches athletes a powerful lesson that the team comes before the individual – a mantra they hope athletes will carry with them into their adult life. For example, Sakuranomiya's Komura told the Osaka Board of Education that, 'I have often hit my students for their own sake … I thought I could hit my students without incident because we had a good relationship' (quoted in Osaka Board of Education 2013). Athletes, meanwhile, are expected to accept corporal punishment without complaint, accepting it for their own sake and for the sake of the group.

Japanese education authorities rarely challenge such behaviour. Remarkably, sports coaches and teachers in Japan have a high chance of avoiding punishment for acts carried out in the name of corporal punishment, even when they admit to MEXT to having beaten, injured, or killed an athlete (Miller 2013). Moreover when such acts are prosecuted, sentences have, until recently, tended to be lenient or suspended, as the case of Totsuka Hiroshi illustrates.

Totsuka was a former Olympic yachtsman and principal at the Totsuka Yacht School in the district of Aichi, around 160 miles west of the capital Tokyo. He was also an avid proponent of corporal punishment. At the school he 'reigned over a regime of extreme discipline that was intended to "improve" the anti-social behaviour of the children, several of whom were autistic, who had been placed in his care' (Goodman 2003: n.44). Several students at the school died or went missing, and Totsuka was eventually tried for murder in relation to at least one child's death. He was convicted but received a non-custodial sentence on the grounds that he had the children's best interests at heart (Miller 2013). Upon his release from prison in 2006, Totsuka was unrepentant, famously telling the Japanese media that 'corporal punishment *is* education'. He returned to managing the yacht school, which continues to receive considerable support from certain elements of Japanese society such as conservative businessmen and politicians.

Few Japanese and even fewer foreigners realize that corporal punishment has been illegal in educational settings in Japan since the end of World War II, or that there were laws enacted against its use as early as the Meiji Period (1868–1912). In fact, Japan was the sixth nation in the world to ban corporal punishment, in 1879 (Miller 2013). And although this ban was vigorously debated, even repealed for a time, the government's official policy since World War II has been that corporal punishment has no place in Japanese schools or sports. Yet cases of corporal punishment, sometimes with tragic consequences, continue because the government does little about educators who insist corporal punishment is the best way to guide Japan's youth. Indeed, many Japanese parents are willing to accept that their children suffer corporal punishment in sport because they see such 'education' as a way of instilling discipline and beneficial to them and wider society.

Modern Japan, then, appears to have developed a striking ambivalence toward corporal punishment. This ambivalence is what the sociologist of education Imazu Koujiro (Imazu 2006) identifies as the difference between 'tatemae', or 'what one says in public', versus 'honne', or 'what one truly believes' about corporal punishment. The Japanese government may have a law against the use of corporal punishment but many teachers and coaches in Japan still believe such behaviour is a necessary evil that they may sometimes have to use (Miller 2013).

Conclusion

For relatively minor corporal punishment offences Japanese coaches stand a good chance of evading punishment altogether. However more serious cases, mainly where the consequences are severe, are increasingly resulting in criminal convictions for perpetrators, suggesting the government and local authorities are beginning to take the issue seriously.

The Sakuranomiya incident discussed at the start of this chapter is one such example. Komura was fired for his behaviour, was tried and found guilty by the Osaka District Court and sentenced to three years in prison (*Asahi Shimbun* 2013). While Komura was therefore held responsible for playing a direct role in the student's death, he did not serve jail time (*Japan Times* 2013).

The points raised in this chapter beg the following questions: Who has sovereignty over a child's body? Is a child's body solely the child's domain over which he/she and he/she alone must reign, or is it, until a certain age, his/her parent's or guardian's property to protect as well as discipline? If the child holds this right, under what conditions, if any, can it be taken away? If his/her parents hold this right, under what conditions can the state take it away from them? If the school or state holds this right, under what conditions, if any, can it be taken away, and by whom? Finally, is the physical sovereignty of one's body – adult or child – a basic human right, or does one only maintain the privilege of sovereignty if he/she obeys the laws and rules of his/her home, school, sports team, or nation? In short, who does, and who should, safeguard the Japanese child athlete from abuse?

While recent actions taken by the Japanese government hold the promise of stricter enforcement of existing anti-corporal punishment laws in the future, it is unclear whether renewed interest in this issue will be enough to stop future tragedies like that at Sakuranomiya High School. Only time will tell.

In the meantime, it is our job to help protect children from danger when they take part in sport. Our research has led us to conclude that young students and athletes crave both attention and structure, and that they want firm but fair as well as stern but supportive teachers and coaches. Corporal punishment, no matter how it is rhetorically justified, constitutes no part of this equation. MEXT needs to begin consistently punishing coaches and teachers when they admit to having broken Japanese law, and Japanese judges need to punish such lawbreakers as well. Suspended sentences like the one given to Komura do not deter future teachers from raising their own hand against a child.

Corporal punishment is an issue that challenges us to think through what the idea of safeguarding children in sport means, and while agenda-led research is a patent methodological mistake, now that we have completed nearly a decade of research on corporal punishment in Japan, should we not offer our own reasoned, empirically based suggestions to the public? If we as scholars do not help the public think critically about the ways in which our actions as adults impact on our children's lives, and whether these actions are right or wrong, who will? If Japanese authorities are unwilling or unable to do their part to protect Japanese children in sport, somebody must.

References

Aquino, F. (2013) *Osaka Basketball Coach who Bullied Student to Suicide to Face Criminal Prosecution*. Online. Available HTTP: <www.japandailypress.com/osaka-basketball-coach-who-bullied-student-into-suicide-to-face-criminal-prosecution-0631806/> (accessed 25 October 2013).

Asahi Shimbun (2013) 'Guilty verdict handed down in case of corporal punishment at Sakuranomiya High School', *Asahi Shimbun Newspaper*, 11 October.

Donnelly, M. and Straus, M. (2005) *Corporal Punishment of Children in Theoretical Perspective*, New Haven: Yale University Press.

Goodman, R. (2003) 'On introducing the UN Convention on the Rights of the Child into Japan', in R. Goodman and I. Neary (eds) *Case Studies on Human Rights in Japan*, Oxon: RoutledgeCurzon.

Imazu, K. (2006) 'Corporal punishment is necessary', in K. Imazu and D. Hida (eds) *How Should we Read Educational Discourse?*, Tokyo: Shinyosha.

Japan Times (2013) 'No jail for hoops coach who triggered suicide in Osaka', *Japan Times*, 26 September. Online. Available HTTP: <www.japantimes.co.jp/news/2013/09/26/national/no-jail-for-hoops-coach-who-triggered-suicide-in-osaka/#.UnKYl-Dj_ZQ> (accessed 31 October 2013).

Miller, A. L. (2009) 'Taibatsu: corporal punishment in Japanese socio-cultural context', *Japan Forum*, 21: 233–54.

— (2013) *Discourses of Discipline: an anthropology of corporal punishment in Japan's schools and sports*, Berkeley: University of California, Berkeley.

Ministry of Education, Culture, Sports, Science and Technology (2013a) *Report from Survey Research Regarding the Activity of Sports*. Online. Available HTTP: <www.mext.go.jp/a_menu/sports/jyujitsu/__icsFiles/afieldfile/2013/05/27/1335529_1.pdf> (accessed 15 October 2013).

— (2013b) *Regarding Thorough Efforts Aimed at the Eradication of Corporal Punishment*. Online. Available HTTP: <www.mext.go.jp/a_menu/shotou/seitoshidou/1338620.html> (accessed 15 October 2013).

— (2013c) *Regarding our Survey on the Actual State of Corporal Punishment Affairs, 2nd Report*. Online. Available HTTP: <www.mext.go.jp/a_menu/shotou/seitoshidou/__icsFiles/afieldfile/2013/08/09/1338569_01_2_1.pdf> (accessed 15 October 2013).

— (2013d) *Appendix 1: Bullying Prevention Countermeasure Promotion Act*. Online. Available HTTP: <www.mext.go.jp/a_menu/shotou/seitoshidou/1337288.htm> (accessed 15 October 2013).

— (2013e) *Regarding the Prohibition of Corporal Punishment and Thorough Instruction Based on Students' Understanding*. Online. Available HTTP: <www.mext.go.jp/a_menu/shotou/seitoshidou/1331907.htmL> (accessed 15 October 2013).

Ministry of Internal Affairs and Communications (1947a) School Education Act. Online. Available HTTP: <http://law.e-gov.go.jp/cgi-bin/idxselect.cgi?IDX_OPT=1&H_NAME=%8A%77%8D%5a%8B%B3%88%E7%96%40&H_NAME_YOMI=%82%A0&H_NO_GENGO=H&H_NO_YEAR=&H_NO_TYPE=2&H_NO_NO=&H_FILE_NAME=S22HO026&H_RYAKU=1&H_CTG=1&H_YOMI_GUN=1&H_CTG_GUN=1> (accessed 31 March 2014).

— (1947b) Child Welfare Act. Online. Available HTTP: <http://law.e-gov.go.jp/cgi-bin/idxselect.cgi?IDX_OPT=1&H_NAME=%8E%99%93%B6%95%9F%8E%83%96%40&H_NAME_YOMI=%82%A0&H_NO_GENGO=H&H_NO_YEAR=&H_NO_TYPE=2&H_NO_NO=&H_FILE_NAME=S22HO164&H_RYAKU=1&H_CTG=1&H_YOMI_GUN=1&H_CTG_GUN=1> (accessed 31 March 2014).

— (2000) Child Abuse Protection Act. Online. Available HTTP: <http://law.e-gov.go.jp/cgi-bin/idxselect.cgi?IDX_OPT=1&H_NAME=%8B%73%91%D2&H_NAME_YOMI=%82%A0&H_NO_GENGO=H&H_NO_YEAR=&H_NO_TYPE=2&H_NO_NO=&H_FILE_NAME=H12HO082&H_RYAKU=1&H_CTG=1&H_YOMI_GUN=1&H_CTG_GUN=1> (accessed 31 March 2014).

— (2011) Basic Act on Sport. Online. Available HTTP: <http://law.e-gov.go.jp/cgi-bin/idxselect.cgi?IDX_OPT=1&H_NAME=%83%58%83%7c%81%5b%83%63%8A%EE%96%7b%96%40&H_NAME_YOMI=%82%A0&H_NO_GENGO=H&H_NO_YEAR=&H_NO_TYPE=2&H_NO_NO=&H_FILE_NAME=H23HO078&H_RYAKU=1&H_CTG=1&H_YOMI_GUN=1&H_CTG_GUN=1> (accessed 31 March 2014).

— (2013) Bullying Prevention Countermeasure Promotion Act. Online. Available HTTP: <http://law.e-gov.go.jp/cgi-bin/idxselect.cgi?IDX_OPT=1&H_NAME=%82%A2%82%B6%82%DF&H_NAME_YOMI=%82%A0&H_NO_

GENGO=H&H_NO_YEAR=&H_NO_TYPE=2&H_NO_NO=&H_FILE_
NAME=H25HO071&H_RYAKU=1&H_CTG=1&H_YOMI_GUN=1&H_CTG_
GUN=1> (accessed 31 March 2014).

Osaka Board of Education (2013) *Board of Education Response Regarding the Death of
a Student at Osaka Sakuranomiya High School.* Online. Available HTTP: <www.city.
osaka.lg.jp/kyoiku/page/0000204927.html> (accessed 15 October 2013).

The Office of the Prime Minister of Japan and his Cabinet (2013) *Regarding Responses
to Bullying and other Problems.* Online. Available HTTP: <www.kantei.go.jp/jp/singi/
kyouikusaisei/pdf/dai1_1.pdf> (accessed 15 October 2013).

Part II
Developing fields of enquiry

15 Safeguarding athletes from emotional abuse

Ashley Stirling and Gretchen Kerr

In December 2012 Rutgers University (New Jersey, United States of America) head basketball coach Mike Rice was fined $50,000 (approximately £30,000) and suspended for three games for 'physically and verbally assaulting his own players during team practices'. He was subsequently fired in 2013 when further video emerged showing Coach Rice hurling basketballs at his players and yelling derogatory remarks (Terbush 2013). Commenting on this case, Gary Parrish from College Basketball Sports stated, 'I've sat in on hundreds of college basketball practices. I've seen coaches yell, scream, and cuss at players. I've seen players buckle, cry, and walk out' (Parrish 2013). A similar case emerged where Seton Hall's softball coach, Paige Smith, allegedly used a pattern of 'verbally abusive and capricious behaviour' (Busbee 2013). Likewise, in 2012 US speed skating coach Jae Su Chun was placed on administrative leave after being accused of a range of harmful behaviours including calling his female athletes 'fat' and 'disgusting' (Ghanbari 2012).

Although the above examples are anecdotal news stories, they highlight the widespread occurrence of emotionally harmful coaching practices. Without further information on the persistence of the emotional ill-treatment and the type of relationship in which these behaviours took place, it would be problematic to label such stories as emotional abuse. Instead, these cases are presented to highlight the pervasive nature of harmful coaching practices and the need to include the issue of athlete emotional harm as an important part of the safeguarding/athlete protection agenda.

This chapter addresses the issue of athlete emotional abuse and its emergence as a developing agenda for sport. In this chapter, we define athlete emotional abuse, review present research on emotional abuse in the coach-athlete relationship and offer some recommendations.

Defining emotional abuse

Emotional abuse refers to the persistent emotional ill-treatment of a person within a critical relationship. Such behaviour is frequently normalized, whilst also occurring alongside sexual and physical abuse, it often goes unrecognized and is, therefore, the most prevalent form of abuse (Glaser 2002). Emotional abuse may be expressed in acts of omission or commission, including physical behaviour (e.g. punching walls or throwing athletic equipment in a threatening manner), verbal behaviour (e.g. degrading remarks, name-calling, belittling comments, threats), and the denial of attention and support (e.g. intentionally ignoring or isolating an athlete) (Stirling and Kerr 2008). These categories of athlete emotional abuse have also been grouped into verbal and non-verbal behaviour (Stirling 2009). Such examples of emotional ill-treatment can make an athlete feel worthless or unloved, inadequate, or valued only insofar as he or she meets the needs of another person. They can cause an athlete to feel frightened or in danger, or may lead to exploitation or corruption of an athlete (Evans 2002).

Congruency in definitions of emotional abuse is one of the greatest challenges to addressing this safeguarding concern in sport (Stirling 2009). In some situations, cases of athlete emotional abuse may go unrecognized, while in others, the term 'emotional abuse' is applied inappropriately (Stirling 2009). According to Iwaniec (1995) a lack of consensus over definition 'has created so many difficulties for practitioners and so much confusion for researchers and theorists alike' (Iwaniec 1997: 371). As research on emotional abuse has evolved, so has the process of defining it. Variability in definitions is now most often attributed to the purpose for which the emotional abuse is being defined – e.g. legal vs. safeguarding (Porter et al. 2006).

Within the context of sport, we define emotional abuse as 'a pattern of deliberate non-contact behaviours by a person within a critical relationship role that has the potential to be harmful' (Stirling and Kerr 2008: 178). It refers to a persistent emotional ill-treatment and not just a one-off event. While there is frequently a lack of malicious intent on the part of the coach and/or understanding of the harmful effects of emotionally abusive behaviour, in cases of emotional abuse the coach is aware that he/she is exerting the behaviour. Emotional abuse is non-contact in nature, and occurs within a relationship in which the athlete depends on the coach for his/her sense of safety, trust and fulfillment of needs. This type of relationship is often referred to as analogous to that of a parent-child relationship in order to capture the dependence and significant influence therein. Finally, there is no age limitation to which an athlete may experience emotional abuse.

Distinguishing emotional abuse from other forms of emotional maltreatment

The term emotional abuse is often used interchangeably with the terms verbal assault, verbal abuse, emotional assault, emotional bullying, and psychological abuse. While each of these concepts is related, they are not equivalent. A similar form of emotional maltreatment in sport that is frequently mislabelled as emotional abuse is that of emotional harassment. Athlete emotional abuse and emotional harassment are both forms of emotional ill-treatment that may occur in the coach-athlete relationship, however, it is the nature of the coach-athlete relationship which determines how the behaviour is defined (Stirling 2009). The term 'harassment' is used to describe emotional ill-treatment that occurs within

Table 15.1 Similarities and differences in definitions of emotional abuse and emotional harassment

Emotional abuse	Emotional harassment
Potential to be harmful	
Behaviours are deliberate	
Behaviours are non-contact in nature	
Occurs by a person with a prescribed position of authority over the athlete	
Pattern of harmful behaviors	Single or multiple acts of unwanted or coerced behaviours
Occurs within a critical relationship	Occurs within a non-critical relationship

Adapted from Dietz 2013

a relationship in which the coach is in a position of prescribed authority over the athlete, but does not possess a *critical* relationship role. Furthermore, a single act of ill-treatment is sufficient to meet the definition of emotional harassment.

It is important to emphasize that the difference between these constructs is not based on the intensity of the behaviour or the severity of the harm experienced, but the nature of the *relationship* between the coach and the athlete. This distinction is adopted from the definition of emotional abuse within parent-child literature as that which occurs within a *critical* relationship role (Crooks and Wolfe 2007). This distinction is highlighted as there has been no research to date on emotional harassment in sport. Much of our understanding of athlete emotional *abuse* may also apply to emotional *harassment*, but further research is required before this assertion can be made.

Research on emotional abuse in sport

The first study specifically on emotional abuse in the coach-athlete relationship was conducted in 2004 by Gervis and Dunn on the prevalence of emotional abuse of elite athletes by their coaches. Exploratory, semi-structured interviews were conducted with 12 former elite child athletes. Data indicated that shouting, belittling, threats, and humiliation are the most common forms of athlete emotional abuse, with more abusive behaviour reported at the elite level (Gervis and Dunn 2004).

While this research is the first conducted specifically on athlete emotional abuse, it is limited in several ways. In particular, the application of Garbarino et al.'s (1986) list of key behaviours indicative of 'emotional abuse' (in parent-child relations) to the examination of emotional abuse in sport is problematic. Garbarino et al. (1986) developed indicators to identify different categories of psychological maltreatment; a concept related to, but not the same as, emotional abuse, as it includes both intentional *and* unintentional acts and considers the behavioural, cognitive, affective and physical outcomes of the behaviour (Binggeli et al. 2001). Garbarino et al.'s (1986) framework has itself been criticized in more recent literature (Binggeli et al. 2001; Glaser 2002). Furthermore, the study claims to investigate the prevalence of emotional abuse of elite child athletes by their coaches, yet the numerical frequencies provided are based on the retrospective accounts of only 12 athletes.

Extending the work of Gervis and Dunn (2004), the authors have confirmed that emotional abuse does occur in the coach-athlete relationship, reporting that it may occur in both public and private settings and that more than one athlete may experience emotional abuse from a coach simultaneously (Stirling and Kerr 2008). Furthermore, emotional abuse is often normalized by athletes as a required part of the training process (Stirling and Kerr 2007). Given the power disparity between the coach and athlete, athletes may be reluctant to question their coaches' harmful behaviour and to report abusive experiences (Stirling and Kerr 2009).

However, this work is also limited in several ways, principally by a small, female-only sample and a lack of diversity in the type of sports represented (individual sports characterized by the young age of elite competition) (Stirling and Kerr 2007, 2008, 2009). In addition, the specific research questions asked were quite preliminary in nature, focusing almost exclusively on gleaning descriptive knowledge about the occurrence of emotional abuse in the coach-athlete relationship. Furthermore, these studies examine athletes' perspectives on their experiences but exclude the perspectives of other stakeholders.

Addressing some of these shortcomings, nine coaches from a variety of sports were surveyed on their previous use of emotionally harmful coaching practices (Stirling 2013). The main findings from this research were that coaches are often well-intentioned in their use of emotionally abusive coaching practices, and that there are two main reasons why athlete emotional abuse occurs: (1) attempting to push an athlete to a higher level of functioning (*instrumental* emotional abuse); and (2) out of anger and a loss of emotional control (*expressive* emotional abuse) (Stirling 2013). Parents were also interviewed on their perceptions of their child's experiences of athlete emotional abuse. In this study, it was found that similar to athletes, parents are also socialized into the culture of elite sport and can come to accept problematic coaching practices, thus becoming silent bystanders to their children's experiences of emotional abuse (Kerr and Stirling 2012). This lack of recognition of athlete emotional abuse has also been reported among other authorities in sport such as coaches (Stirling 2013), sport psychology consultants (Stirling and Kerr 2010) medical practitioners and sport administrators (Stirling 2011).

Furthermore, interviews with both male and female athletes from a diverse range of sports on the experience of emotional abuse in the coach-athlete relationship indicated a number of harmful effects including feeling depressed, anxious, low self-worth, low self-confidence, loneliness, anger and emotional withdrawal (Stirling and Kerr 2013). This research advances our understanding of athlete emotional abuse by providing insight into multiple stakeholders' perspectives across a greater diversity of sports, however, the qualitative nature of these investigations limits the generalizability of the findings. Large-scale quantitative investigation of athlete emotional abuse is required.

Although a large-scale prevalence study of emotional abuse in sport remains to be conducted, preliminary survey-based investigations suggest significant and long-term harm resulting from these experiences (Gervis 2009), and that emotional ill-treatment may be the most frequently occurring form of harm in sport (Alexander et al. 2011). Gervis (2009) surveyed 543 undergraduate students on their childhood experiences of harm in the coach-athlete relationship, focusing specifically on their emotional responses to the experience of negative coach behaviour. Gervis (2009) reported increasing negative effects over time, with residual effects lasting as long as ten years.

A recent online survey of more than 6,000 students reported childhood experiences of harm in sport including emotional, sexual, physical and self-harm, and body image issues (Alexander et al. 2011). Emotional harm was the most commonly reported type of harm experienced, with 75 per cent (n=4,554) of respondents reporting having experienced emotional harm in some form in sport (e.g. from a coach, parent or teammate). Looking specifically at emotional harm by coaches (e.g. emotional abuse or emotional harassment), 34 per cent of the athletes indicated that their coach or trainer was involved in treating them in an emotionally harmful manner. It was reported that coaches become an increasingly frequent source of emotionally harmful behaviour as young athletes moved through the competitive ranks – with greater percentages of athletes from individual sports (e.g. dance, swimming, athletics) compared to athletes from team sports (e.g. netball, football, hockey, rugby) reporting emotionally harmful coaching experiences. Both male (29 per cent, n=328) and female (36 per cent, n=1,056) athletes reportedly experienced emotional harm from their coach.

It should be noted, however, that neither of these studies considered the nature of the coach-athlete relationship in which the harm occurred, and thus failed to differentiate between different types of emotional harm experienced. Future research specifically on the prevalence of emotional abuse in the coach-athlete relationship is required. These prevalence studies are also limited by the fact that they were conducted solely with student athletes. These students were all over 18 years old and were asked to reflect on previous experiences in sport that occurred as children/youth before the age of 16 years. Future research should also consider non-student athletes and aim to reduce the degree of retrospection.

Given the reasons outlined above – namely, the potential for harm, significant power of the coach, and the widespread normalization of these harmful coaching practices – it is paramount that athletes are safeguarded from experiences of emotional abuse.

Safeguarding recommendations

The widespread normalization of emotionally harmful coaching practices means they are not recognized for what they are. It is paramount that safeguarding initiatives begin by addressing the historical and political context of sport that has led to the common acceptance of emotional abuse as an appropriate method for athlete development. Those who want to safeguard athletes from emotional abuse face considerable challenges; these include: the military-based foundation of athletic training; culturally accepted violence and aggression in the sport environment; the competitive and performance-based climate of sport; the power of the coach/submission of athletes; and the perceived necessity of authoritarian-based coaching practices (Stirling 2011).

Given these challenges, an important first step in safeguarding athletes from emotional abuse may be to re-define/re-emphasize the purpose of sport participation. We propose that while competition is inherent to sport, the primary reason for an athlete's sport participation should be personal development, including the enhancement of physical, emotional and social well-being. Accordingly, the delivery of sport programmes should be holistic, values-based, and delivered with a focus on positive athlete development.

Five Cs of positive youth development

To assure that athletes are optimizing benefits from their sport participation, it is critical that professionals in sport engage in practices consistent with the core foundations of positive youth development. According to Lerner et al. (2005) these are: competence, confidence, character, connection, and caring and compassion. Each one will be briefly discussed.

The *competence* foundation includes the social, cognitive, physical and vocational skill acquisition of the athlete (Lerner et al. 2005). This may be done in sport by structuring athletic training programmes so that athletes learn the physical skills of their respective sport as well as skills such as decision making, and exploration of potential career choices. A few recommendations include involving athletes in the decision-making process (e.g. deciding what warm-up exercise to run), encouraging the athletes to think creatively and imaginatively about how to play each game by discussing game strategy, and providing athletes with information on the career paths of various professionals in sport (e.g. coach, manager, athlete, athletic therapist, sport psychology consultant, etc.).

It is important that the development of athletes' competence be paired with *confidence* development, referring to the athletes' feelings of self-efficacy and global self-regard (Lerner et al. 2005). Age and stage appropriate competition in sport and an emphasis on consistent positive feedback are a few examples of ways in which athletes' confidence may be enhanced through their participation in sport (Fraser-Thomas et al. 2005). The *character* dimension of Lerner et al.'s (2005) core foundations of positive youth development includes the development of integrity, morality, and respect for societal and cultural rules. Promoting and modelling of the sporting philosophies of fair play and sportsmanship by authorities in sport may enhance the character development of athletes. *Connection* refers to the development of positive bonds with others (Lerner et al. 2005) which may include athletes' relations with peers, coaches and family. Some ways to enhance athletes' bond with others may be through the facilitation of team bonding events and positive mentoring relations with coaches in sport.

Finally the *caring* and *compassion* foundation of positive youth development refers to the compassionate and empathic treatment of athletes. It also includes teaching athletes to be sympathetic and empathic towards others. Consistent with this foundation of positive youth development, effective coach-athlete relationships characterized by mutual respect, trust, care, concern, support, open communication, shared knowledge and understanding, and clear, corresponding roles and tasks, have been found to contribute positively to the health and development of athletes (Jowett 2005).

This review of the Five Cs is an example of one theoretical model that can be used to inform the delivery of sport programmes so that they may be holistic and values-based. An applied sport-programming model of positive youth development incorporating the important roles of policy makers, sport organizations, coaches and parents in fostering positive youth development has also been proposed (Fraser-Thomas et al. 2005).

Ethic of care

As a part of the safeguarding initiative it is important to promote an ethic of care among all sporting stakeholders. Promoting ethical care of athletes includes the development of universal codes of conduct that may be used to guide professional behaviour in the sport environment. Within these codes of conduct, autonomy, beneficence, non-maleficence and justice may serve as the major ethical principles underpinning the appropriate care for athletes in sport (Kasar and Clark 2000). Consistent with these ethical principles, it is important that each athlete has the right to make decisions about her or his life. The actions of all sporting stakeholders should aim to benefit athletes and enhance their health in sport, and it is important to ensure fair and equitable distribution of goods and services across all athletes.

Advocacy

Finally, referring specifically to problematizing the use of emotionally abusive coaching practices, the education of all sporting stakeholders (coaches, parents, athletes, sport therapists/medical practitioners, administrators, policy makers, etc.) about the negative consequences of these practices on athletes' health is recommended. This includes advocating against the current acceptance of emotionally abusive coaching practices as a required part of the athlete development process. For example, this could be done through the creation of an International Olympic Committee (IOC) consensus statement on the prevention of emotional abuse in sport, as per their consensus statement on sexual harassment and abuse in sport (Brackenridge and Fasting 2011). It is also important to develop and promote education programmes on preventing athlete emotional abuse using the positive developmental approaches described in this chapter. A coach education module was recently developed in Canada entitled 'Empower+: Creating Positive and Healthy Sport Experiences' (Stirling and Wheeler 2012).

In this module, coaches are educated on the topic of athlete maltreatment, with a focus on cases of emotional abuse and emotional harassment in the coach-athlete relationship. Importantly, a large focus of the module is on educating coaches on positive strategies to develop athletic talent in sport and enhance athlete wellbeing. It is recommended that such ongoing education and professional development of coaches be strongly encouraged.

Conclusion

The prevention of athlete emotional abuse is an integral part of the safeguarding in sport agenda. It is paramount that safeguarding initiatives begin by addressing the context of sport that has led to the common acceptance of athlete emotional abuse as an accepted athlete development strategy. More specifically, it is recommended that personal development should be emphasized as the primary reason for an athlete's sport participation. With this, an ethic of care among all sporting stakeholders should be promoted along with education and advocacy on the harmful effect of emotionally abusive coaching and alternative, positive athlete development approaches. These initiatives should be directed towards all sporting stakeholders including coaches, parents, athletes, sport therapists/ medical practitioners, administrators, and policy makers. We propose that the recognition and problematization of emotional abuse in sport is the first step required to safeguard athletes from these harmful experiences.

References

Alexander, K., Stafford, A. and Lewis, R. (2011) *The Experiences of Children Participating in Organized Sport in the UK*, Edinburgh: University of Edinburgh/NSPCC. Online. Available HTTP: <http://www.nspcc.org.uk/Inform/research/findings/experiences_children_sport_main_report_wdf85014.pdf> (accessed 1 June 2013).

Binggeli, N. J., Hart, S. N. and Brassard, M. R. (2001) *Psychological Maltreatment of Children: the APSAC study guides 4,* Thousand Oaks, CA: Sage Publications.

Brackenridge, C. and Fasting, K. (2011) *Consensus Statement: sexual harassment and abuse in sport*. Online. Available HTTP: <http://www.olympic.org/Documents/Reports/EN/en_report_1125.pdf> (accessed 1 June 2013).

Busbee, J. (2013) 'Seton Hall softball coach accused of verbally abusive, insensitive behaviour', *The Turnstile*. Online. Available HTTP: <http://ca.sports.yahoo.com/blogs/the-turnstile/seton-hall-softball-coach-accused-abusive-insensitive-behavior-150558231.html> (accessed 24 May 2013).

Crooks, C. V. and Wolfe, D. A. (2007) 'Child abuse and neglect', in E. J. Mash and R. A. Barkley (eds) *Assessment of Childhood Disorders,* 4th edn, New York: Guilford Press.

Deitz, C. (2013) '*College athletes' experiences of emotional maltreatment by a head coach*', unpublished thesis, Alliant International University.

Evans, H. (2002) *Emotional Abuse Factsheet.* Online. Available HTTP: <https://www.nspcc.org.uk/Inform/research/briefings/emotionalabuse_wda48215.html> (accessed 7 August 2012).

Fraser-Thomas, J., Côté, J. and Deadkin, J. (2005) 'Youth sport programmes: an avenue to foster positive youth development', *Physical Education and Sport Pedagogy,* 10: 19–40.

Garbarino, J., Guttman, E. and Seeley, J. (1986) *The Psychologically Battered Child: strategies for identification, assessment and intervention,* San Francisco, CA: Jossey-Bass.

Gervis, M. (2009) '*An investigation into the emotional responses of child athletes to their coach's behaviour from a child maltreatment perspective*', unpublished thesis, Brunel University.

Gervis, M. and Dunn, N. (2004) 'The emotional abuse of elite child athletes by their coaches', *Child Abuse Review,* 13: 215–23.

Ghanbari, H. N. (2012) 'US short track speedskating coach accused of physical, verbal abuse', *The Associated Press.* Online. Available HTTP: <www.cbc.ca/sports/speedskating/story/2012/09/16/sp-short-track-chu-coach-abuse-investigation.html> (accessed 24 May 2013).

Glaser, D. (2002) 'Emotional abuse and neglect (psychological maltreatment): a conceptual framework', *Child Abuse and Neglect,* 26: 697–714.

Iwaniec, D. (1995) *The Emotionally Abused and Neglected Child,* Chichester: Wiley.

—— (1997) 'An overview of emotional maltreatment and failure-to-thrive', *Child Abuse Review,* 6: 370–88.

Jowett, S. (2005) 'The coach-athlete partnership', *The Psychologist,* 18: 412–5.

Kasar, J. and Clark, E. N. (2000) *Developing Professional Behaviors,* Thorofare, NJ: SLACK Incorporated.

Kerr, G. A. and Stirling, A. E. (2012) 'Child protection in sport: implications of an athlete-centred philosophy', *Quest,* 60: 307–23.

—— (2012) 'Parents' reflections on their child's experiences of emotionally abusive coaching practices', *Journal of Applied Sport Psychology,* 24: 191–206.

Lerner, R. M., Lerner, J. V., Almerigi, J. B., Theokas, C., Phelps, E., Nadeau, S. et al. (2005) 'Positive youth development, participation in community youth development programmes, and community contributions of fifth-grade adolescents: findings from the first wave of the 4–H study of positive youth development', *Journal of Early Adolescence,* 25: 17–71.

Parrish, G. (2013) 'Mike Rice practice video shows a coach whom Rutgers should fire', *EYE ON College Basketball.* Online. Available HTTP: <www.cbssports.com/collegebasketball/blog/eye-on-college-basketball/21996252/video-of-rutgers-mike-rice-shows-a-man-in-practice-who-should-be-fired> (accessed 24 May 2013).

Porter, M. R., Antonishak, J. and Reppucci, N. D. (2006) 'Policy and applied definitions of child maltreatment', in M. M. Feerick, J. F. Knutson, P. K. Trickett, and S. Flanzer (eds), *Child Abuse and Neglect: definitions, classifications, and a framework for research.* Baltimore, Maryland: Brooks Publishing.

Stirling, A. E. (2009) 'Definition and constituents of maltreatment in sport: establishing a conceptual framework for research practitioners', *British Journal of Sports Medicine,* 43: 1091–9.

—— (2011) '*Initiating and sustaining emotional abuse in the coach-athlete relationship: athletes', parents, and coaches' reflections*', unpublished thesis, University of Toronto.

—— (2013) 'Understanding the use of emotionally abusive coaching practices', International Journal of Sports Science and Coaching, 8: 625–40.

Stirling, A. E. and Kerr, G. A. (2007) 'Elite female swimmers' experiences of emotional abuse across time', *Journal of Emotional Abuse,* 7: 89–113.

—— (2008) 'Defining and categorizing emotional abuse in sport', *European Journal of Sport Science,* 8: 173–81.

—— (2009) 'Abused athletes' perceptions of the coach-athlete relationship', *Sport in Society,* 12: 227–39.

— (2010) 'Sport psychology consultants as agents of child protection', *Journal of Applied Sport Psychology,* 22: 305–19.

— (2013) 'The perceived effects of elite athletes' experiences of emotional abuse in the coach-athlete relationship', *International Journal of Sport and Exercise Psychology,* 11: 87–100.

Stirling, A. and Wheeler, G. (2012) *Empower+: creating positive and healthy sport experiences, Coach Workbook, Reference Material, and Learning Facilitator Guide,* Ottawa: Coaching Association of Canada.

Terbush, J. (2013) 'Rutgers coach's abuse of players caught on video', *The Week.* Online. Available HTTP: <http://theweek.com/article/index/242211/watch-rutgers-coachs-abuse-of-players-caught-on-video> (accessed 24 May 2013).

16 Safeguarding the welfare of disabled people in sport

Some policy issues and considerations

Andy Smith

Detailed empirical and theoretical analysis of attempts to safeguard the welfare of disabled people, whether in sport or other aspects of the wider society, is a relatively recent phenomenon. The objective of this chapter is to examine some of the safeguarding-related issues that merit careful consideration if we are to arrive at a more adequate understanding of policy responses and their outcomes for young disabled people and adults. More particularly, the chapter will: (1) examine individual and social explanations of disability; (2) consider some of the difficulties of defining and identifying the scope of the terms 'vulnerable' and 'vulnerability'; (3) discuss the increased vulnerability of disabled people to maltreatment and abuse; and (4) outline some key policy issues associated with attempts to safeguard the welfare of disabled people in sport in Britain.

Understanding impairment and disability

It is generally accepted that definitions of disability can be grouped into two broad categories: medical or social. The medical (or individual) model of disability dominated thinking about disability for most of the twentieth century, particularly in Western societies, and conceptualized disability as the consequence of an impairment believed to be located within the individual that can only be 'cured' through medical intervention and rehabilitative therapy (Barnes and Mercer 2003; Thomas and Smith 2009). This individualized view of disability began to be widely criticized from the late 1960s by several political campaigns led by the disabled people's movement across Europe and North America who argued that it focused exclusively on the personal limitations of disabled people and presented impairment as the sole cause of disability (Oliver and Barnes 2012; Thomas and Smith 2009).

In the early 1980s, however, Oliver (1983) introduced the social model of disability that paid closer attention to the disabling barriers faced by disabled people in society, and which he argued needed to be identified and eradicated to improve disabled people's lives (Oliver 1983, 2013). In doing so, the social model emphasized 'the impact of social and environmental barriers, such as inaccessible buildings and transport, discriminatory attitudes and negative cultural stereotypes, in "disabling" people with impairments' (Barnes and Mercer 2003: 1). Although the social model of disability is thought to have helped enable disabled people to take greater control over their own lives than they did previously (Barnes and Mercer 2003; Oliver and Barnes 2008), and helped stimulate some change in government policy in fields such as sport (Smith and Haycock 2011; Thomas and Smith 2009), it has not been without criticism. Indeed, although Oliver (2013: 1024) never suggested the individual model should be abandoned, or presented the social model as 'an all-encompassing framework within which everything that happens to disabled people could be understood or explained', it has nevertheless been criticized for failing to acknowledge the centrality of impairment and for ignoring the differences that exist between disabled people (e.g. Hughes and Paterson 1997; Shakespeare and Watson 1997). Regardless of the veracity of these claims, how disability and impairment have been conceptualized in both policy and practice, and prevailing social attitudes towards disabled people (Oliver and Barnes 2012), are vital pre-requisites for understanding the welfare of disabled people in sport and other aspects of the wider society (Smith and Thomas 2012; Thomas and Smith 2009), including their vulnerability to abuse and maltreatment of various kinds.

'Vulnerable' and 'vulnerability': definition and scope

It is not possible in this chapter to capture adequately the sheer complexity and diversity of policy contexts intended to safeguard the welfare and needs of disabled people in sport and the wider society. These vary – often considerably so – including in the definitions and terms used, the legislative frameworks which underpin them, the populations for whom they are relevant, the proposed sanctions for those who violate accepted laws, and in both the reporting and handling of cases (Dunn et al. 2008; Larkin 2009; Morris et al. 2008). It is clear, though, that much policy – in and beyond sport – and the practices it informs continue to be underpinned by inadequate and deterministic assumptions about what constitutes vulnerability, which groups are deemed vulnerable, and on what basis interventions intended to protect vulnerable groups can be appropriately justified. This is particularly the case because there are no universally accepted definitions of the socially constructed terms 'vulnerable' or 'vulnerability', nor are these terms well understood, clearly defined, or used consistently in both policy and practice. As Sherwood-Johnson (2013: 910) has noted, vulnerability is a universal experience of social life, has multiple meanings, and 'is often used by professionals and policymakers in nebulous ways and without definition'. Indeed, precisely which groups are considered to be vulnerable, from whom, from what kinds of behaviours, and with what outcomes for individuals and social groups, is difficult to determine. Among other things, this is because the term 'vulnerable' and definition of a 'vulnerable group' are context specific, are often subjectively defined, have a variety of contested meanings that vary across different societies and time periods, and are shaped by the understandings more dominant and powerful groups have of behaviours which are deemed to be more or less socially acceptable or unacceptable.

Notwithstanding the inherent ambiguities involved in both defining and understanding the social position of vulnerable groups, it has been suggested that the term 'vulnerable' can be used variously to include 'a person [who] is in danger, at risk, under threat, susceptible to problems, helpless, and in need of protection and support' (Larkin 2009: 1). Larkin (2009: 3) has also argued that the criteria often used 'in the construction of groups as being "vulnerable"' are typically based on 'the ways in which they are marginalized, socially excluded, have limited opportunities and income, and suffer abuse (physical, sexual, psychological and financial) hardship, prejudice and discrimination'. Disabled people and, in particular, disabled children and young people, are considered to be among those at increased risk of vulnerability, maltreatment and abuse (National Working Group on Child Protection and Disability 2003).

Increased vulnerability of disabled people

The association between impairment and disability and the experiences of maltreatment among disabled people has been widely discussed (see Sullivan and Knutson 2000), but there have been a number of difficulties in estimating reliably 'the extent or rate of abuse among children with disabilities' and whether impairments 'were present before the abuse or were the direct result of maltreatment' (Hibbard, Desch and the Committee on Child Abuse and Neglect and Council on Children with Disabilities 2007: 1018). Indeed, obtaining reliable data on the incidence and prevalence of maltreatment of disabled people, particularly disabled children and young disabled people, is 'limited by varying definitions of disability and lack of uniform methods of classifying maltreatment' (Hibbard, Desch and the Committee on Child Abuse and Neglect and Council on Children with Disabilities 2007: 1018). A Canadian study of sexual harassment and abuse among disabled, lesbian, gay, bi-sexual and transgender athletes in sport also concluded that, for disabled people, 'the information about the actual nature and scope of sexual harassment and abuse remains unclear, particularly in the sport context' (Kirby et al. 2008: 410), a point which appears to confirm the picture internationally (Brackenridge 2001).

Although there are a number of difficulties involved in establishing the prevalence of maltreatment and abuse among disabled people, it has been argued that there is a:

> …strong association between disability and child maltreatment, indicating that disabled children are significantly more likely to experience abuse than their non-disabled peers … the interaction of age, gender and/or socio-cultural factors with impairment results in different patterns of abuse to those found among non-disabled children.
>
> (Stalker and McArthur 2012: 24)

The findings of a study of maltreatment among children in the United States confirmed that disabled children are indeed at increased risk of maltreatment

(Sullivan and Knutson 2000). The overall rate of maltreatment among children in the study was 11 per cent compared to 31 per cent of disabled children, a rate of more than three times that of non-disabled children (Sullivan and Knutson 2000). Neglect was reported as the most common form of maltreatment among all children, and most children experienced multiple forms of maltreatment with disabled children being more likely to be 'maltreated multiple times and multiple ways' (Sullivan and Knutson 2000: 1262) than their non-disabled peers. The study concluded that while there were no significant associations between types of impairment and type of maltreatment, 'neglect was clearly the predominate form of maltreatment, followed by physical abuse, emotional abuse, and sexual abuse' (Sullivan and Knutson 2000: 1262). In relation to the prevalence of abuse, Sullivan and Knutson (2000) also noted that disabled children were up to four times more likely to be experience neglect (3.8 times) and be abused physically (3.8 times), emotionally (3.9 times) and sexually (3.1 times). Immediate family members were reported to account for the majority of cases of neglect (92.4 per cent), physical abuse (82.2 per cent), and emotional abuse (89.5 per cent), while sexual abuse (59.3 per cent) was most likely to be committed by extra-familial perpetrators (Sullivan and Knutson 2000).

That disabled children are especially vulnerable to abuse is perhaps unsurprising for, as the Child Protection in Sport Unit (CPSU) (2011: 1) have noted, deaf and disabled children are more likely to be at increased risk of social isolation; have fewer outside contacts than non-disabled children; be dependent on others for practical assistance with daily living (including intimate personal care); have an impaired capacity to resist, avoid and understand abuse; have additional speech and language communication needs which prevent them from discussing their experiences with others; be particularly vulnerable to bullying.

Safeguarding disabled people in sport: policy contexts

Since the 1970s, in particular, the promotion and development of sporting opportunities for key target groups, including vulnerable disabled people, has become an increasingly central feature of government sport policy and sport development-related activity in many countries (Smith and Haycock 2011; Thomas and Smith 2009). In Europe, for example, the White Paper on Sport (European Commission 2007), supported by Article 165 of the Lisbon Treaty (European Commission 2008, C115/120) and the inclusion of sport in the European Disability Strategy 2010–2020 (European Commission 2010), emphasized the need to address the 'needs and situation of underrepresented groups' such as disabled people and pointed to the alleged 'special role that sport can play for young people, people with disabilities and people from less privileged backgrounds' (European Commission 2007: 7). The Commission also suggests that, 'persons with disabilities have the right to participate on an equal basis with others in sporting activities' (European Commission 2011: 6) and notes that having signed the UN Convention on the Rights of Persons with Disabilities, the

European Union and its Member States are obliged to 'take appropriate measures to make these rights effective' (European Commission 2011: 6).

In Britain, the promotion of sport participation among disabled people (particularly those aged 14–25 years old) is also emphasized in the government document Creating a Sporting Habit for Life, published in 2012 (Department of Culture Media and Sport, [DCMS] 2012), while the English Federation of Disability Sport (EFDS) lists among its strategic aims for 2012–2017 the provision of 'strategic leadership and direct support to get more disabled people participating in sport and physical activity' (EFDS 2012: 15). This is not altogether surprising for, as the findings of Sport England's Active People Survey indicate, in 2013 seven in ten disabled people (71.4 per cent) had not participated in any sport in the last month compared to just under one-half (48.4 per cent) of the non-disabled population (Sport England, 2013). In the period April 2012–April 2013, the monthly and weekly sport participation rates of disabled people were also reported to be half those of non-disabled people (a finding reported since 2007), though these differences varied by key social divisions including age, gender and impairment type. Indeed, reflecting the participation patterns of other members of the population, participation among disabled people was more common among disabled men and those aged 16–19 years old, while those with hearing and visual impairments were the least likely sport participants (Sport England 2013; see also EFDS 2013).

Despite the alleged commitment to enhancing sport and physical activity participation of disabled people, concern about safeguarding the welfare of disabled people in sport is a relatively recent phenomenon and little is currently known about the welfare-related experiences of disabled people in sport. Indeed, there is currently a dearth of systematically collected and reliable data on the involvement of disabled people in training and competing in sport, their relationships with significant others (e.g. coaches, friends, parents), and the degree to which their individual and collective circumstances makes them additionally vulnerable to the risks (e.g. of abuse) associated with sport, particularly at the higher levels of sport. In the absence of these data, it is not uncommon for organizations such as the CPSU to suggest that sports authorities need to recognize the 'additional vulnerabilities' (CPSU 2011: 1) that groups including deaf and disabled children and young people experience and the constraints these have on their sport participation. The provision of safeguarding training is thus regarded 'an essential aspect of protecting deaf and disabled children and young people' since 'a lack of understanding about safeguarding can result in failure to recognize the signs of abuse or neglect' (CPSU 2011: 3).

It is also clear that while there has been increasing political interest in disability sport, in Britain at least it has historically been a marginal policy priority, is at best loosely integrated into the sport development activities of national governing bodies (NGBs) of sport and local authorities, and responsibility for its organization and provision has traditionally been kept at arms length from direct government involvement (Thomas and Smith 2009). This has been particularly the case from the early 1990s when the Sports Council (now Sport England) began to play an increasing role in the policy process, a point which was articulated in its policy statement People with Disabilities and Sport: Policy and Current/Planned Action, where the need for a strategic approach to the planning and development of sport for disabled people was among its key policy priorities (Sports Council 1993). In particular, the Sports Council expressed an alleged commitment to equity, which it defined as 'fairness in sport, equality of access, recognizing inequalities and taking steps to address them' (Sports Council 1993: 4). The Sports Council (1993: 4) went on to claim that:

> This will require the providers of sport, as a matter of principle, to consult, represent, involve and employ people with disabilities. It is this principle of sports equity that the Sports Council is determined to promote both in its own work and that of its partners.

The overarching aim of the policy was to 'ensure equality of opportunity for people with a disability to take part in sport and recreation at the level of their choice' (Sports Council 1993: 7) and that it would be the responsibility of NGBs for delivering disability sport. The alleged commitment to encouraging sports organizations to achieve equality in all aspects of their work was reinforced in the Equality Standard for Sport first introduced by the UK Sports Councils in 2004 and updated eight years later by the Sports Councils Equality Group (SCEG) (SCEG 2012). As well as providing sports organizations with a framework 'for widening access and increasing the participation and involvement in sport and physical activity by under-represented individuals, groups and communities' (SCEG 2012: 5), it is also intended to protect vulnerable groups from discrimination and harassment in sport.

The recent introduction of welfare-related legislation, including the Safeguarding Vulnerable Groups Act 2006 (Department for Education and Skills 2006) and the Equality Act introduced on 1 October 2010 (Equality and Human Rights Commission 2010), has at least constrained NGBs (albeit to varying degrees) to make the safeguarding of vulnerable groups a more prominent feature of their policies. In its Safeguarding Children: Policy and Procedures, for example, the English Football Association (no date) noted that disabled children and young people might be additionally vulnerable because they may:

- lack a wide network of friends who support and protect them;
- have significant communication differences – this may include very limited verbal communication or they may use sign language or other forms of non-verbal communication;
- require personal intimate care;
- have a reduced capacity to resist either verbally or physically;
- not be believed;
- depend on the abuser for their involvement in sport;
- lack access to peers to discover what is acceptable behaviour;
- have medical needs that are used to explain abuse.

British Gymnastics (2011: 55) have similarly emphasized that its commitment to safeguarding and promoting the welfare of vulnerable adults involves the protection of those groups from 'abuse or neglect, preventing impairment of their health and development, and ensuring they are growing up in circumstances consistent with the provision of safe and effective care that enables vulnerable adults to have optimum life chances'. As part of their Duty of Care to safeguard athletes for whom they are responsible, all clubs and coaches of gymnastics are required to adhere to all aspects of British Gymnastics' (2011) Safeguarding Vulnerable Adults Policy, which provides a variety of best practice recommendations intended to protect athlete welfare. These include, *inter alia*, the avoidance of one-to-one communication between coach and a vulnerable adult, including by text message, through internet chat rooms and social networking sites (e.g. Facebook and Twitter), and by email. All communication by these means are expected to be undertaken through the parent/carer and where direct communication between a coach and vulnerable adult over the age of 16 does take place, this must be with the prior consent of a parent/carer, be limited to training-related matters, and a copy must be sent either to a welfare officer or senior official (British Gymnastics 2011).

These safeguarding policies and those of other NGBs in Britain, as elsewhere, are of course underpinned by the demands of national legislation which, in turn, is frequently underpinned by international policy and legislature. Since the needs of vulnerable groups are thought to be similar across national contexts and in settings such as social care and other welfare services, this is not surprising. It is interesting to note, however, that the universal adoption of policy and legislation such as the Safeguarding Vulnerable Groups Act 2006 and the Equality Act are unlikely to impact uniformly on the welfare of vulnerable groups in sport in the same way. This is because how *sports* are characterized vary – often very considerably indeed – in terms of their cultures, the pattern of relationships involved, the demands and pressures of participation, opportunities for close physical, psychological, and social contact, and in a whole variety of other ways that have implications for the welfare of its participants. In this regard, might the development of policy which is more differentiated on a sport-by-sport basis involve the imposition in one sport of sanctions which do not apply in other sports? Is there value in differentiating policy which has the protection and welfare of vulnerable groups as a central objective in such a way that it is appropriately tailored to the requirements of each sport? Might it be suggested that what is required is harmonization along certain axes of policy, together with differentiation along other axes, so that safeguarding policy is *appropriate* to the needs of vulnerable groups in each sport, for policy which is not appropriate is hardly likely to be effective?

Conclusions and future research

The policy developments discussed in this chapter have, at least rhetorically, given a higher profile to the need to safeguard the welfare of vulnerable groups such as disabled people in sport than previously. However, policy talk of 'equality' and 'equity' does not translate straightforwardly and unproblematically into effective practice. This is especially important in a policy climate in which the promotion of sport participation among disabled people is ostensibly a priority of government and other organizations (DCMS 2012). Accordingly, we should be rather cautious about drawing firm conclusions about the efficacy of prevailing policy controls intended to safeguard the welfare of disabled people in sport. In this regard, it would appear fruitful to ask in future research a series of questions to advance knowledge in this area. In the sporting context, these might include: To what extent are the needs of disabled people being, and perhaps can be, met in sport? How is policy effectiveness influenced by sports-specific cultures at all levels, including at higher levels of sport where the constraints towards success are often disproportionately higher? What impact does the existence of (often quite separate) policies which focus specifically on issues of safeguarding, child protection, and other aspects of welfare limit the degree to which principles of equity and equality are embedded meaningfully in other areas of sport policy? And since sport does not exist in a social vacuum, to what degree do prevailing social attitudes towards disabled people shape subsequent political and policy responses to breaches of safeguarding controls by those inside and outside the sporting community?

On a more general level, it is important to answer several other equally important questions, because until they are answered it will be difficult to determine the degree to which governments and other organizations are able to achieve their policy goals: Are the policy responses appropriate and based on a relatively detached analysis of the realities of safeguarding practices and the more-or-less subjective experiences of disabled people? To what extent are organizations achieving their goals as intended? Or are the policies being pursued resulting in outcomes which may not be welcome by the relevant groups involved?

These are just some of the many questions that merit careful consideration in this incredibly difficult and complex policy area if the needs of disabled people, at all levels of sport and in other aspects of wider society, are to be safeguarded effectively in the future.

References

Barnes, C. and Mercer, G. (2003) *Disability*, London: Polity Press.

Brackenridge, C. (2001) *Spoilsports: understanding and preventing sexual exploitation in sport*, London: Routledge.

British Gymnastics (2011) *Safeguarding Vulnerable Adults Policy*, Shropshire: British Gymnastics.

Child Protection Support Unit (2011) *Safeguarding Deaf and Disabled Children and Young People*, Leicestershire: CPSU.

Department of Culture, Media and Sport (2012) *Creating a Sporting Habit for Life*, London: DCMS.

Department for Education and Skills (2006) Safeguarding Vulnerable Groups Act, London: Department for Education and Skills.

Dunn, M., Clare, I. and Holland, A. (2008) 'To empower or to protect? Constructing the "vulnerable adult" in English law and public policy', *Legal Studies*, 28: 234–58.

English Federation of Disability Sport (2012) *Active for Life: the English Federation of Disability Sport strategy*, Loughborough: EFDS.

Equality and Human Rights Commission (2010) *Equality Act 2010*, London: Equality and Human Rights Commission.

— (2013) *Active People 7: interim factsheet*, Loughborough: EFDS.

European Commission (2007) *White Paper on Sport*, Brussels: European Commission.

— (2008) 'Consolidated Version of the Treaty on the Functioning of the European Union', *Official Journal of the European Union*, C115/120. Brussels: European Commission

— (2010) *European Disability Strategy 2010–2020: A Renewed Commitment to a Barrier-Free Europe. Initial Plan to Implement the European Disability Strategy 2010–2020. List of Actions 2010–2015. SEC(2010)1324 Final*, Brussels: European Commission.

— (2011) *Communication from the Commission to the European Parliament, the Council, the European Economic and Social Committee and the Committee of the Regions: Developing the European Dimension in Sport*, Brussels: European Commission.

Football Association (no date) *Safeguarding Children Policy and Procedures*, London: Football Association.

Hibbard, R., Desch, K. and the Committee on Child Abuse and Neglect and Council on Children with Disabilities (2007) 'Maltreatment of children with disabilities', *Pediatrics*, 119: 1018–25.

Hughes, B. and Paterson, K. (1997) 'The social explanation of disability and the disappearing body: towards a sociology of impairment', *Disability and Society*, 12: 325–40.

Kirby, S., Demers, G. and Parent, S. (2008) 'Vulnerability/prevention: considering the needs of disabled and gay athletes in the context of sexual harassment and abuse', *International Journal of Sport and Exercise Psychology*, 6: 407–26.

Larkin, M. (2009) *Vulnerable Groups in Health and Social Care*, London: Sage.

Morris, M., Rutt, S., Kendall, L. and Mehta, P. (2008) *Overview and Analysis of Available Datasets on Vulnerable Groups and the Five ECM Outcomes (Narrowing the Gap in Outcomes for Vulnerable Groups)*, Slough: National Foundation for Educational Research.

National Working Group on Child Protection and Disability (2003) *It Doesn't Happen to Disabled Children: child protection and disabled children*, London: NSPCC.

Oliver, M. (1983) *Social Work with Disabled People*, Basingstoke: Macmillan.

— (2013) 'The social model: thirty years on', *Disability and Society*, 28: 1024–26.

Oliver, M. and Barnes, C. (2008) 'Talking about us without us? A response to Neil Crowther', *Disability and Society*, 23: 397–99.

— (2012) *The New Politics of Disablement* (2nd ed.), Basingstoke: Palgrave Macmillan.

Shakespeare, T. and Watson, N. (1997) 'Defending the social model', *Disability and Society*, 12: 293–300.

Sherwood-Johnson, F. (2013) 'Constructions of "vulnerability" in comparative perspective: Scottish protection policies and the trouble with "adults at risk"', *Disability and Society*, 28: 908–21.

Smith, A. and Haycock, D. (2011) 'Sport development and disability', in B. Houlihan and M. Green (eds) *Routledge Handbook of Sports Development*, London: Routledge.

Smith, A. and Thomas, N. (2012) 'The politics and policy of inclusion and technology in Paralympic sport: beyond Pistorius', *International Journal of Sport Policy and Politics*, 4: 397–410.

Sport England (2013) *Active People Survey 7*. Online. Available HTTP: <archive. sportengland.org/research/active_people_survey/active_people_survey_7.aspx> (accessed 11 December 2013).

Sports Council (1993) *People with Disabilities and Sport: policy and current/planned action*, London: Sports Council.

Sports Council Equality Group (2012) *Guidance for Sports Organizations: UK equality standard resource pack*, London: SCEG.

Stalker, K. and McArthur, K. (2012) 'Child abuse, child protection and disabled children: a review of recent research', *Child Abuse Review*, 21: 24–40.

Sullivan, P. and Knutson, J. (2000) 'Maltreatment and disabilities: a population-based epidemiological study', *Child Abuse and Neglect*, 24: 1257–73.

Thomas, N. and Smith, A. (2009) *Disability, Sport and Society: an introduction*, London: Routledge.

17 Physical training as a potential form of abuse

Jon L. Oliver and Rhodri S. Lloyd

It is now widely accepted that children can safely engage in various forms of physical conditioning, with academic, professional and sports medicine organizations promoting the use of resistance training (Lloyd et al. 2012), plyometric training (Faigenbaum and Chu 2001), high-intensity training (Williams and Bond 2012) and endurance training (Baxter-Jones and Maffulli 2003) in children. In fact, the authors of this chapter have recently developed a model to help promote the physical development of youth athletes (Lloyd and Oliver 2012), reflecting our belief that physical training that is appropriately structured and delivered can provide many benefits for child athletes.

The positive benefits physical training can offer children should not be assumed. Unless training is appropriately designed and implemented it can also be associated with many negative consequences. Sports systems are placing a substantial emphasis on the physical conditioning of youth athletes (Ford et al. 2011). Dangers of this approach include exposing children to too much training, exposing children to inappropriate training regimes and allowing coaches to employ inappropriate training practices. Consequently, this chapter will seek to identify undesirable training methods that could potentially be considered to constitute a form abuse. The International Olympic Committee (Mountjoy et al. 2008) and the Child Protection in Sport Unit (CPSU) in the United Kingdom (UK) (CPSU 2011) have identified the need to consider training volumes and regimes of elite child athletes. However, safeguarding policies need to extend beyond this to consider a greater range of issues relating to training methods employed with children, with a further need to apply such policies to all children and not just those at an elite level (a point noted by the CPSU).

Currently a dichotomy exists between the positive benefits that sports participation and physical conditioning can provide children, and the potential for this to (inadvertently or intentionally) overspill into excessive and inappropriate training practices. The situation is further complicated by the consideration that providing too much training may lead to a negative state of being 'overtrained', whereas failing to provide adequate physical conditioning to prepare and protect the child athlete for the rigours of sport may also be considered a form of neglect. This is reflected in the view of the CPSU (2011) that overtraining or dangerous training could constitute physical abuse. Consequently, child protection and safeguarding policies need to consider the types of training methods that should be avoided and those that should be promoted to ensure children are able to fully enjoy their experiences in sport.

Forced physical exertion

There is a very thin line that divides intensive training from that in which children can be abused and exploited (David 2005). Recently the term 'forced physical exertion' has been offered to denote movement from legitimate physical conditioning to abusive practice (Kerr 2010). Forced physical exertion can be denoted where one or more of four possible criteria are evident:

- exercise that could cause potential harm;
- where there is no actual or perceived benefit;
- where there is an absence of consent;
- where exercise is used as a form of punishment.

(Kerr 2010)

As well as anecdotal evidence and media reports, research has identified the existence of such types of abusive practice in Eastern societies like China (Hong 2004). Within the United States there is the example of a physical education teacher who punished disruptive pupils by forcing them to complete between 250 and 500 repeated squat jumps, which led to one 12–year-old boy experiencing exertional rhabdomyolysis, requiring seven days of hospitalization (Clarkson 2006). Lin et al. (2005) reported a case of a gymnastic teacher in Taipei who instructed 17–18–year-old students to perform vigorous exercise in cold conditions, resulting in 20 students being submitted to hospital for treatment of rhabdomyolysis. A further case study has been presented for a 16–year-old Italian national swimmer who experienced rhabdomyolysis, which was attributed to a combination of his large training load and inappropriate diet (Borrione et al. 2009).

From a large (n = 6,000) retrospective study of experiences in youth sport in the UK, Alexander et al. (2011) found that a large proportion of children in organized youth sport reported being forced to train when injured or exhausted. The incidence rate of such negative experiences increased as performance standards moved towards the elite level. The report also highlighted anecdotal experiences of children being made to train excessively when injured, or training with such volume and intensity they would vomit or pass out. This demonstrates the widespread occurrence of inappropriate training practices in organized youth sport.

Symbolic violence is characterized by actions that are exercised on a population that is complicit but whereby those subjected to the actions do not necessarily recognize the negative act as it is seen to be legitimate (Bourdieu 1998). Such a scenario may well apply to a youth population who cannot recognize the potential abuse of being forced to exercise without consent, when injured or exhausted or where training could lead to harm. Symbolic violence has been observed in elite

UK youth soccer, with coaches seeking to assert their dominance over players with, amongst other things, the use of exercise as a form of punishment (Cushion and Jones 2006). Similarly, symbolic violence has been shown to lead to the drop-out of children participating in sport and physical activity in both the UK (Thompson et al. 2003) and Spain (Beltran-Carrillo et al. 2012).

There are few child safeguarding and protection policies which specifically identify the issue of forced physical exertion as a form of abuse. This situation needs addressing. Safeguarding and child protection policies need to state clearly that using physical training that could potentially cause harm, or in any way that provides no perceived or actual benefit to the child, or where there is an absence of consent, are all forms of abuse (Kerr 2010). Such guidelines should also explicitly state that using exercise as a form of punishment is not acceptable. Where such practices are identified, child protection policies should make provisions for removing the child from the situation and placing sanctions on the perpetrator.

Overtraining as a form of abuse

It is recognized that for an individual to reach their sporting potential, a certain amount of training, including physical training, will be required. However, there is much debate regarding the amount of training that is required during childhood (Balyi and Hamilton 2000; Ford et al. 2011; Moesch et al. 2012). An undesired consequence of too much training is overtraining. The overtraining syndrome is difficult to define and diagnose but is suggested to be identified by prolonged impairments in performance accompanied by prolonged maladaptation of biological, neurochemical and hormonal systems (Meeusen et al. 2013). A defining characteristic is that these negative consequences are not restored within months of recovery and cannot be attributed to other clinical conditions. The overtraining syndrome can be preceded by non-functional overreaching, whereby decreases in performance and impaired function may recover within weeks or months of rest (Matos et al. 2011; Meuusen et al. 2013). In a joint position statement from the European College of Sport Science and the American College of Sports Medicine (Meeusen et al. 2013) it is stated that like a massive orthopaedic injury, overtraining is just as debilitating and takes a substantial amount of time for recovery to occur spontaneously. Non-functional overreaching (the initial undesirable state that precedes overtraining) and overtraining are serious conditions which are associated with negative physiological, psychological and sociological consequences in children (Matos et al. 2011).

It has been reported that talent development programmes for swimming in the UK require adolescents to accumulate up to 24 hours of swimming training per week, covering weekly distances of approximately 52 kilometres (Lang and Light 2010). Similarly, in the United States it has been suggested that swimmers as young as 14 years are being made to swim in excess of 40 miles per week (Leonard 2006). A study observing elite German gymnasts reported that female gymnasts aged 13.6 ± 1.0 were training on average 22.1 ± 1.7 hours per week (Weimann 2002). In comparison, a typical professional adult athlete in the UK has been reported to train for 21.8 hours per week (UK Sport 2007). Therefore, while it is widely recognized that physiologically children are not miniature adults, it is apparent that sport systems exist in highly successful sporting nations that impose what can be considered adult training volumes on child athletes.

The desire to promote a large accumulation of training hours in child athletes may come from the belief that it takes 10 years or 10,000 hours of training to achieve mastery (Ericsson 1993). This philosophy is embedded within the Long-Term Athlete Development (LTAD) model of Balyi and Hamilton (2000); a model developed in Canada that has gained global popularity including implementation by nearly all national governing bodies within UK sport and many others globally. The LTAD model proposes increased training volumes around adolescence, together with a focus on the training of physical fitness qualities in this period. The model proposes that this period of increased training volume and physical fitness training 'makes or breaks the athlete' (Canadian Sport for Life 2013). However with limited supporting empirical evidence, such claims have been heavily criticized in recent literature (Bailey et al. 2010; Ford et al. 2011; Lloyd and Oliver 2012). Clearly a goal of training children should not be to 'break' young athletes with a view that the fittest who survive will go on to be the best competitors. Conversely, contemporary evidence from Denmark suggests accumulation of training in childhood is not a determinant of attaining elite senior status (Moesch et al. 2011).

Although terms and definitions associated with overtraining differ between studies, consistent findings have been found in child populations. In an international study of young swimmers, Raglin et al. (2000) reported 35 per cent of athletes experienced symptoms linked with overtraining. A UK study reported a similar prevalence of 29 per cent of children involved in sport having experienced at least one bout of non-functional overreaching or overtraining (Matos et al. 2011), while a study of youth sport in Sweden suggested that 37 per cent of athletes across a range of sports experienced overtraining (Kentta et al. 2001). Athletes involved in individual sports, females, those exposed to higher training volumes and those competing at a higher standard are all at increased risk of experiencing overtraining during childhood. The initial marker of overtraining is an unexplained drop in performance and persistent fatigue (Meeusen et al. 2013). Additional potential markers of overtraining in children are shown in Table 17.1, where physical symptoms are approximately twice as likely to be experienced compared to psychological symptoms.

The evidence reveals a high prevalence of overtraining in youth sport and this is associated with negative symptoms. Excessive training may be part of the problem that contributes to the prevalence of overtraining. It should be noted that overtraining represents the accumulation of both training and non-training stress (Matos and Winsley 2007; Meeusen et al. 2013), although both are likely to be related. For instance, a high training volume and demanding competitive schedule may not only provide high levels of physical stress but also contribute indirectly to non-training stress by limiting time available for children to complete school work, to socialize with peers and family, to maintain an adequate

Table 17.1 Most frequently reported physical and psychological symptoms of overtraining in children. Symptoms are presented in order of reported prevalence.

Physical symptoms	Psychological symptoms
Loss of appetite	Apathy
Often get injured	Feel intimidated by opponents
Frequently tired	Bad mood
Inability to cope with training loads	Often sad
Frequent respiratory infections	Lack of confidence in future
Heavy and stiff muscles	Lack of confidence in competition
Sleep problems	Do not enjoy training

(adapted from Matos et al. 2011)

diet or to achieve enough sleep (e.g. having to get up for early morning training sessions). Overtraining in childhood is also associated with increased injury occurrence (Matos et al. 2011; Olsen 2006). Reduced performance and fatigue may be accompanied by mood swings, lethargy, reduced social interaction and an inability to cope with demands of life, which have led to the symptoms of overtraining being likened to depression in children (Matos and Winsley 2007).

It has been suggested for some time that children are encouraged to train harder than is necessary (Gerrard 1993). It is also unlikely that children will be able to recognize that they are becoming overtrained (Oliver et al. 2011) and the responsibility for preventing overtraining should rest with the coach. A well-informed coach should be able to recognize early the potential signs of a child becoming overtrained and intervene appropriately; this would likely include initiating a period of rest and recovery with closer monitoring and possible referral to a clinician to screen for any confounding factors (such as viral diseases, bacterial infections and other conditions). In a position statement on the training of elite child athletes, the International Olympic Committee (IOC) recommend that national sports governing bodies monitor training volumes and intensities (Mountjoy et al. 2008). Similarly, the CPSU (2011) states that governing bodies should consider the emotional, social and physical impact of the training requirements set for elite young athletes. However, safeguarding policies need to go beyond this to protect the welfare of all child athletes.

Sports clubs and governing bodies need to educate children, coaches and parents on the symptoms of overtraining to allow for early detection and intervention; campaigns and marketing that raise awareness of this issue need initiating. Safeguarding and child protection strategies should also require sports organizations to consider a child's involvement in other sports and adjust training schedules accordingly to ensure total training load is appropriate, and that periods of recovery are planned throughout the year. Child protection policies should incorporate actions for dealing with suspected overtraining as this is associated with many negative outcomes for the child.

Injury risk and physical conditioning

In the US 3.5 million children under the age of 14 receive medical treatment for sports-related injuries each year (SafeKids 2012). Negative consequences of injury can include reduced wellbeing (Oliver et al. 2011), drop-out from sport (Maffulli et al. 2010), and short-term and potential long-term negative health implications (Maffulli et al. 2010). A position statement from the National Athletic Trainers' Association suggests that 50 per cent of youth sport overuse injuries are avoidable with preparatory conditioning (Valovich-McLeod et al. 2011). A survey from the US reveals that both children and their parents rely on the coach to implement injury-prevention strategies, yet nearly half of coaches feel they do not have enough time to focus on injury prevention (Mickalide and Hansen 2012).

This suggests sport systems are failing to correctly prioritize the needs of child athletes and are consequently placing them at unnecessary risk. Coaches are failing to protect children from injury risk by not implementing appropriate physical conditioning strategies. Such a scenario is likely to be the by-product of poor coach education and sports systems that are heavily focused on short-term performance outcomes (e.g. winning) in youth sport, rather than long-term development of the individual. The Youth Physical Development Model (YPDM) supports the use of physical conditioning throughout childhood and adolescence (Lloyd and Oliver 2012). However, contrary to previous athlete development models, the YPDM identifies that physical training should have a clear focus on injury prevention in child athletes (Lloyd and Oliver 2012).

Gender, growth and maturation can all increase the risk of particular types of injuries during childhood and adolescence. For instance, adolescent female athletes are at increased risk of suffering non-contact anterior cruciate ligament (ACL) injury, with physical conditioning in this population shown to reduce ACL injury occurrence by ~80 per cent (Mandlebaum et al. 2005). While physical training can play an important role in safeguarding children from avoidable injuries, current sports systems neglect to prioritize injury prevention within their training programmes. Consequently, athlete development systems and safeguarding policies should explicitly state that strength and conditioning of children should incorporate injury prevention as a primary focus, and that training for performance should not occur at the expense of training to prevent injuries. To facilitate this process, coaches should be educated regarding the potential that simple strength and conditioning programmes can have in reducing injury occurrence in child athletes.

Conclusion

There is considerable evidence that children involved in sport are being made to train when exhausted or injured, being forced to perform exercise that could cause harm and has no benefit, or being forced to exercise as a form of punishment. There is also a trend for sports to encourage early sports specialization and adopt development systems that promote the accumulation of large volumes of training during childhood. Evidence demonstrates a consequence of this is a high prevalence of overtraining in child athletes, which is associated with long-term maladaptation leading to negative physiological and socio-psychological consequences. Improving coach and athlete education on these matters would begin to address the problem. What needs to be recognized is exactly how physical training can benefit and safeguard a child. There is considerable evidence to support the role of strength and conditioning in reducing the risk of injury in child athletes, yet this opportunity may not be recognized by coaches or it becomes marginalized where there is a desire to achieve short-term performance success. Safeguarding and protection policies need to prevent physical training practices that put children at unnecessary risk from inappropriate or excessive training regimes, while proactively promoting practices which help to ensure the safeguarding of children.

References

Alexander, K., Stafford, A. and Lewis, R. (2011) *Summary Report: the experiences of children participating in organized sport in the UK*, London: NSPCC.

Bailey, R., Collins, D., Ford, P., MacNamara, A., Toms, M. and Pearce, G. (2010) *Participant Development in Sport: an academic review*, Leeds: Sports Coach UK.

Balyi, I. and Hamilton, A. (2000) 'Key to success: long-term athlete development', *Sport Coach*, 23.

Baxter-Jones, A. D. and Maffulli, N. (2003) 'Endurance in young athletes: it can be trained', *British Journal of Sports Medicine*, 37: 96–7.

Beltran-Carrillo, V. J., Devis-Devis, J., Peior-Velert, C. and Brown, D. H. K. (2012) 'When physical activity participation promotes inactivity: negative experiences of spanish adolescents in physical education and sport', *Youth and Society*, 44: 3–27.

Borrione, P., Spaccamiglio, A., Salvo, R. A., Mastrone, A., Fagnani, F. and Pigozzi, F. (2009) 'Rhabdomyolysis in a young vegetarian athlete', *American Journal of Physical Medicine and Rehabilitation*, 88: 951–4.

Bourdieu, P. (1998) *Practical Reason: on the theory of action*, Stanford, CA: Stanford University Press.

Canadian Sport for Life (2013) *Train to Train*. Online. Available HTTP: <http://www.canadiansportforlife.ca/ltad-stages/train-train> (accessed 15 March 2013).

Child Protection in Sport Unit (2011) *Briefing: safeguarding the elite young athlete*. Online. Available at HTTP: <www.thecpsu.org.uk/resource-library/2013/safeguarding-the-elite-young-athlete> (accessed 10 May 2013).

Clarkson, P. M. (2006) 'Case report of exertional rhabdomyolysis in a 12–year-old boy', *Medicine and Science in Sports and Exercise*, 38: 197–200.

Cushion, C. and Jones, R. L. (2006) 'Power, discourse, and symbolic violence in professional youth soccer: the case of Albion football club', *Sociology of Sport Journal*, 23: 142–61.

David, P. (2005) *Human Rights in Youth Sport: a critical review of children's rights in competitive sports*, New York: Guilford Press.

Ericsson, K. A., Krampe, R. T. and Tesch-Romer, C. (1993) 'The role of deliberate practice in the acquisition of expert performance', *Psychological Review*, 100: 363–406.

Faigenbaum, A. D. and Chu, D. A. (2001) 'Plyometric training for children and adults', *American College of Sports Medicine*. Online. Available HTTP: <www.acsm.org/docs/current-comments/plyometrictraining.pdf> (accessed 10 May 2013).

Ford, P. A., De Ste Croix, M. B. A., Lloyd., R. S., Meyers, R., Moosavi, M., Oliver, J., Till, K. and Williams, C. A. (2011) 'The long-term athlete development model: Problems with its physiological application', *Journal of Sports Science*, 29: 389–402.

Gerrard, D. F. (1993) 'Overuse injury and growing bones: the young athlete at risk', *British Journal of Sports Medicine*, 27: 14–8.

Hong, F. (2004) 'Innocence lost: child athletes in China', *Sport in Society: cultures, commerce, media, politics*, 7: 338–54.

Kentta, G., Hassmen, P. and Raglin, J. S. (2001) 'Training practices and overtraining syndrome in swedish age-group athletes', *International Journal of Sports Medicine*, 22: 460–65.

Kerr, G. (2010) 'Physical and emotional abuse of elite child athletes: the case of forced physical exertion', in Brackenridge, C. H. and Rhind, D. (eds) *Elite Child Athlete Welfare: international perspectives*, London: Brunel University.

Lang, M. and Light, R. (2010) 'Interpreting and implementing the long-term athlete development model: English swimming coaches views on the (swimming) LTAD in practice', *International Journal of Sports Science and Coaching*, 5: 389–402.

Leonard, J. (2006) 'Age-group training volumes in the USA', *American Swimming Coaches Association Newsletter*, 4: 1–2.

Lin, A. C., Lin, C. M., Wang, T. L. and Leu, J. G. (2005) 'Rhabdomyolysis in 119 students after repetitive exercise', *British Journal of Sports Medicine*, 39: e3.

Lloyd, R. S. and Oliver, J. L. (2012) 'The youth physical development model: a new approach to long-term athletic development', *Strength and Conditioning Journal*, 34: 61–72.

Lloyd, R. S., Faigenbaum, A. D., Myer, G. D., Stone, M. H., Oliver, J. L., Jeffreys, I., Moody, J., Brewer, C. and Pierce, K. (2012) 'UKSCA position statement: youth resistance training', *Professional Strength and Conditioning*, 26: 26–39.

Maffulli, N., Longo, U. G., Gougoulias, N., Loppini, M. and Denaro, V. (2010) 'Long-term health outcomes of youth sports injuries', *British Journal of Sports Medicine*, 44: 21–5.

Mandelbaum, B. R., Silvers, H. J., Watanabe, D. S., Knarr, J. F., Thomas, S. D., Griffin, L. Y., Kirkendall, D. T. and Garrett, W., Jr. (2005) 'Effectiveness of a neuromuscular and proprioceptive training program in preventing anterior cruciate ligament injuries in female athletes: 2–year follow-up', *American Journal of Sports Medicine*, 33: 1003–10.

Matos, N. and Winsley, R. J. (2007) 'Trainability of young athletes and overtraining', *Journal of Sports Science and Medicine*, 6: 353–67.

Matos, N. F., Winsley, R. J. and Williams, C. A. (2011) 'Prevalence of nonfunctional overreaching/overtraining in young english athletes', *Medicine and Science in Sports and Exercise*, 43: 1287–94.

Meeusen, R., Duclos, M., Foster, C., Fry, A., Gleeson, M., Nieman, D., Raglin, J., Rietjens, G., Steinacker, J. and Urhausen, A. (2013) 'Prevention, diagnosis, and treatment of the overtraining syndrome: joint consensus statement of the European College of Sport Science and the American College of Sports Medicine', *Medicine and Science in Sports and Exercise*, 45: 186–205.

Mickalide, A. D. and Hansen, L. M. (2012) *Coaching Our Kids to Fewer Injuries: a report on youth sports safety*. Washington, DC: Safe Kids Worldwide.

Moesch, K., Elbe, A. M., Hauge, M. L. and Wikman, J. M. (2011) 'Late specialization: the key to success in centimeters, grams, or seconds (cgs) sports', *Scandinavian Journal of Medicine and Science in Sports*, 21: e282–90.

Mountjoy, M., Armstrong, N., Bizzini, L., Blimkie, C., Evans, J., Gerrard, D., Hangen, J., Knoll, K., Micheli, L., Sangenis, P. and Van Mechelen, W. (2008) 'IOC consensus statement: "training the elite child athlete"', *British Journal of Sports Medicine*, 42: 163–4.

Oliver, J. L., Lloyd, R. S. and Meyers, R. W. (2011) 'Training elite child athletes: welfare and well-being', *Strength and Conditioning Journal*, 33: 73–9.

Olsen, S. J., 2nd, Fleisig, G. S., Dun, S., Loftice, J. and Andrews, J. R. (2006) 'Risk factors for shoulder and elbow injuries in adolescent baseball pitchers', *American Journal of Sports Medicine*, 34: 905–12.

Raglin, J., Sawamura, S., Alexiou, S., Hassmen, P. and Kentta, G. (2000) 'Training practices and staleness in 13–18 year-old swimmers: a cross-cultural study', *Pediatric Exercise Science*, 12: 61–70.

SafeKids (2012) Coaching Our Kids to Fewer Injuries: a report on youth sport safety (April 2012). Online. Available HTTP: <http://www.safekids.org/sportsresearch> (accessed 15 March 2013).

Thompson, A. M., Humbert, M. L. and Mirwald, R. L. (2003) 'A longitudinal study of the impact of childhood and adolescent physical activity experiences on adult physical activity perceptions and behaviors', *Qualitative Health Research*, 13: 358–77.

UK Sport (2007) *2007 World Class Athlete Survey: executive summary*, London: UK Sport.

Valovich McLeod, T. C., Decoster, L. C., Loud, K. J., Micheli, L. J., Parker, J. T., Sandrey, M. A. and White, C. (2011) 'National athletic trainers' association position statement: prevention of pediatric overuse injuries', *Journal of Athletic Training*, 46: 206–20.

Williams, C. A. and Bond, B. (2012) 'High intensity training in young athletes', *Professional Strength and Conditioning*, 26: 3–8.

Weimann, E. (2002) 'Gender-related difference in elite gymnasts: the female athlete triad', *Journal of Applied Physiology*, 92: 2146–52.

18 Safeguarding, injuries and athlete choice

Elizabeth C. J. Pike and Andrea Scott

The health benefits of engagement in physical activity are well documented. However, the assumption of an inherently positive relationship between exercise and health, particularly given the paradox of injury risk in sport, has been the focus of more critical attention in recent years. Research has confirmed that athletes all too frequently normalize injury and other forms of ill-health, prioritizing sports performance efficiency over their welfare (David 2005; Pike 2005, 2010; Weber 2009; Young 2004).

Concerns have been expressed that the training and lifestyles of young athletes sometimes resemble child labour, often within authoritarian and abusive coach-athlete relationships (Brackenridge et al. 2010; Donnelly and Petherick 2004). Such training regimes have been described by various authors as a 'culture of risk', within which athletes 'over-conform' to norms of a sporting ethic which requires a mechanical view of the body (Howe 2004) and makes them willing to play in pain, return from injury before they are fully recovered and vilify other athletes who do not conform to such expectations (Hughes and Coakley 1991). The pressures to engage in such behaviours are particularly significant for young elite athletes whose sports participation is often subject to considerable control by leadership figures, and who may be susceptible to images and behaviours of sporting role models and their mediated pain and injury. Despite this, the physically and emotionally painful ramifications of injury, and the other ways in which sport may be abusive for young athletes, continue to be under-explored (Donnelly 2003; Pike 2010). This chapter attempts to make a contribution to redressing this balance by drawing on the lived experiences of young (under 18) elite gymnasts in the United Kingdom (UK).

Experiences of elite gymnasts in the United Kingdom

The following discussion on safeguarding in sport is informed by semi-structured interviews with eight female gymnasts and four head gymnastic coaches (two male, two female) within the UK. Gymnasts were asked about their experiences of pain and injuries, the ways in which they managed these during their gymnastic careers and their relationships with coaches and support staff (including medical staff). Coaches were asked about how they managed injured child gymnasts, their expectations of injured gymnasts, their relationships with other members of the gymnastics network, and the constraints that they experienced in their role. The findings raise important safeguarding issues; we discuss these and offer concluding comments in relation to the development of policy and practice.

Normalization of injury and impairment of athletes' health

At the elite level in particular, key safeguarding issues tend to be highlighted when examining the achievement-oriented focus of significant people in sport, such as coaches. This case study is not dissimilar to this as coaches search for gymnasts who they feel have the potential to 'make it' to the Olympics. Thus, coaches follow a meritocratic model of training where gymnasts are dispensable if they fail to conform to the dominant values of the sport. It became clear from the interviews conducted that elite-level coaches look for particular characteristics in gymnasts that are considered to be the attributes of a 'good' gymnast. This follows research by Fitzclarence and Hinkley (2001) on the dynamics of personal responsibility of athletes. Here, coaches of gymnasts consistently refer to discipline, mental and physical toughness and general resilience as characteristics they believe make gymnasts more likely to achieve at the elite level, and it is expected that gymnasts demonstrate such characteristics for the coach to consider them as having elite potential (see Anver 2007; Fitzclarent and Hickey 2001). Such characteristics are important to coaches in part because of the physically challenging nature of gymnastics and also because they are considered the attributes necessary to improve athletes' chances of achieving success in a sport that has a relatively short career span. The following coach demonstrates these ideals in a discussion about one gymnast's attitude to pain and injury:

> We had one; she was tough…she wouldn't admit to an injury until she broke her leg and she fell over. You get one like that in a million who doesn't let it knock them back, that's the one that sticks out.
>
> (Simon)

Coaches believe that the demonstration of these characteristics is an indication that gymnasts 'want it', that is that they desire to reach the highest echelons of the sport. All four coaches expressed that gymnasts 'have to want it' and 'if [they] don't want it, then there's the door'. Indeed, the notion that it is gymnasts' responsibility to 'want it enough' is often used to provide a counter for those gymnasts who did not 'make it'.

Such strategies and beliefs serve to legitimize measures to prioritize short-term performance over longer-term athletic well-being (Malcolm 2006; Scott 2012; Theberge 2008). Research with athletes identifies various strategies for normalizing and rationalizing these expected behaviour patterns. In particular, athletes learn to suppress the signs of ill-health by way of coping with such challenges to their athletic identity and career (Allen-Collinson and Hockey 2001). For many, this involves hiding pain or playing with and through painful injuries (Pike and Maguire 2003; Roderick et al. 2000). This is illustrated in the following gymnast's story after sustaining a significant injury at the age of 14:

> Well, after I broke my arm coming off the bars, they [the doctors at the hospital] said don't do anything for six months. Well, I came back far earlier than six months, it was probably three months after I got my pot [plaster cast] off. Looking back on it now, I probably should have stayed away for the time that they told me for the arm to heal properly. Maybe if I had, I wouldn't have as much pain with it now.
>
> (Rachael)

Restorative narratives are also used whereby athletes rationalize their injury as a necessary aspect of the athletic experience. As one gymnast states: 'It wouldn't be right if something didn't hurt, it wouldn't be gymnastics' (Caroline).

In other cases, athletes learn to depersonalize their pain and injuries such that the damaged body is experienced as 'othered' from the athlete themselves, enabling them to maintain engagement in their sport (Charlesworth and Young 2006; Smith and Sparkes 2005). One gymnast described how she had learned disciplinary techniques that enabled continued training:

> Pain is good as it keeps you going. It helps you to stop going backwards in your training, it teaches you to make yourself keep going and you learn to work through the pain. When you train it hurts, it's like, if you get through this session where it hurts, next time it won't be as bad because you have disciplined your body to do it.
>
> (Zoe)

To facilitate the process whereby gymnasts learn appropriate attitudes and behaviours, measures to 'train' young gymnasts into accepting pain and injuries occur within a framework that is ostensibly to ensure care and well-being. In the main, this relates to the messages provided by significant others in the lives of young gymnasts, which, rather than ensuring the safety and well-being of young gymnasts, often encourages risk taking. It is to a discussion of these messages and the implications for safeguarding young athletes that we now turn.

Provision of safe and effective care

A variety of systems and personnel are available to safeguard athletes from injury, and yet it is apparent that these personnel are often complicit in the injurious processes. For example, one coach states that gymnasts 'don't have time off, even if they have a pot on. They come and do the programme, even if it's just a couple of hours of conditioning' (Sarah).

Coaches frequently reject attempts by gymnasts to disclose accounts of pain and injury reinforcing dominant messages that disclosing pain and injury is not acceptable. Gymnasts are thereby coerced into risking their physical and emotional health, effectively securing their complicity. This is clearly indicated in the following discussion with a coach:

> Sometimes you have a little kid that will come to you and say something is hurting…but then you look at them and say, 'well, is it really hurting or is it just something you don't like doing?' With the little ones you have to take what they say with a pinch of salt. I mean, if a kid is coming up to the bars and I know they don't like the bars and their hands hurt, *I don't accept it.*
>
> (Simon, emphasis added)

It is important to coaches that these measures of controlling gymnasts' attitudes to pain and injury are enforced while they are young and, therefore, still vulnerable to accepting without question the instructions and practices of authority figures (Farstad 2007; Pike 2010; Reynolds 2000). One coach explains the importance of gymnasts obediently accepting the coach's word:

> It's better when they are young, perhaps 10 or 11. They need to be *learning quickly about working through pain from a young age* because, very quickly, they get to an age, perhaps 13 or 14, where they become fearful of getting an injury. With younger gymnasts it really is a case of where *you say 'jump' and they say 'how high'.*
>
> (Sarah, emphasis added)

Thus, coaches' constructions of what they consider to be acceptable and unacceptable management of pain and injury means that gymnasts learn over time that experiencing pain and injury is a necessary and worthwhile component of being an elite-level gymnast. This is expressed by one gymnast who states that, 'you have to keep going; you don't have a choice. You have to be happy with what the coaches say. Even if it really hurts, you have to go through the pain because they have told you' (Katie).

Indeed, not only does this extract demonstrate gymnasts' acceptance of risk, pain and injury in their sporting lives, it also raises questions about the agreements young gymnasts make with their significant others about the risks they take with their physical and emotional health. Some scholars have questioned whether minors are fully aware of the consequences of their decision making and the implications of their training regimes (both short and long term) or if we should accept that young athletes are free and able to make appropriate assessments (Farstad 2007; Pike 2010; Reynolds 2000). Gymnasts also describe how these mechanisms of control are a feature of their relationships with other significant people in their lives in a way that compromises the safeguarding of athletes outside the training and competition arena. In this regard, not only do coaches serve to manipulate gymnasts' behaviours within the sports context, gymnasts also highlight how significant others outside of the sport serve to reinforce messages that promote risk taking. In the following two extracts, gymnasts explain how their parents also tend not to believe them when they think they are injured or when something hurts:

> When I go home my dad will always ask how training has gone. If I say it has gone alright he will be fine but if I tell him something is hurting, which I did one time, he says to me *'well I don't think it is'*. He won't listen if I tell him I'm telling the truth and it's hurting loads. He will just tell me to get ready for training the next day.
>
> (Lisa, emphasis added)

Similarly, another gymnast states:

> I went over on my ankle at school and I came home and told my mam. She just *told me I was lying* and to get ready to go to the gym. I had to do everything in training with the pressure on that foot and it made it worse then, all because *nobody believes me.* It got worse and worse until I couldn't do anything on it. I told the coach before training and she just said to get on with it, it's fine, but I was in so much pain. *They just kept saying for me to stop lying and to just get on with it.*
>
> (Marie, emphasis added)

These extracts indicate the importance of gymnastics for parents as well as their children. In the second example, Marie describes a process where both adults (coach and parent) collude in rejecting her pain narrative, leaving her with little capacity to resist.

To manage the ramifications of these behaviours, authority figures often place responsibility for decisions to train with pain and injury on the gymnast. For example, one coach says that he would 'throw it back at them [the gymnast]. I will say "well, can you cope with this injury when you're training?"'(Keith). In sum, the natural pairing of 'injury' and 'training', and the associated criticism of those who do not conform, compel young gymnasts to accept the principles advocated by the coach.

Gymnasts' awareness that coaches have the power to enhance, restrict or even terminate their progression in the sport impacts upon the choices they make about how to manage their experiences of pain and injury. Importantly, the dominance of coaches in particular constrains gymnasts into accepting their doctrine if they wish to remain in the sport. Most importantly, the ways in which gymnasts see themselves and the ways in which they want others to see them are central to their motives for training when injured and in pain. They often look for recognition and praise from their coaches and peers and, as such, gymnasts constantly work at being noticed by the coach in order to justify their status. As a result, gymnasts invest heavily in the gymnastics 'role' to the extent where gymnastics is not something that they 'do' but is a major part of their identity. In the following case, one gymnast describes how gymnastics forms a central part of her identity as well as the frightening prospect of being, in her words, 'free' from the sport:

[Gymnastics] has always been a part of me and I don't know any different. It would be weird if I didn't do it, I would feel weird, and I wouldn't feel like me. I wouldn't know what to do with myself if I gave up. I would be totally lost. That would be scary. If I gave up I would be scared. I guess I would be free, but the freedom would scare me too much.

(Donna)

Another consequence of this is that gymnasts make decisions about which medical professionals to talk to regarding the management of pain and injury so as to secure advice that will facilitate a prompt return to training and competition. In the following example, one gymnast discusses how she took the medical advice about her injury that served to minimize her time out from training. Understanding the rationales for such decision making is central to our knowledge of safeguarding issues in sport given the role that medical professionals have in overseeing injuries, monitoring recovery and protecting young people from potential impairments to their health (Mountjoy 2010), as one gymnast explained:

At Lilleshall [the national gymnastics centre] though, they would say, 'just have a little rest' 'cause they deal with things like that every day and they just say, 'take it easy but don't cut it out completely'. The physios at home are saying, 'cut it out completely because it's never going to get better'. At the end of the day though, those physios don't know about the sport as much as the physios at the national gymnastics centre. It's good to know from the physios there that you can still train, so you have your hopes up and then you feel like you're not going to risk falling too far behind. I would usually ignore the physios at home and just take advice from the physios at Lilleshall.

(Rachael)

All gymnasts interviewed describe how they prefer medical advice that returns short-term benefits for their progression in gymnastics above advice regarding the potentially long-term costs to their health. The gymnast in this example makes it clear that physiotherapists who are not aware of the time-related constraints of gymnastics cannot meet the needs of gymnasts. This supports existing literature that demonstrates clinicians heightened awareness of time-related constraints and the implications that time away from sport can have for athletes' development (see Roderick 2006; Scott 2012). As a result, clinicians have discussed the pressures they face to take greater medical risks when working in elite-level sport (see Malcolm and Scott 2011; Roderick et al. 2000). Thus, it is not surprising that those working within the context of gymnastics provide gymnasts with advice that they want to hear rather than advice that may be more suitable for their complete physical recovery from injury.

Implications and recommendations

It is clear from the findings of this study that these gymnasts perform their sport in an environment that compromises their welfare. They are influenced by, but also contribute to, a culture in which performance takes precedence over health. In recent years, various high-level initiatives have been introduced to safeguard athletes from injurious behaviour (e.g. International Olympic Committee's Olympic Charter 2007; Olympic Movement Medical Code 2009). We have witnessed the introduction of the European EUROSAFE task force for sports safety (www.eurosafe.eu.com) to improve knowledge and inform prevention of acute and overuse injuries; and, in the United States, a scheme entitled STOP (Sports Trauma and Overuse Prevention) is a national effort to educate athletes, coaches and others involved in sport for elite children regarding what can be done to prevent sports injuries (www.stopsportsinjuries.org).

There are signs that such developments can have a positive impact. For example, some coaches in our study indicated that they now take athletes' expressions of pain more seriously: 'Before [the child protection guidelines] we would have said "come on, it's not bleeding, it's fine, keep working"' (Joan). However, for others, the introduction of policies and guidelines are seen as a hindrance:

> You see problems all over the place and what you've got to keep reminding yourself of is, you are in the box and the prosecution is asking you, 'where were you when that child broke her neck?' It has impacted. In many cases, these kids are losing out because you are constantly worried about what you can or can't do or what may be seen as something that isn't quite right. I mean, when I was a young coach I would shout or push a kid and if a parent saw it they would no doubt say to me, 'make sure you're working them hard now'. It wasn't an issue. Yesterday I had some young ones in and they were doing a running warm up around the gym and I had one kid crying. Now, 10 years ago I would have let her cry and kept on going, but yesterday I pulled her out. My attitude is if you want to do this sport and you can't run around the track 10 times you are wasting your time. Now I'm forced to back off.
>
> (Simon)

These comments illustrate the complexity of balancing the demands of elite-level sport with the protection of athletes (see also Lang 2010; Piper et al. 2012). The process of making recommendations to safeguard athletes and reduce their likelihood of injury risk is further complicated by theoretical debates regarding the paternalistic desire to protect the child contrasted with the liberalist position that children should have freedom to make their own decisions (see Pike 2010). These considerations have also raised the issue of the age at which children should be: (a) considered able to make such decisions; and (b) exposed to intensive training and competition (see Donnelly 1997; Farstad 2007).

This study has illustrated that there is still some way to go in safeguarding athletes from the risks of injury in their sports. It remains difficult to see how such work will be effective when the dominant sporting model views athletic success in terms of pushing the frontiers of human performance (see Pike 2010). There needs to be a sharing of information and good practice from international policies, schemes and guidelines; continued review of appropriate levels of training, competition and judging criteria; and further research such as that cited in this chapter that enables the voice of the athlete to be heard in informing future practice.

References

Allen-Collinson, J. and Hockey, J. (2001) 'Runners' tales: autoethnography, injury and narrative', *Auto/Biography*, IX, 1 and 2: 95–106.

Anver, Z. (2007) 'Knowledge for sports coaching', in J. Denison (ed.) *Coaching Knowledges: understanding the dynamics of sports performance,* London: A and C Black.

Brackenridge, C., Fasting, K., Kirby, S. and Leahy, T. (2010) *Protecting Children from Violence in Sport: a review with a focus on industrialized countries,* Florence: United Nations Innocenti Research Centre Review.

Charlesworth, H. and Young, K. (2006) 'Injured female athletes: experiential accounts from England and Canada', in S. Loland, B. Skirstad and I. Waddington (eds) *Pain and Injury in Sport: social and ethical analysis,* London: Routledge.

David, P. (2005) *Human Rights in Youth Sport: a critical review of children's rights in competitive sport,* London: Routledge.

Donnelly, P. (1997) 'Child labour, sport labour: applying child labour laws to sport', *International Review for the Sociology of Sport*, 32: 389–406.

Donnelly, P. (2003) '*Marching out of step: sport, social order and the case of child labour*', keynote address presented at the 2nd World Congress of Sociology of Sport, Cologne, Germany, June 2003.

Donnelly, P. and L. Petherick (2004) 'Workers' playtime?: Child labour at the extremes of the sporting spectrum', *Sport in Society*, 7: 301–21.

Farstad, S. (2007) *Protecting Children's Rights in Sport: the use of minimum age.* Online. Available HTTP: <www.nottingham.ac.uk/hrlc/publications/humanrightslawcommentary.aspx> (accessed 18 July 2013).

Fitzclarence, L. and Hickey, C. (2001) 'Real footballers don't eat quiche: old narratives in new times', *Men and Masculinities*, 4: 118–39.

Howe, P. D. (2004) *Sport, Professionalism and Pain: ethnographies of injury and risk,* London: Routledge.

Hughes, R. and Coakley, J. (1991) 'Positive deviance among athletes: the implications of overconformity to the sport ethic', *Sociology of Sport Journal*, 4: 307–25.

IOC (2007) *The Olympic Charter.* Online. Available HTTP: < http://www.olympic.org/Documents/Olympic%20Charter/Olympic_Charter_through_time/2007-Olympic_Charter.pdf> (accessed 25 March 2014).

IOC Medical Commission (2009) *The Olympic Movement Medical Code.* Online. Available HTTP: <http://www.olympic.org/PageFiles/61597/Olympic_Movement_Medical_Code_eng.pdf (accessed 25 March 2014).

Lang, M. (2010) 'Surveillance and conformity in competitive youth swimming', *Sport, Education and Society,* 15: 19–37.

Maffuli, N., Baxter-Jones, A. and Grieve, A. (2005) 'Long term sport involvement and sport injury rate in elite young athletes', *Archives of Disease in Childhood*, 90: 525–27.

Malcolm, D. E. (2006) 'Unprofessional practice? The power and status of sports physicians', *Sociology of Sport Journal*, 23: 376–95.

Malcolm, D. E. and Scott, A. (2011) 'Professional relations in elite sport healthcare: workplace responses to organizational change', *Social Science and Medicine*, 72: 513–20.

Mountjoy, M. (2010) 'Protecting the elite child athlete: the IOC perspective,' in C. H. Brackenridge and D. Rhind (eds) *Elite Child Athlete Welfare*, Uxbridge: Brunel University Press.

Murphy, P. and Waddington, I. (2007) 'Are elite athletes exploited?', *Sport in Society*, 10: 239–55.

Pike, E. (2005) 'Doctors just say "rest and take Ibuprofen": a critical examination of the role of non-orthodox health care in women's sport', *International Review for the Sociology of Sport*, 40: 201–19.

— (2010) 'The elite child athlete and injury risk', in C. Brackenridge and D. Rhind (eds) *Elite Child Athlete Welfare: international perspectives,* Uxbridge: Brunel University Press.

Pike, E. and Maguire, J. (2003) 'Injury in women's sport: classifying key elements of "risk encounters"', *Sociology of Sport Journal*, 20: 232–51.

Piper, H., Taylor, B. and Garratt, G. (2012) 'Sports coaching in risk society: no touch! no trust!' *Sport, Education and Society*, 17: 331–45.

Reynolds, M. J. (2000) 'A theoretical explanation of the relationship between the expectations of sports coaches and the physical and emotional health of athletes', *Journal of Science and Medicine in Sport*, 3 (Supp.): 51–7.

Roderick, M. J. (2006) 'Adding insult to injury: workplace injury in English professional football', *Sociology of Health and Illness*, 28: 76–97.

Roderick, M., Waddington, I. and Parker, G. (2000) 'Playing hurt: managing injuries in English professional football', *International Review for the Sociology of Sport*, 35: 165–80.

Scott, A. (2012) 'Making compromises in sports medicine: an examination of the health-performance nexus in British Olympic sports', in D. E. Malcolm and P. Safai (eds) *The Social Organization of Sports Medicine*, London: Routledge.

Smith, B. and Sparkes, A. (2005) 'Men, sport, spinal cord injury, and the narrative of hope', *Social Science and Medicine*, 61: 1095–105.

Theberge, N. (2008) '"Just a normal bad part of what I do": elite athletes' accounts of the relationship between sport participation and health', *Sociology of Sport Journal*, 25: 206–22.

Weber, R. (2009) 'Protection of children in competitive sport: some critical questions for London 2012', *International Review for the Sociology of Sport*, 44: 55–70.

Young, K. (2004) 'Sports-related pain and injury: sociological notes', in K. Young (ed.) *Sporting Bodies, Damaged Selves: sociological studies of sports-related injury,* London: Elsevier.

19 Evaluation in safeguarding and child protection in sport

Mike Hartill and Jimmy O'Gorman

As we have seen, during the past two decades research has begun to establish the nature and scope of the abuse, maltreatment and exploitation of children and young people in sport (e.g. Brackenridge 1994; Brackenridge and Fasting 2002; David 2005; Donnelly 1997; Krasnow et al. 1999) as well as establishing the extent to which governing agencies within sport acknowledge these problems and are prepared to address them (e.g. Brackenridge 2002; Malkin et al. 2000; Parent and El Hlimi 2012). The international sport community's response, therefore, has a relatively short history. However, well over a decade ago Brackenridge (2001: 216) raised two key concerns about child protection policy in sport: (1) 'very wide variation in the efficacy of' policies; and (2) 'very little evidence that many of them are evaluated or monitored on a continuous improvement basis'. Being able to address the first point clearly requires that action is taken on the second. According to Brackenridge (2001: 217) 'monitoring provides data about progress towards targets; evaluation is the process by which these data are judged as successful or not'.

In 2014, Brackenridge's concerns remain highly pertinent and there is little evidence that sports organizations or umbrella agencies have attempted to evaluate the efficacy of the policy interventions they have introduced. However there are important exceptions, including: the Netherlands Olympic Committee and National Sports Federation (NOC*NSF) (Serkei et al. 2012; Vertommen et al. 2013; Weber et al. 2006); the German Sports Ministry of North Rhine-Westphalia (Rulofs 2007; Rulofs and Emberger 2011); the Coaching Association of Canada (Stirling et al. 2012); the English Football Association (Brackenridge et al. 2005, 2007); and the English Rugby Football League (Hartill and Prescott 2007).

Nevertheless in charting many of the major developments within safeguarding and child protection in sport, a common feature throughout this collection (and in wider debates) is a concern for the lack of robust evaluation to accompany such developments. Given the substantial (publicly funded) policy developments within the United Kingdom (UK) since 2001 in relation to safeguarding children in sport, the lack of UK-based evaluation studies in this field is a concern. In this chapter we begin by offering a critique of the situation in England (based on the authors' knowledge of this context). We then outline some wider issues and principles that we view as important for the advancement of useful evaluation in this field.

Evaluation in the English approach to safeguarding children in sport

According to the Child Protection in Sport Unit (CPSU) the English Standards for Safeguarding and Protecting Children in Sport 'are based on current good practice and are informed by legislation and guidance, evidence from research and experience of what works from the fields of child protection and from sport' (CPSU 2003: 4; CPSU 2012: 1 – see Chapter 1 for more on the Standards and the CPSU). However, we are required to take this on trust and no detail or reference to the research evidence on 'what works' is offered. As recent critiques of the wider child protection system in England demonstrate (e.g. Munro 2011), the evidence on what works in this field is highly contested. Indeed, according to a global expert on child *sexual* abuse 'as yet, no true evidence-based programmes or policies exist in the area of preventing child sexual abuse' (Finkelhor 2009: 170). In addition, some critics see the approach taken in English sport (and the rest of the UK) as misguided and 'weaken[ing], corrupt[ing] and undermin[ing]' the adult-child relation in sport and the positive aspects of children's sports participation (Piper et al. 2013: 596). It is, therefore, crucial that policy devised to address the issue of child abuse in sport, especially policies implemented on the scale that English sport has introduced, are monitored and evaluated.

Importantly, however, monitoring and evaluation was, in fact, built in to the English system from the start. Standard Nine of the national standards (CPSU 2003, 2007) – 'Implementation and Monitoring' – is described as 'action taken to ensure that the organization's intentions in relation to safeguarding children are taking place, and to monitor and evaluate action and effectiveness' (CPSU 2007: 13). As 89 of 95 centrally funded sport agencies have achieved the (final) Advanced level of the national standards (as of October 2013, see CPSU 2013a), the vast majority of national sport organizations in England are officially considered to have appropriate processes and criteria in place for monitoring (their own) action and evaluating its effectiveness. We would suggest, however, that independent research is required if this position is to be convincingly validated.

However, it is in fact the CPSU itself that constitutes a national-level monitoring and evaluation mechanism for safeguarding children policy in English sport. That is, in order to retain their funding, national governing bodies (NGBs) and regional sport agencies (such as County Sport Partnerships [CSPs]) have been required to present evidence of progress to the CPSU; where progress is inadequate, a remedial action plan is agreed. At the centre of the English approach to safeguarding children in sport, then, is the CPSU, which is ultimately responsible, through Sport England, to the Department of Culture, Media and Sport (DCMS). Therefore, the CPSU currently assumes a dual role, acting as both a supporting body for governing agencies in sport as well as an evaluating one.

According to the CPSU 'robust research … has been, and continues to be, integral to the work of the CPSU' (CPSU 2013c). Such a positive stance towards research is to be welcomed (indeed, the first author has provided voluntary consultancy to the CPSU since 2004) but it also demands examination by the research community. First, it must be observed that this national intervention was implemented without an associated programme of independent evaluation. As a consequence, many important opportunities to develop a greater understanding of 'what works' for children and young people as well as adult volunteers, professionals and their organizations – within the sport context – were missed. Thus, opportunities to disseminate such knowledge to a wider audience were also missed. So whilst organizational compliance by sport agencies is monitored and measured by the CPSU (coupled with the threat of a reduction in funding for poor performance), robust, systematic evaluation of safeguarding and child protection in sport programmes is not evident.

One exception is the research commissioned by the English Football Association (FA) to evaluate its policy on child welfare (Brackenridge et al. 2007). Designating a 'change in culture' as the definition of 'impact', Brackenridge and colleagues developed the 'Activation States' model to measure 'shifts' in *knowledge, feelings, actions* and *discourses* of key stakeholders. The results generally pointed towards positive changes in attitude, knowledge and practice in relation to child protection issues across the range of stakeholders in football. However, this project was curtailed after two years of what was intended to be a five-year study due to changes of FA staff in key leadership positions and shifting priorities. Hartill and Prescott (2002, 2006, 2007) have also conducted evaluations of the British Rugby Football League's (RFL) implementation of child protection and safeguarding policy. As this work continues (Hartill, Lang and Ashley 2014) it is anticipated that a comprehensive picture of one governing body's implementation of policy in this area will emerge.

Nevertheless, whilst a great deal of activity has taken place in English sport in relation to safeguarding children (and vulnerable adults), we know very little about that activity. As the UK system is often held up as an international model of best practice, this is an important point. In this context MacDonald and Roberts' (1995) conclusion from their review of child abuse prevention programmes in the UK (roughly two decades after the issue of child maltreatment became widely acknowledged) seems to be relevant; they found 'that the vast majority of interventions had not been evaluated prior to introduction, and to all intents and purposes had the status of uncontrolled experiments' (Tomison 2000: 4).

According to Coalter (2007), Pawson's (2006) conclusion that 'a wide range of social policy interventions can be characterized as "ill-defined interventions with hard-to-follow outcomes"' is also true of UK-based sport policy in general (Coalter 2007: 31). Coalter argues 'the various UK-based sports-related reviews concluded that the definitions of desired outcomes were very vague and extremely ambitious' (Coalter 2007: 31). Clearly, policy aimed at safeguarding children in sport must also be considered in light of such critique.

The most recent policy development in England – the 'Framework for maintaining and embedding safeguarding for children in and through sport' (CPSU 2012), or 'Sports Safeguarding Framework' (see Chapter 1) – is in the early stages of implementation. At the heart of the new Framework is a self-assessment process whereby NGBs are supplied with detailed criteria against which they must monitor, evaluate and document their own progress through four ascending stages (CPSU 2013b). Several NGBs and CSPs participated in a pilot of this new framework. However, no evidence of what was piloted or how it influenced the final framework and its implementation has been published. The lack of external evaluation and transparency immediately raises concerns about rigour and objectivity. Given that this work underpinned the implementation of such an important piece of (publicly funded) sports policy, it is surprising that more robust processes were not employed.

The objectives of the Framework are stated as follows:

1 Ensure high-quality experiences of sport for children and young people;
2 Maintain and build on the positive outcomes arising from the application of the Safeguarding Standards;
3 Embed good safeguarding practice at all levels within sport;
4 Integrate the involvement of children and young people in the development and implementation of safeguarding processes.

(CPSU 2012)

Arguably these objectives fall foul of Coalter's critique. For example, what is meant by 'high-quality experiences' and how will we know that these have been 'ensured' for children? Furthermore, without robust evidence on exactly what 'positive outcomes' arose from the application and achievement of the original Safeguarding Standards, it will surely be impossible to ascertain (with any degree of rigour) the *extent* to which these are built upon through the application of the new Framework. The vague nature of such objectives increases ambiguity as well as the potential for conflict within the implementation process, although a more focused analysis would be beneficial (see Matland 1995). Certainly, without more specific, measureable aims/objectives, it is difficult to know how the CPSU can (robustly) gauge its own progress or, more importantly perhaps, how external observers are able to do this.

Nevertheless, the Framework criteria by which sport organizations must assess themselves is extensive, indeed 'assessing implementation and impact at delivery/local level' (CPSU 2012: 2) is stated as a key requirement. Thus, the new framework also includes four evaluation stages: (1) (initial) 'self-assessment'; (2) 'impact assessment'; (3) 'development of implementation safegurading plan'; and (4) 'monitoring and evaluation' (CPSU 2014). According to the CPSU (2012: 2) the underpinning principle 'is that the assessment considers how well good practice has become embedded throughout an organisation and specifically has filtered through to a local delivery level.' Issues around what exactly constitutes 'good practice' notwithstanding, critical self-reflection based on empirical data is to be encouraged. However, it must be observed that this process seems to anticipate that sport organizations will have the requisite skills, experience and resources (or funds to obtain them) to assess, in robust fashion, the extent to which safeguarding 'good practice' has become embedded within their own processes and mechanisms. Indeed, governing bodies are required to 'develop their own monitoring and evaluation systems', assisted by the CPSU who 'will also develop resources and place them on [its] website' (CPSU 2014). This approach clearly places a model of continuous assessment at the heart of the policy process for safeguarding children in English sport and it will be interesting to see how it unfolds. However, it would certainly be problematic if such in-house assessment were confused with a comprehensive and robust evaluation of the extent to which overarching programme aims are achieved and the impact of the various programme 'inputs', 'processes' and 'outputs' on the subsequent outcomes (see Tomison 2000). Thus, while the detailed criteria within the new Framework will no doubt be effective in stimulating and directing further action, including potentially valuable data collection, this mechanism will tell us little about the contexts in which change does or does not occur or what are the effects of that change – planned and unforeseen.

In its most recent initiative – the 'Sport Safeguarding Children Initiative' (see NSPCC 2013; Sport England 2013) – it is regrettable, then, that Sport England, the NSPCC and their partners have, again, failed to identify, as a central aim, the need to generate empirical evidence and understanding about the policies *they* have initiated within sport. Once again (as of the time of writing) it seems that a large programme for 'safeguarding' in English sport will be undertaken (implemented) without any plan for systematic external evaluation. Relying heavily on self-monitoring and in-house evaluation, whilst not to be dismissed as a potentially important mechanism for change, does not represent a robust approach to evaluation; certainly this situation seems to mitigate against the 'classic model of evidence-based policy in which evaluation precedes implementation' (Walker 2000: 155). The absence of an associated *research* framework capable of generating information 'not only on [the] programme's *level* of effectiveness but also the *reasons* for its effectiveness' (Tomison 2000: 10) is a considerable shortcoming of the centralized, publicly funded approach to child protection and safeguarding in English sport. There is surely much to be proud of, however, as Tomison (2000: 6) argues 'a failure to evaluate means that a programme is operating without clear evidence that it is effective.'

Developing a more robust approach

The absence of robust, comprehensive evaluation not only means there has been no systematic, rigorous attempt to determine whether designated outcomes have been achieved, there has also been no systematic attempt to understand which mechanisms – within the sports context and across different cultural contexts – are (most) effective and why. As Coalter (2008: 3) argues:

> Without information on process and implementation, we will be unable to understand the vitally important questions relating to *why* our programmes have or have not achieved the desired outcomes. This vital information is necessary to understand better what does and does not work and in what circumstances.

For Brackenridge (2001: 203) 'policy without implementation is like a car with no engine; it may look good but it's going nowhere.' However, (continuing the metaphor) global sport has now developed a range of cars, with varying engine capacities. Yet if implementation proceeds without appropriate evaluation, whilst multiple destinations will undoubtedly be reached, clear understanding of *how* they were reached (e.g. process) and *how* we might proceed more effectively, will prove illusive. Unless safeguarding interventions in sport, designed to address problems such as child abuse, begin to employ more meaningful and substantive evaluations, service providers and policy makers will be 'driving blind' – whatever the destination, clear descriptions of the journey and the associated messages key to developing more effective systems, will always be vague at best and at risk of being dominated by the ideology of funding bodies and their agents. Evaluation research must, then, be the foundation from which future 'road maps' for children's welfare in sport are designed.

In her 'action plan for protection against sexual exploitation in sport organizations', Brackenridge (2001: 218) stipulated that organizations should 'commission research and use the results to improve practice'. Such contextualized knowledge is not easily generated but is sorely needed and sought after (see Chroni et al. 2012) as more sport organizations around the world, with little previous experience of this area, begin to consider how they can most effectively (and efficiently) address problems such as child maltreatment.

However, exactly what is meant by *context* must be considered, especially in relation to cross-cultural evaluation (see Fitzpatrick 2012). Greene (2005) identifies five specific dimensions to context in evaluation: (1) demographic characteristics of the setting and the people in it; (2) material and economic features; (3) institutional and organizational climate; (4) interpersonal dimensions or typical means of interaction; and (5) norms for relationships in the setting, and political dynamics of the setting, including issues and interests (from Fitzpatrick 2012: 9). As safeguarding and child protection increasingly become features of international sport, it is imperative that researchers are able to document contextual information across all these dimensions. Clearly, the difficulty of cross-cultural evaluation should not be underestimated but our capacity to conduct such studies, and to generate more substantive messages for policy development and implementation, will be crucial to the improvement of children's experiences in sport over the coming decades.

In beginning the process of establishing a more robust, substantive and appropriately contextualized evidence base for safeguarding and child protection in sport, we would agree with Schram (2012: 20) and colleagues that research should:

> ... privilege producing knowledge that improves the ability of those people [being studied] to make informed decisions about critical issues confronting them ... producing knowledge that can challenge power not in theory but in ways that inform real efforts to produce change.

Researchers could do much more to understand what these critical issues are in relation to safeguarding and child protection policy implementation and those within sport governance could certainly do more to facilitate such understanding.

According to Flyvbjerg (2001: 162) social science should focus on answering four critical questions: (1) where are we going?, (2) who gains, and who loses, by which mechanisms of power?, (3) is it desirable? and (4) what should be done? These seem to be pertinent and urgent questions for researchers (and policy makers) concerned about children's welfare in sport. Flyvbjerg and colleagues go on to argue that social science must 'concentrate on producing research that helps make a difference in people's lives by focusing on what it would really take to make that difference on the issues that matter to them most and which most crucially affect them' (Flyvbjerg et al. 2012: 20). Such a focus is essential if research wishes to remain relevant to the needs of children and the individuals charged with developing and delivering safeguarding in sport policy. It is also crucial if research is to positively influence both the nature of that policy, organizational cultures within sport, the efficient allocation of resources, implementation strategies and individual practice within sports environments.

Conclusion

According to Brackenridge (2001), following a number of high-profile cases of child sexual abuse in British sport the climate within which the CPSU was established (via a national 'task force' and a partnership between Sport England and the National Society for the Prevention of Cruelty to Children or NSPCC – see Chapter 1) in 2001 was characteristic of a 'moral panic' (for a wider discussion see Critcher 2002; Meyer 2007). Child protection initiatives in sport have often (though not always) developed in environments characterized by a heightened public awareness of child sexual abuse, often prompted, or at least accompanied, by media reports of 'sex beasts' preying on children within sports contexts (e.g. Cunningham 2007). In such circumstances the political objective of taking action (and being seen to do so) may supersede all other concerns, perhaps especially those around monitoring and evaluation (Coalter 2007). According to Weiss (1997) 'a considerable amount of ineffectiveness may be tolerated if a programme fits well with prevailing values, if it satisfies voters, or if it pays off political debts' (quoted in Coalter 2007: 42).

The systematic introduction of individuals with an increased knowledge of the issues facing children and young people in sport, via safeguarding/child protection training or other means, who fulfil designated roles within the delivery of children's sport, supported by governing agencies and agreed policies and guidelines, is to be greatly welcomed. However, unless we know much more about the impact of developments such as these on the experiences of children in sport (as well as those that provide sport), it might be argued that the appearance of doing something counts for more than understanding whether that 'thing' in fact makes a (positive) difference – and how much difference, to whom and under what circumstances.

Regardless of the socio-political environment within which safeguarding emerges, if outcomes related to improved experiences for children in sport are to be achieved, governing agencies must establish clear, measurable outcomes by which their interventions can be evaluated. Requiring all state-funded sports agencies to achieve a set of outputs says little about the impact of generating these outputs on the individuals who work with children or the experiences of children themselves, and even less about the impact they have (intended and otherwise) on child maltreatment in sport. Such an approach to policy implementation raises the concern that powerful organizations may feel able to operate unchecked, trumpeting their own perceived successes, and thereby justify their own existence, without any external evaluation.

This is not an issue confined to the sports context and messages from the wider field of research on child protection should be considered. According to Carter et al. (2006: 742):

> An unquantifiable amount of effort and resource is devoted to raising awareness of the principles of safeguarding children ... While many of the studies described interesting programmes of training ... most were limited because of poor design and lack of objective evaluation.

Substantial, meaningful and holistic approaches to safeguarding in sport policy development and implementation will view research evaluation as an *integral* and indispensable element of all phases and aspects of the policy process rather than an annexed sub-group to be called upon to deliver evidence for predetermined themes, initiatives and activities. Organizations across the globe, now considering their approach to the problem of child abuse, would do well to engender such an approach from the outset. However, as Coalter (2007: 117) warns, and as the CPSU has frequently pointed out, 'limited project funding is concentrated on provision rather than evaluation'. Clearly, the strategic thinking behind safeguarding and child protection in sport initiatives and programmes determines (funding) priorities.

Finally, (and in the hope of prompting further discussion) we offer the following points as a starting position for the development of a more robust policy framework in this field.

- Independent evaluation research is built into key interventions with a designated role for evaluators within all aspects of the policy development and implementation process, including assisting with the process of setting aims and objectives and establishing monitoring mechanisms.
- Research design aims to capture the specific challenges and difficulties faced by sports organizations/communities (including policy makers) and appropriate mechanisms for these to be voiced are embedded within the research process.
- Evaluations are peer-reviewed, published and disseminated widely with mechanisms for community feedback/commentary on process and findings embedded within the research design.
- Organizational responses to evaluations are published (and to a timetable of no more than six months) and disseminated, especially to the groups most affected by those responses.

References

Brackenridge, C. H. (1994) 'Fair play or fair game: child sexual abuse in sport organisations', *International Review for the Sociology of Sport*, 29: 287–99.

— (2001) *Spoilsports: understanding and preventing sexual exploitation in sport,* London: Routledge.

— (2002) '"… so what?" Attitudes of the voluntary sector towards child protection in sports clubs', *Managing Leisure*, 7: 103–23.

Brackenridge, C. H. and Fasting, K. (2002) *Sexual Harassment and Abuse in Sport: international research and policy perspectives*, London: Whiting and Birch.

Brackenridge, C. H., Pitchford, A., Russell, K. and Nutt, G. (2007) *Child Welfare in Football: an exploration of children's welfare in the modern game,* London: Routledge.

Brackenridge, C. H., Pawlczek, Z., Bringer, J. D., Cockburn, C., Nutt, G., Pitchford, A. and Russell, K. (2005) 'Measuring the impact of child protection through Activation States', *Sport, Education and Society,* 10: 239–56.

Carter, Y. H., Bannon, M. J., Limbert, C., Docherty, A. and Barlow, J. (2006) 'Improving child protection: a systematic review of training and procedural interventions', *Archives of Disease in Childhood*, 91: 740–43.

Child Protection in Sport Unit (2003) *Standards for Safeguarding and Protecting Children in Sport*, 1st edn, Leicester: CPSU.

— (2007) *Standards for Safeguarding and Protecting Children in Sport*, 2nd edn, Leicester: CPSU.

— (2012) *The Framework for Maintaining and Embedding Safeguarding for Children in and through Sport*, Leicester: CPSU.

— (2013a) *Sports Safeguarding Children Initiative: mid-project progress report*, London: NSPCC/CPSU. Online. Available HTTP: <thecpsu.org.uk/resource-library/2013/sports-safeguarding-children-initiative-report/> (accessed 6 January 2014).

— (2013b) *Safeguarding Framework Self-Assessment Tool SAT (with guidance).* Online. Available HTTP: <thecpsu.org.uk/resource-library/2013/safeguarding-framework-self-assessment-tool-sat-(with-guidance)/> (accessed 20 July 2013).

— (2013c) *Research on Child Protection and Child Abuse.* Online. Available HTTP: <thecpsu.org.uk/help-advice/related-information/research-on-child-protection-and-child-abuse/> (accessed 20 November 2013).

— (2014) *Develop and Improve Standards.* Online. Available HTTP: <thecpsu.org.uk/help-advice/develop-and-improve-standards-and-framework/> (accessed 2 January 2014).

Chroni, S., Fasting, K., Hartill, M., Knorre, N., Martin, M., Papaefstathiou, M., Rhind, D., Rulofs, B., Toeftgaard Støckel, J., Vertommen, T. and Zurc, J. (2012) *Prevention of Sexual and Gender Harassment and Abuse in Sports: initiatives in Europe and beyond*, Frankfurt: Deutsche Sportjugend.

Coalter, F. (2007) *A Wider Social Role for Sport: who's keeping the score?* London: Routledge.

— (2008) *Sport-in-Development: a monitoring and evaluation manual*, London: UK Sport. Online. Available HTTP: <www.sportanddev.org/toolkit/?uNewsID=17> (accessed 4 January 2014).

Critcher, C. (2002) 'Media, government and moral panic: the politics of paedophilia in Britain 2000–1', *Journalism Studies,* 3: 521–35.

Cunningham, (2007) 'Perverted: Ireland's paedo shame sex beast O'Rourke goes into hiding after his early release from jail', *The Mirror*: 1.

David, P. (2005) *Human Rights in Youth Sport: a critical review of children's rights in competitive sports,* London: Routledge.

Davies, H. T. O., Nutley, S. M. and Smith, P. C. (2000) *What Works? Evidence-based policy and practice in public services,* Bristol: The Policy Press.

Donnelly, P. (1997) 'Child labour, sport labour: applying child labour laws to sport', *International Review for the Sociology of Sport,* 32: 389–406.

Finkelhor, D. (2009) 'The prevention of childhood sexual abuse', *The Future of Children,* 19: 169–94.

Fitzpatrick, J. L. (2012) 'An introduction to context and its role in evaluation practice', in D. J. Rog, J. L. Fitzpatrick and R. F. Conner (eds) *Context: a framework for its influence on evaluation practice – new directions for evaluation,* 135, 7–24.

Flyvbjerg, B. (2001) *Making Social Science Matter: why social inquiry fails and how it can succeed again,* Cambridge: Cambridge University Press.

Flyvbjerg, B., Landman, T. and Schram, S. (2012) (eds) *Real Social Science: applied phronesis,* Cambridge: Cambridge University Press.

Greene, J. C. (2005) 'Context', in S. Mathison (ed.) *Encyclopedia of Evaluation,* Thousand Oaks, CA: Sage.

Hartill, M., Lang, M. and Ashley, N. (2014) *Safeguarding and Child Protection in Rugby Football League: final report,* Ormskirk: Edge Hill University.

Hartill, M. and Prescott, P. (2002) *An Evaluation of BARLA's Child Protection Policy Pilot Implementation,* unpublished report for the British Amateur Rugby League Association (BARLA), Ormskirk, UK: Edge Hill University.

—— (2006) *An Evaluation of the Rugby Football League's Child Protection Policy (phase 1),* unpublished report for the Rugby Football League (RFL), Ormskirk, UK: Edge Hill University.

—— (2007) 'Serious business or "any other business"?: safeguarding and child protection policy in British rugby league', *Child Abuse Review,* 16: 237–51.

Krasnow, D., Manwaring, L. and Kerr, G. (1999) 'Injury, stress, and perfectionism in young dancers and gymnasts', *Journal of Dance Medicine and Science,* 3: 51–8.

MacDonald, G. and Roberts, H. (1995) *What Works in the Early Years? Effective interventions for children and their families in health, social welfare, education and child protection,* Essex: Barnardos.

Malkin, K., Johnston, L. and Brackenridge, C. H. (2000) 'A critical evaluation of training needs for child protection in UK sport', *Managing Leisure,* 5: 151–60.

Matland, R. E. (1995) 'Sytnthesizing the implementation literature: the ambiguity-conflict model of policy implementation', *Journal of Public Administration Research and Theory,* 2: 145–74.

Meyer, A. (2007) *The Child at Risk: paedophiles, media responses and public opinion,* Manchester: Manchester University Press.

Munro, E. (2011) *The Munro Review of Child Protection: final report – a child-centred system,* London: Department for Education.

National Society for the Prevention of Cruelty to Children (2013) *Sport Safeguarding Children Initiative: mid-term report,* Leicester: NSPCC.

Parent, S. and El Hlimi, K. (2012) 'Athlete protection in Quebec's sport system: assessments, problems and challenges', *Journal of Sport and Social Issues.* Online. Available HTTP: <http://jss.sagepub.com/content/37/3/284.short> (accessed 9 August 2013).

Pawson, R. (2006) *Evidence-Based Policy: a realist perspective,* London: Sage.

Piper, H., Garratt, D. and Taylor, B. (2013) 'Child abuse, child protection, and defensive "touch" in PE teaching and sports coaching', *Sport, Education and Society,* 18: 583–98.

Rulofs, B. (2007) 'Prevention of sexualized violence in sport – an analysis of the preliminary measures in North Rhine-Westphalia', in B. Rulofs (ed.) *Silence Protects the Wrong People: sexualized violence in sport – situation analysis and opportunities for action*, Dusseldorf: Ministry of North Rhine-Westphalia.

Rulofs, B. and Emberger, D. (2011) *Prevention of Sexual Violence in Sport – between voluntarism and commitment? Analysis of the perception and acceptance of specific prevention measures of the sports federation in North Rhine-Westphalia from the perspective of functionaries in sport*, unpublished report to the Sports Ministry of North Rhine-Westphalia.

Schram, S. (2012) 'Phronetic Social Science: an idea whose time has come', in B. Flyvbjerg, T. Landman and S. Schram (2012) (eds) *Real Social Science: applied phronesis,* Cambridge: Cambridge University Press.

Serkei, B., Goes, A. and de Groot, N. (2012) *From Blind Confidence to Responsible Policy: usefulness and effectiveness of NOC*NSF policy instruments sexual harassment*, Utrecht: MOVISIE.

Sport England (2013) *Sport England Boosts Funding to Help More Young People Enjoy Sport in a Safe Environment*. Online. Available HTTP: <www.sportengland.org/media-centre/news/2013/january/10/sport-england-boosts-funding-to-help-more-young-people-enjoy-sport-in-a-safe-environment/> (accessed 9 August 2013).

Stirling, A. E., Kerr, G. A., and Cruz, L. C. (2012) 'An evaluation of Canada's National Coaching Certification Programme's "Make Ethical Decisions" coach education module', *International Journal of Coaching Science*, 6: 45–60.

Tomison, A. M. (2000) 'Evaluating child abuse prevention programs', *Issues in Child Abuse Prevention,* 12: 1–20.

Vertommen, T., Schipper-van Veldhoven, N., Hartill, M. J. and Eede, F. Van Den (2013) 'Sexual harassment and abuse in sport: the NOC*NSF Helpline', *International Review for the Sociology of Sport*. Online. Available HTTP: <irs.sagepub.com/content/early/recent> (accessed 20 August 2013).

Walker, R. (2000) 'Welfare Policy: tendering for evidence', in H. T. O. Davies, S. M. Nutley and P. C. Smith (2000) *What works? Evidence-based policy and practice in public services*, Bristol: The Policy Press.

Weber, M., Bruin, A. P. de and Moget, P. (2006) *The Dutch Programme Against Sexual Harassment in Sports, 1996–2006*, Arnhem: NOC*NSF.

Weiss, C. H. (1997) 'How can theory based evaluation make greater headway?', *Education Review*, 21: 501–24.

Conclusion

Mike Hartill and Melanie Lang

Whilst the recognition of child abuse as a serious and widespread social problem dates to only the 1970s (Gil 1975; Helfer and Kempe 1968; Kempe 1978), the abuse, maltreatment and neglect of children and youth is not a new problem (Jackson 2000; Radbill 1968). Rather, it is a widespread, persistent, historical practice which has been recognized, relatively recently, as a serious global issue. Thus, the last 30 years or so have seen a seismic increase in international efforts to address this situation. Nevertheless, it would seem apparent that our various societies and communities have persistently reproduced conditions in which the abuse and neglect of children is able to flourish.

The story of our recognition of child maltreatment in the late-twentieth century continues to unfold and is shaped by our shifting understandings, or social constructions, of the 'the child' and 'childhood' and the adult-child relation (Prout and James 1997). Thus, activities or practices between adults and children that may have been considered relatively unremarkable (for example, a parent 'smacking' a child for being 'naughty' or a sports coach humiliating a child to evoke an increase in effort) may now, in some contexts, be considered abusive and detrimental to a child's development. Whilst in some cultural contexts (often in spite of legal prohibitions) 'sparing the rod' is still viewed as a recipe for 'spoiling the child', in others the 'rod' has largely been outlawed; similarly, the notion that 'children should be seen but not heard' and should 'do as they are told' has been replaced by the view that children's voices should be heard and they should participate in the decision-making process (James and James 2004).

Indeed, when children's rights are taken as the essential starting point for the evaluation of the social spaces and activities that adults provide for children, many traditional cultural practices are called into question. As a key social space for children and youth – and one which frequently emphasizes a strict corporeal discipline – sport is clearly a field requiring careful examination. One of the intentions of this book has been to contribute to that examination. In this concluding chapter, we begin by considering the key term around which this book was devised – *safeguarding* – before summing up what we see as the key issues and debates emerging from the contributions within this text.

Protection, prevention and safeguarding

The idiom 'prevention is better than cure' is never more apparent than when applied to the abuse and neglect of children. Therefore, those societies that have recognized the abuse of children as a serious social problem have, relatively quickly, looked for ways to prevent abuse before it happens. This is, of course, an immensely complex problem that we are a long way from solving, as prevalence figures indicate (e.g. Gilbert et al. 2009; Pereda et al. 2009). Within a sports context, whilst researchers and other critical commentators are often (rightly) sceptical about some of the claims made on behalf of the 'power' of sport to deliver socio-political outcomes, sport, like other sectors, has an important role to play in the wider effort to prevent the abuse of children and young people. Initiatives such as those established by the Netherlands Olympic Committee since 1996 (Chapter 4); the Regional Sports Federation of North-Rhine-Westphalia since 1997 and, more recently, the German Olympic Sports Confederation (Chapter 5); and by Sport England (with the United Kingdom's [UK] largest children's charity, the National Society for the Prevention of Cruelty to Children or NSPCC) since 2001 (Chapter 1), illustrate the sport sectors' engagement with wider concerns around child (sexual) abuse and indicate the considerable experience that some sport agencies now have in this field.

As we noted in the Introduction, prevailing attitudes about the abuse and neglect of children have shifted, reflecting a turn to a more holistic approach to child welfare and an increasing demand that organizations explicitly recognize children's rights. In the UK, no sooner had the sports community begun to establish mechanisms to 'protect' children from abuse, it was informed it must 'safeguard' their welfare and their rights. As noted in Chapter 1, the term 'safeguarding', as it is understood in England, foregrounds children's rights over the rights of adults, in line with Gilbert et al.'s (2011) child-focused approach to children's welfare (see Introduction Chapter). This perspective promotes early intervention and preventative services as a positive way of helping maximize children's developmental opportunities, educational attainment and overall health and well-being (Parton 2010). Sport in England, then, as well as other parts of the UK, has begun to incorporate this more proactive, preventative approach to children's welfare into its policies and practices (see Chapter 1 for more details).

Safeguarding

Of course, the degree to which broader 'safeguarding' agendas have been adopted within national sport systems varies greatly. Whilst the *term* 'safeguarding' is largely confined to the UK, similar shifts towards the proactive prevention of negative outcomes for children have been adopted elsewhere. For example in Australia (Chapter 12), all states and territories have endorsed the National Framework for Protecting Australia's Children (Commonwealth of Australia 2009), which calls on the country to move away from reactively protecting children specifically from abuse and maltreatment and move towards the more proactive and holistic approach of promoting the safety and wellbeing of children. Similarly, in Belgium (Chapter 3) the Panathlon Declaration on Ethics in Youth Sport prompted the regional government to adopt legislation that requires sports organizations to have in place 'preventative and curative measures ... to safeguard and promote the ethical dimension in sports' (Council of Europe 2009: 2).

In the Netherlands (Chapter 4) the programme Together for Sportsmanship and Respect also adopted a broader approach to tackling unwanted behaviour within sport. Most recently, in the United States (US) the US Olympic Committee now requires affiliated National Governing Bodies of Sport (NGBs) to adopt an athlete welfare strategy (see Chapter 10). Other chapters in this book document similar developments.

However, despite important international reports and statements (e.g. Brackenridge et al. 2010), it is clear that sports governance within some countries has, somewhat surprisingly, remained inactive in relation to abuses against children, at least until very recently. For example, whilst media reports of sexual abuse in Spanish sport have been documented since the 1980s, it was not until a high-profile disclosure of sexual abuse in 2013 that Spain's governing sport agency began to consider its responsibilities in this area (see Chapter 7). Cyprus has apparently not yet reached this stage, and for other countries, such as Denmark, Greece, Japan and South Africa, acceptance of the problem could be characterized as begrudging and reluctant even though, in some cases, laws and even sport-based policies may be in place (see Brackenridge 2001 for a discussion of the various responses that organizations may exhibit).

Clearly, we may point to the wider cultural context of countries that retain highly patriarchal and deeply masculinist political and social systems where the daily experience of sexual harassment faced by many women garners little substantial attention. In such contexts, where the rights of the (patriarchal) family to raise children without intrusive government intervention are prioritized, child abuse (especially sexual abuse) remains a largely taboo topic. Nevertheless, whilst the wider political system will always be reflected within sports governance, especially where systems are highly centralized, ignorance of, or lack of, engagement with wider international developments within sport is surely also the product of a wilful refusal to acknowledge events and issues that may prove difficult or uncomfortable for those in positions of privilege and high status.

International dialogues that are beginning to move children's rights and gender equality agendas forward within sport will certainly require the political allegiance of those within the (mostly male) corridors of power. Equally, those who seek to delay the process by refusing to acknowledge sport-based violations of human and children's rights conventions to which they are signed up must be 'called out'. The fact that some boardrooms of deeply conservative, male-dominated organizations, responsible for the vast majority of sports governance, appear reluctant to acknowledge that valued adults in trusted positions within their sport may abuse children (let alone that their systems and processes may not be aligned with the 'best interests' of children), or stay silent even when they are party to such knowledge, should increasingly be addressed by academic researchers as well as international sports bodies.

High-level efforts to address this situation are evident and ongoing: for example, a recent Enlarged Partial Agreement on Sport (EPAS) conference highlighted the issue of child abuse in sport at a pan-European level (Council of Europe 2013); the European Commission has emphasized 'the fight against sexual violence and harassment in sport' within its funding priorities for 2014–2020 (European Commission 2013); and the United Nations Office for Sport for Development and Peace (UNOSDP) has also designated 'child protection' as a key theme within its programme 'encouraging' member states to 'implement plans to prevent the exploitation and abuse of children and youth in sport contexts' (UNOSDP 2014).

Equally, the development of national and international networks are vital to support the early advocacy work of those individuals and agencies willing to put their head above the parapet and engage with such challenging issues. The work of the Support Group to Prevent Sexual Abuse in Sport in Spain, known as GAPAS(D) (see Chapter 7) is a good example of how committed individuals can initiate agendas for change from within social systems that have been seemingly reluctant to acknowledge the abuse of children's rights. However, access to resources, including current knowledge, is vital if such ground-level initiatives are to be sustainable and effective. The recommendations made to the European Commission by the German Sport Youth and ENGSO Youth project (see German Sport Youth 2013) and the draft proposals presented by Professor Kari Fasting at the European Commission's 2013 conference on gender equality in sport (European Commission 2013) in Vilnius, Lithuania (3–4 December 2013) both call for the development of (European) international networks which might provide much-needed support and facilitate collaboration.

Panic, resistance and critique of current approaches

The English Child Protection in Sport Unit (CPSU) has now taken on a more international role through its collaboration with other international agencies in establishing international standards for safeguarding children in sport (see sportanddev.org 2013). Yet it has also faced substantial and important criticism for adopting a 'narrow and selective focus' 'in which the idea of the predatory adult is central' (Piper et al. 2013: 596) with 'negative implications for ... the development of healthy relationships between adults and children through participation in sport' (Piper et al. 2012: 342). It must be observed, however, that a strategy which incorporates a requirement that 'managers and senior staff promote a culture that ensures children are listened to and respected as individuals' (CPSU 2007: 17) is at least attempting to go well beyond the confines of a strictly protectionist approach.

A growing awareness of the reality of sexual violence against children (in sport) has been accompanied by a particular representation of abuse (see Meyer 2007). For example, Steven Downes (2002) writes:

Youngsters in Britain face a growing danger of being sexually abused by their sports coaches ... this special report ... asks how we can best protect children from *the menace that may lurk at the poolside and in the changing rooms*. (emphasis added)

In addition, the reality of sexual violence, including that against children and young people, is that it is an overwhelmingly male crime (Wykes and Welch 2009). Clearly, the recent recognition that men have for generations used spaces such as churches, schools, care facilities and sports settings as sites for subjecting children to sexual activity has served to shatter previously held confidences in such extra-familial spaces, and those that provide them, as *inherently* safe places for children. Unsurprisingly, then, the (hyper) masculinist and extremely powerful field of sport, which outside of the family remains a key space in which men and children (especially boys) interact on a regular basis, has felt threatened.

Whilst there may well be concern amongst sports coaches over whether they can touch children and how this may be perceived (in a 'surveillance society' – see Lang 2010, 2014), concerns around the sexist, homophobic, racist, violent and abusive narratives that frequently permeate the practice of (children's) sport cannot be conjured away. Increased regulation, 'surveillance' and 'disciplinary mechanisms' within youth sport may well cause concerns for those adults who are subject to them, and whilst those concerns should be taken very seriously, so should the many years of critical inquiry that has revealed so much about the disciplinary and surveillance culture that exists within youth sports and to which children and young people have been subject (e.g. Johns and Johns 2000; Johnson and Holman 2004; Lang 2010).

The history of the concealment of sexual violence and other abuses of children's rights that the masculinist field of sports (and male communities within it) has housed – not unwittingly (Hartill 2012a) – for so many generations, indicates that the anguish expressed by adults for their own interests has been too frequently absent when the wellbeing of a child has been at stake. This would seem to be a feature of sport (as well as other contexts) across national boundaries, as is well illustrated by recent cases of sexual abuse in sport in Spain (Ayala and Ayala 2013; Iríbar 2013), the US (Quinn and Amante 2010) and Germany (*Die Tageszeitung* 2012). As Kelly Curran Davies puts it, in the wake of her allegations against her former swimming coach Rick Curl (subsequently imprisoned for seven years), 'these [other] coaches knew and yet ... they're still coaching for him' (National Public Radio 2012).

Beyond sexual abuse

The field of sports has undoubtedly moved out of neutral in its response to the problem of adult sexual violence against children; what is much less clear, however, is the extent to which sport governance is prepared to recognize and challenge behaviour that is *physically* or *emotionally* abusive or neglectful. This task represents, perhaps, an even greater challenge for the delivery of children's sport. As a recent promotional film by the CPSU (2013) illustrates, when children put on their 'magic sports kit' they are euphemistically (thus literally) transformed into 'athletes' and 'players': 'footballers', 'swimmers', 'gymnasts', even officials – that is, their status as *children* is diluted or transfigured and, therefore, the 'rules of the game' appear to change (Bourdieu 1990). It will surprise few people to learn that sports coaches have been found to use physical punishment as a standard method of instilling 'discipline' in child athletes, as illustrated in Chapter 14 (Japan), although this is a practice far from confined to a particular cultural context. Meanwhile, other authors show how emotional abuse and injury to children within sport can often be overlooked or accepted as just 'part of the game' (see Chapters 8, 15, 17 and 18).

From our perspective, without underpinning systems that prioritize a children's rights agenda – preferably initiated through mutual consent and built from the ground up rather than simply imposed from above – codes of ethical conduct and suchlike will have little impact on children's experiences in organized sport.

Research

Fundamental research

According to Brackenridge and Rhind (2010: 159) 'significant strides have been made over recent years in our efforts to promote and protect the welfare of elite child athletes. Despite this progress, there remains considerable scope for future research.' Research in the 1990s and 2000s did a great deal to pull back the veil of privilege, secrecy, complicity and denial that had shrouded and continues to shroud the exploitation and abuse of women and children within sport (e.g. Brackenridge 2001; Leahy et al. 2002). We will not rehearse the findings of this research here, but as the chapters in this book indicate, this work must continue and with some urgency.

The sports organizations that will distinguish themselves in this field in the 2010s will be those that campaign for and commission fundamental research within their own specific contexts. Any organization that is able to state – based on *robust* data – a prevalence rate for, say, sexual violence within their sport, will be rewarded from all sectors (especially from those with broad social aims) and will ultimately be able to make justifiable claims to being child-focused and socially responsible.

Those sports that wish to demonstrate they have broken free of the denial and concealment that has surrounded sexual abuse and that wish to adopt proactive and informed approaches to this problem will be the first to take this opportunity. However, as the chapters in the second part of this collection clearly demonstrate, fundamental research is required across a range of issues in relation to children and young people's sports participation. The rewards, in terms of organizational learning and development, as well as public confidence, may be considerable for those agencies that can exhibit a strong research (learning) agenda. Similarly, the organizations that not only make appropriate provision for the reporting of issues such as abuse, but actively encourage the telling of abuse stories (by 'victims' and bystanders), providing appropriate and substantial support services for those that may wish to, will also distinguish themselves.

In the search for answers, even solutions, to the problem of child abuse, the examination of clinical (often incarcerated) populations, in order to uncover 'offender profiles', may seem an expedient avenue for politicians and funders of research to follow. We certainly do not dismiss such efforts, however, the very focus on abuse and maltreatment *in* sport (as within the Church) demands a cultural analysis. Research must be prepared to (further) engage in rigorous and substantial socio-cultural analyses of the myriad sports environments that children and young people encounter. Those sports organizations most proactive in the field of safeguarding and child protection will support, champion and value such analyses.

Applied research

Whilst the lack of large-scale, robust studies on the rates of prevalence and incidence of child abuse within sport seems increasingly unacceptable, it is equally important that the systems and processes put in place to safeguard children and vulnerable adults are evaluated to increase efficacy as well as efficiency. In this regard, research evaluations of specific training/education interventions in Canada (Stirling et al. 2012) and Germany (Rulofs 2007; Rulofs and Emberger 2011) have recently produced some positive findings.

However, the funds committed to advocacy and policy development through the 2000s were not accompanied by – or did not make provision for – evaluation; indeed, the vast majority of interventions in this field have never been evaluated. This error should not be repeated when new programmes are commissioned and developed. The work of Celia Brackenridge with, for example, the English Football Association (Brackenridge et al. 2007) clearly leads the way in this regard. But it is the commitment of organizations such as the NOC*NSF in the Netherlands (Chapter 4) and the sports ministry of North Rhine-Westphalia in Germany (Chapter 5), who are collaborating with researchers and publish evaluations of their own policies (e.g. Lucassen and Kalmthout 2012), that seems to offer the model of current best practice and perhaps the most sustainable approach to establishing key messages from which future policy development and implementation can benefit. The English Rugby Football League has also shown a long-term desire to engage with critical academic research and feed messages back into its own planning and education strategies (Hartill 2012b; Hartill, Lang and Ashley 2014)) as well as to disseminate them for wider benefit (Hartill and Prescott 2007). This evaluation work continues – recently with the support of the CPSU (Hartill, Lang and Ashley 2014) – and perhaps also offers a model that could be replicated elsewhere. More recently, the International Safeguarding Children in Sport Working Group, which in 2013 began piloting a set of 11 standards to protect children in international sport and sport-for-development, have commissioned evaluation research alongside piloting of these standards.

Practitioners and policy makers must do more to communicate with researchers about their particular contexts, and researchers must do more to establish critical collaborations with practitioners to understand better the challenges they face. Neither side need sacrifice the interests and values that underpin their work but each must understand and respect the fact that these may both converge as well as differ. Certainly, as prevention measures and children's rights become more embedded within sport (a long process in itself), publicly accountable governing agencies and funding bodies within the sports sector must be more discerning in recognizing and valuing programmes and instruments that are underpinned by robust research. A stronger engagement with impartial evaluation will do much to stem criticism that powerful organizations are implementing policy from 'on high' and then cherry-picking their successes – with no acknowledgment of their failures – and amplifying them to justify their own existence and budgets.

The absence of children from policy making, practice and research

The participation of children and young people within all dimensions of safeguarding and child protection is essential. Whilst all organizations must strive to include the voices of children and young people within their systems and processes, taking children's rights seriously also means providing them with the knowledge required to arrive at informed opinions about issues on which they are asked to contribute. Children should be both *participants within* research as well as the *beneficiaries of* research; as well as participating in research design and implementation, children and young people should be given appropriate access to relevant research data and findings so that they are able to approach the policy making process on a more equal footing. Finally, sport organizations should seek the interpretations of children and young people in relation to the research conducted on their behalf so that these views can be incorporated into action plans and the decision-making process. Thus, research should be: *informed* by children's perspectives; *include* children as participants; and *deliver* research to children in an appropriate format according to age and ability.

Final thoughts

This book represents the most recent entry in a short list of academic texts that are committed to illuminating the abuse of children in sport and the political, organizational and local responses that have emerged to date. The intention has been to provide an international text of sufficient scope to enable a good grasp of the major developments in this field. The space limitations of this text mean that much of the detail, especially in relation to local initiatives, cannot be included. While there now appears to be some forward momentum in some sport contexts, given the many abuses of children's rights across the globe, both within and beyond sport, finding second gear is not inevitable. Certainly, the abuse and neglect of children and children's rights is not an issue that is going to disappear quickly or indeed a problem that will be solved 'once and for all'.

The mainstreaming of children's rights within sport (as with gender, ethnicity and disability – perhaps even more so) will be a constant endeavour, not a journey with an end. So it is important that the struggles faced by those working to move the agenda in sport forward are, where possible, acknowledged and supported. Thus, the story behind the changes that have and continue to take place in sport must be documented and considered so that the valuable lessons to be gleaned from them are preserved. In compiling and editing this collection we have sought to provide both a critical overview of the arrangements for safeguarding children's welfare in the international context of sport, whilst also encouraging authors to provide something of a narrative for developments within their own contexts. We hope this will be of interest and value in and of itself, but we also see this documenting of the current picture as a crucial step towards enhancing inter-cultural learning within sport and, ultimately, enhancing the experience of sports for all.

References

Ayala, M. F. and Ayala, M. (2013) *The Karate Sect*, Madrid: Mercurio Editorial.

Bourdieu, P. (1990) *The Logic of Practice,* Cambridge: Polity Press.

Brackenridge, C. H. (2001) Spoilsports: understanding and preventing sexual exploitation in sport, London: Routledge.

Brackenridge, C. H. and Rhind, D. (eds) (2010) *Elite Child Athlete Welfare: international perspectives*, Uxbridge: Brunel University Press.

Brackenridge, C. H., Pitchford, A., Russell, K. and Nutt, G. (2007) *Child Welfare in Football: an exploration of children's welfare in the modern game,* London: Routledge.

Brackenridge, C. H., Fasting, K., Kirby, S. and Leahy, T. (2010) *Protecting Children from Violence in Sport: a review with a focus on industrialized countries*, UNICEF Innocenti Research Centre, Florence, Italy: UNICEF.

Child Protection in Sport Unit (2007) *Standards for Safeguarding and Protecting Children in Sport*, 2nd edn, Leicester: Child Protection in Sport Unit.

—— (2013) *My Magic Sports Kit.* Online. Available HTTP: <thecpsu.org.uk/resource-library/2013/my-magic-sports-kit/> (accessed 7 January 2014).

Commonwealth of Australia (2009) *Protecting Children is Everyone's Business – National Framework for Protecting Australia's Children 2009–2020: understanding the approach*, Canberra: Commonwealth of Australia. Online. Available HTTP: <www.fahcsia.gov.au/our-responsibilities/families-and-children/publications-articles/protecting-children-is-everyones-business> (accessed 1 July 2013).

Council of Europe (2009) *13 July 2007 Flemish Parliament Act on Medically and Ethically Justified Sports Practice*. Online. Available HTTP: <www.coe.int/t/dg4/sport/doping/antidoping_database/Reports/2009/leg/LEG1–BEL-FLA_EN.pdf> (accessed 10 October 2013).

—— (2013) *Conference: inclusion and protection of children in and through sport, 7 and 8 October 2013, Budapest, Hungary,* Enlarged Partial Agreement on Sport (EPAS). Online. Available HTTP: <www.coe.int/t/dg4/epas/News/News_2013_Budapest_Conf_EN.asp>

Die Tageszeitung (2012) *Abuse Scandal in the Swimming Association: again, no one knew anything.* Online. Available HTTP: <www.taz.de/Missbrauchsaffaere-beim-Schwimm-Verband/!99425/> (accessed 27 May 2013).

Downes, S. (2002) 'Every parents' nightmare', *Observer Sport Monthly*, 7 April. Online. Available HTTP: <observer.theguardian.com/print/0,,4386620–103977,00.html> (accessed 4 January 2014).

European Commission (2013) *EU Conference on Gender Equality in Sport*. Online. Available HTTP: <ec.europa.eu/sport/news/20131129_en.htm> (accessed 21 December 2013).

German Sport Youth (2013) *Safer, Better, Stronger! Prevention of Sexual Harassment and Abuse in Sports: recommendations to the European Commission*. Online. Available HTTP: <www.dsj.de/fileadmin/user_upload/Bilder/Handlungsfelder/Europa/europ_PSG_Projekt_2012/EN-recommendations-psv-20130524.pdf> (accessed 7 January 2013).

Gil, D. (1975) 'Unravelling child abuse', *American Journal of Orthopsychiatry*, 45: 346–56.

Gilbert, N., Parton, N. and Skivenes, M. (2011) *Child Protection Systems: international trends and orientations*, New York: Open University Press.

Gilbert, R., Spatz Widom, C., Browne, K., Fergusson, D., Webb, E. and Janson, S. (2009) 'Child maltreatment 1: burden and consequences of child maltreatment in high-income countries', *The Lancet*, 373: 68–81.

Hartill, M. (2012a) 'Concealment of child sexual abuse in sports', *Quest*, 65: 241–54.

— (2012b) '*Child protection research in Rugby League*', presentation for the Rugby Football League Annual Safeguarding Conference, Warrington, November 2012.

Hartill, M. and Prescott, P. (2007) 'Serious business or 'any other business? Safeguarding and child protection policy in British rugby league', *Child Abuse Review*, 16: 237–51.

Hartill, M., Lang, M. and Ashley, N. (2014) *Safeguarding and Child Protection in Rugby Football League: final report*, Ormskirk: Edge Hill University.

Helfer, R. E. and Kempe C. H. (eds) (1968) *The Battered Child*, London: University of Chicago Press.

Iríbar, A. (2013) 'He wouldn't let us talk to the girls', *El País*, 9 July. Online. Available HTTP: <elpais.com/elpais/2013/07/09/inenglish/1373372172_899333.html> (accessed 9 September 2013).

Jackson, L. A. (2000) *Child Sexual Abuse in Victorian England*, London: Routledge.

James, A. and James, A. L. (2004) *Constructing Childhood: theory, policy and social practice*, Basingstoke: Palgrave Macmillan.

Johns, D. and Johns, J. (2000) 'Surveillance, subjectivism and technologies of power: an analysis of the discursive practice of high-performance sport', *International Review for the Sociology of Sport*, 35: 219–34.

Johnson, J. and Holman, M. J. (2004) *Making the Team: inside the world of sport initiations and hazing*, Toronto: Canadian Scholars Press.

Kempe, H. D. (1978) 'Sexual abuse: another hidden paediatric problem', *Pediatrics*, 62: 382–9.

Lang, M. (2010) 'Surveillance and conformity in competitive youth swimming', *Sport, Education and Society*, 12: 19–37.

— (2014) 'Touchy subject: a Foucauldian analysis of coaches' perceptions of adult-child touch in youth swimming', *Sociology of Sport Journal*.

Leahy, T., Pretty, G. and Tenenbaum, G. (2002) 'Prevalence of sexual abuse in sport in Australia', *Journal of Sexual Aggression*, 2: 16–36.

Lucassen, J. and Kalmthout, J. van (2012) *You Can Only See it, if You Know It: final results monitoring programme 'Together for Sportsmanship and Respect'*, Utrecht: Mulier Instituut.

Meyer, A. (2007) *The Child at Risk: paedophiles, media responses and public opinion,* Manchester: Manchester University Press.

National Public Radio (2012) *Behind Closed Doors: sex abuse haunts former Olympic swim hopeful.* Online. Available HTTP: <www.npr.org/2012/08/06/158199112/sex-abuse-haunts-former-olympic-swim-hopeful> (accessed 20 December 2013).

Parton, N. (2010)'*I*nternational comparison of child protection systems', paper presented at the SFI conference, Copenhagen, Denmark, September.

Pereda, N., Guilera, G., Forns, M and Gómez-Benito, J. (2009) 'The international epidemiology of child sexual abuse: a continuation of Finkelhor (1994)', *Child Abuse and Neglect,* 33: 331–42.

Piper, H., Garratt, D. and Taylor, B. (2012) 'Sports coaching in risk society: no touch! no trust!', *Sport, Education and Society,* 17: 331–45.

— (2013) 'Child abuse, child protection, and defensive "touch' in PE teaching and sports coaching", *Sport, Education and Society,* 18: 583–98.

Prout, A. and James, A. (1997) (eds) *Constructing and Reconstructing Childhood: contemporary issues in the sociological study of childhood,* 2nd edn, London: RoutledgeFalmer.

Quinn, T. J. and Amante, G. (2010) 'Sex abuse pervasive in US swimming', ESPN. Online. Available HTTP: <sports.espn.go.com/espn/otl/news/story?id=5071820> (accessed 1 April 2012).

Radbill, S. X. (1968) 'A history of child abuse and infanticide' in R. E. Helfer and C. H. Kempe (eds) *The Battered Child,* London: University of Chicago Press.

Rulofs, B. (2007) 'Prevention of sexualized violence in sport – an analysis of the preliminary measures in North Rhine-Westphalia', in B. Rulofs (ed.) *Silence Protects the Wrong People: sexualized violence in sport – situation analysis and opportunities for action,* Dusseldorf: Ministry of North Rhine-Westphalia.

Rulofs, B. and Emberger, D. (2011) '*Prevention of Sexual Violence in Sport – between voluntarism and commitment? Analysis of the perception and acceptance of specific prevention measures of the sports federation in North Rhine-Westphalia from the perspective of functionaries in sport'*, unpublished report to the Sports Ministry of North Rhine-Westphalia.

Sportanddev.org (2013) *Child Protection and Safeguarding in Sport.* Online. Available HTTP: <www.sportanddev.org/en/learnmore/safeguarding/> (accessed 7 January 2014).

Stirling, A. E., Kerr, G. A., and Cruz, L. C. (2012) 'An evaluation of Canada's National Coaching Certification Programme's "Make Ethical Decisions" coach education module', *International Journal of Coaching Science,* 6: 45–60.

United Nations Office on Sport for Development and Peace (2014) *Child Protection in Sport.* Online. Available HTTP: <www.un.org/wcm/content/site/sport/home/unplayers/memberstates/sdp_iwg_thematicwgs/pid/6412> (accessed 5 January 2014).

Wykes, M. and Welsh, K. (2009) *Violence, Gender and Justice,* London: Sage.

Index